The Puzzle of Unanimity

The Puzzle of Unanimity

Consensus on the United States Supreme Court

Pamela C. Corley, Amy Steigerwalt, and Artemus Ward

STANFORD
LAW BOOKS
Stanford, California

Stanford University Press
Stanford, California

Printed in the United States of America on acid-free, archival-quality paper

Library of Congress Cataloging-in-Publication Data

Corley, Pamela C., 1967– author.
The puzzle of unanimity : consensus on the United States Supreme Court / Pamela C. Corley, Amy Steigerwalt, and Artemus Ward.
pages cm
Includes bibliographical references and index.
ISBN 978-0-8047-8472-6 (cloth : alk. paper)
1. United States. Supreme Court. 2. Judicial process—United States. 3. Consensus (Social sciences)—United States. I. Steigerwalt, Amy, 1976– author. II. Ward, Artemus, 1971– author. III. Title.
KF8742.C69 2013
347.73'26—dc23

2012049306

ISBN 978-0-8047-8632-4 (electronic)

Typeset by Newgen in 10/13 Electra

For my husband Greg and my daughter Megan—P.C.

For my parents, Arnold and Ronna Steigerwalt—A.S.

For my grandfather, Robert David Azadian—A.W.

Contents

List of Illustrations ix

Acknowledgments xi

Introduction 1

1. The Roosevelt Court: The Critical Juncture from Consensus to Dissensus 14
2. Closing the Jaws of the Decision Making Vise: A Theory and Model of Consensus 49
3. A Function of Design: Consensus in Votes on the Merits 94
4. Monolithic Solidarity: Consensus in Opinion Writing 114
5. An Opportunity to Clarify: Unanimity and Agenda Setting 141
6. Conclusion 160

Appendix 169

Index of Cases 177

Notes 179

Bibliography 185

Index 197

Illustrations

TABLES

Table 1.1.	Institutional dissensus developments of the Roosevelt Court	15
Table 2.1.	Variable descriptions	63
Table 2.2.	Descriptive statistics for independent variables	64
Table 3.1.	Bivariate predictors of unanimous and highly consensual decisions	99
Table 3.2.	Logit models of unanimous and highly consensual decisions	104
Table 3.3.	Predicted probabilities of unanimous and highly consensual decisions	105
Table 3.4.	Logit models of ideological and legal interaction: Unanimous decisions	110
Table 3.5.	Logit models of ideological and legal interaction: Unanimous or highly consensual decisions	111
Table 4.1.	Bivariate predictors of fully unanimous or highly consensual opinions	122
Table 4.2.	Logit models of unanimous and highly consensual opinions	127
Table 4.3.	Predicted probabilities of unanimous and highly consensual opinions	130
Table 4.4.	Summary of main model results from Chapters 3 and 4	133
Table 4.5.	Logit models of ideological and legal interaction: Unanimous opinions	137
Table 4.6.	Logit models of ideological and legal interaction: Unanimous or highly consensual opinions	138
Table 5.1.	Summary of measures of certworthiness	148
Table A.1.	Logit models of unanimous and highly consensual decisions, without Legal Certainty Index	170

Table A.2. Partial proportional odds model of factors explaining level of voting consensus 171
Table A.3. Logit models of unanimous and highly consensual opinions, without the Legal Certainty Index 173
Table A.4. Partial proportional odds model of factors explaining level of opinion consensus 175

FIGURES

Figure I.1. Reaching consensus: Decisions of the U.S. Supreme Court, 1953–2004 3
Figure 1.1. Measures of dissensus in consensus-era courts 17
Figure 1.2. Comparing the Stone Court to its predecessors: Measures of dissensus 19
Figure 1.3. Comparing the Stone Court to its successors: Measures of dissensus 19
Figure 1.4. Measures of dissensus on the Roosevelt Court, 1937–1946 20
Figure 1.5. Dissenting behavior of the Roosevelt Court justices, 1940–1946 21
Figure 2.1. Constrained court 67
Figure 2.2. Unconstrained court 67
Figure 3.1. Comparison of the Warren, Burger, and Rehnquist Courts: Percentage of unanimous and highly consensual decisions 97
Figure 4.1. Separate opinion writing behavior: Supreme Court, 1800–2004 116
Figure 4.2. Comparing the Warren, Burger, and Rehnquist Courts: Percentage of unanimous and highly consensual opinions 120
Figure 5.1. Subjective case characteristics: Unanimous versus nonunanimous cases 153

Acknowledgments

We would like to sincerely thank Lindsey Herbel and Victoria Kikulis for their able research assistance. We would also like to thank the anonymous reviewers, the participants of the Emory University Law School colloquium and workshop series, and the following individuals for their comments, suggestions, and advice on various versions of this project; their input helped strengthen this manuscript immeasurably, although we take full responsibility for any and all errors or surprisingly insightful thoughts. Thanks go to: Brandon Bartels, Brent Boyea, Christopher Brough, Keith Bybee, Suzanne Globetti, Scott Graves, Christian Grose, Marc Hetherington, Robert Howard, Tonja Jacobi, Timothy Johnson, Tom Keck, Kay Levine, Stefanie Lindquist, Michaela Mattes, Kirk Randazzo, Elliot Slotnick, Jeffrey Staton, Jeffrey Yates, and especially Wendy Martinek and Paul Collins, who may have read more iterations of various draft papers and chapters than we have. We really cannot thank all of you enough.

The Puzzle of Unanimity

Introduction

On March 4, 1998, the United States Supreme Court issued a unanimous ruling in the same-sex harassment case *Oncale v. Sundowner Offshore Services* (1998). At issue was whether Title VII's protection against workplace discrimination "because of . . . sex" applies to harassment between members of the same sex. Joseph Oncale was employed as a roustabout on an oil platform in the Gulf of Mexico and was subjected to humiliating sex-related actions by some of his co-workers in front of the rest of the crew. He complained to supervisory personnel, but received no relief and eventually resigned. Oncale filed suit in federal district court, alleging that he was discriminated against because of his sex. The district court, relying on a Fifth Circuit Court of Appeals decision in *Garcia v. Elf Atochem North America* (1994), held that he had no cause of action because same-sex sexual harassment claims are never cognizable under Title VII. The Fifth Circuit affirmed, and the Supreme Court granted certiorari.

Although lower courts "[had] taken a bewildering variety of stances" on whether Title VII prohibits same-sex sexual harassment cases,[1] the Court unanimously held in *Oncale* that "nothing in Title VII necessarily bars a claim of discrimination 'because of . . . sex' merely because the plaintiff and the defendant . . . are of the same sex" (*Oncale*, 79).[2] According to the majority opinion written by Justice Antonin Scalia (ibid., 79), "[w]e see no justification in the statutory language or our precedents for a categorical rule excluding same-sex harassment claims from coverage of Title VII." Thus, *Oncale* definitively and unanimously set the precedent for analyzing same-sex harassment claims.

Why were the justices able to reach complete agreement in *Oncale*? More broadly, how do we explain decisions where conservative justices agree with liberal justices on potentially contentious issues? Media accounts routinely paint a portrait of a deeply ideologically divided Court. For example, a recent article argued that patterns of law clerk hiring "amplify the ideological rifts on a polarized court" (Liptak 2010). Another account, discussing oral arguments during the 2010 term, began with the statement, "An ideologically divided Supreme Court wrestled Wednesday" with an Establishment Clause case (Biskupic 2010). Similarly, a news report on an oral argument during the 2008 term opened with the claim, "The Supreme Court yesterday split along a familiar ideological battle line in its consideration of the Voting Rights Act" (Barnes 2009). And an article about the confirmation of Justice Elena Kagan in the summer of 2010 had this to say: "'I am sorry, but not surprised, to see the partisan split on her nomination, because that reflects the ideological battleground that is going on [on] the Supreme Court today,' [Senator Arlen] Specter [D-PA] said. The court, like Congress, regularly divides along conservative-liberal lines. That split may appear even more political in the year ahead" (Savage 2010).

As these examples demonstrate, most media accounts of the Supreme Court focus on divisions among the justices, and, as we detail, most scholarly studies seek to explain the reasons behind them. Is public discourse about disagreement on the Court misplaced? Notably, Justice Stephen Breyer in an interview on NPR's *Fresh Air* (2010) recently lamented the political tone of most accounts of the Court:

> The press's job is to take those decisions that usually have very great visibility because they're political so they're in the newspaper. But you should remember, first of all, that probably thirty to forty percent of our decisions are unanimous, that the five-fours account for maybe twenty, twenty-five percent, and it isn't always the same five or the same four, and so we discuss and it isn't always a sure thing. . . . Of course, it's understandable that the press in writing about the Court and political scientists in describing the Court want to describe this in ordinary political terms.

In many ways, as Breyer suggested, split decisions are understandable given that the setting in which the justices operate points toward division rather than consensus. On the modern Court, almost all cases decided stem from the certiorari process and are selected precisely because they present difficult, complex legal questions. Moreover, the justices are appointed for life and so are formally insulated from both the public and the elected branches of government. Given their place at the apex of the judicial system, they possess a great deal of power and independence. It is perhaps unsurprising, then, that the prevailing view is of a Court that hears tough cases and hands down correspondingly divided decisions.

Viewing the Court as hopelessly divided is nothing new. An October 8, 1972, article in the *New York Times* about the start of the 1972 term was entitled "Swing Man on the Supreme Court: The Court is in Two Factions Now, and Justice White is in the Middle" (Liebman 1972). Similarly, a June 28, 1987, *Chicago Tribune* article about Justice Lewis Powell's retirement in 1987 suggested that Powell was more influential in shaping the Court's decisions than were either of the two chief justices he served with, William Rehnquist and Warren Burger, "because he so often sat in the middle of the ideological divide of the nine-member court" (Tybor 1987). Such narratives suggest that the Court is bitterly split along ideological lines on most issues and renders its decisions accordingly.

The problem with this view is that it is simply incorrect. Thus, the first contribution this book makes is to demonstrate that, contrary to conventional wisdom, the Court reaches consensus more often than not. In fact, roughly *one-third* of the Supreme Court's decisions have been unanimous each term since 1953. As Figure I.1 shows, between 1953 and 2004 the proportion of unanimously decided cases varied each term but stayed consistently between 30 and 50 percent. During the early years of the Rehnquist Court, the percentage of unanimous cases steadily increased, reaching an all-time high of 51 percent during the 1997 term. Although the rate of unanimity declined to 37 percent during the last year of Rehnquist's tenure, the data

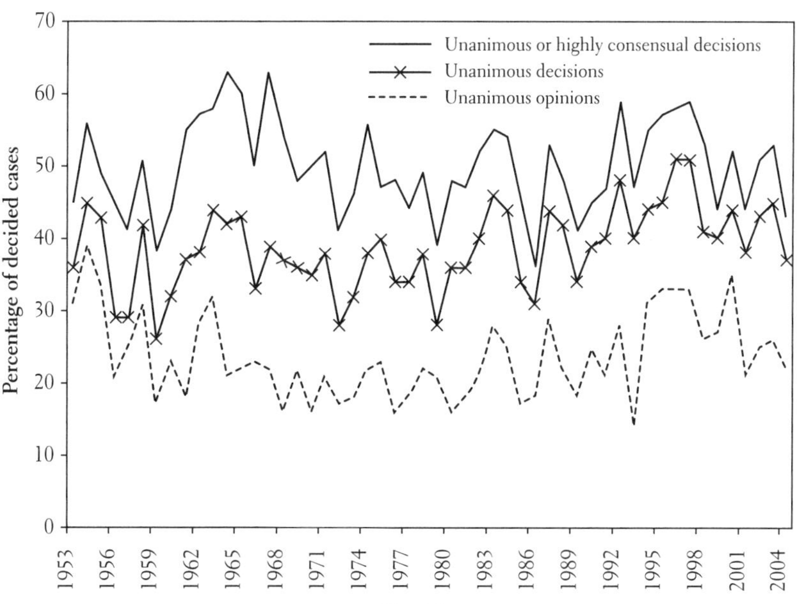

Figure I.1. Reaching consensus: Decisions of the U.S. Supreme Court, 1953–2004

still reveal that a substantial proportion of the Court's decisions were decided without a dissenting vote.

If we examine the Rehnquist Court's cases more closely, we see that many of those that resulted in unanimous outcomes were decidedly important. For example, during the 1996 term the justices unanimously upheld a New York law prohibiting assisted suicide against an Equal Protection challenge (*Vacco v. Quill*, 1997); unanimously determined the standard for when police can constitutionally conduct a "no knock" entry (*Richards v. Wisconsin*, 1997); unanimously agreed that the retroactive cancellation of provisional credits allowing early release for inmates violates the *Ex Post Facto* Clause (*Lynce v. Mathis*, 1997); and unanimously ruled that the Constitution does not require that a lawsuit against a sitting president be deferred until the president's term ends (*Clinton v. Jones*, 1997). In each case, the justices rendered a unanimous decision concerning an important question of constitutional law—including one that affected the sitting president.

Another substantial proportion of cases each term are decided with only one justice dissenting, which we define as a "highly consensual" case. As Figure I.1 reveals, the reality is this: *a majority of the Court's decisions every term are unanimous or highly consensual*. Indeed, while the overall average of unanimous or highly consensual cases for the period under study was 50 percent, in some terms the justices reached complete or near unanimity in nearly two-thirds of the cases decided. These findings suggest that, again, conventional wisdom concerning division on the Court is fairly misplaced.

Whereas a unanimous vote in a case may reflect one type of agreement among the justices, it may also obscure other types of disagreement. When one justice votes with the Court on the outcome of a case but disagrees with the reasoning of the others, he or she may issue a separate opinion—called a concurrence—to express that disagreement. We take into account separate opinions, including concurrences, because of their potential legal and political impact: they "may shake public confidence in the judiciary by bringing into question the certainty of the law" (Walker, Epstein, and Dixon 1988, 387). Any disagreement over the majority opinion "cancels the impact of monolithic solidarity on which the authority of a bench of judges so largely depends" (Hand 1958, 72). And while dissents are more clearly detrimental to the authority of majority opinions, concurrences can be equally damaging. In fact, if a decision of the Court is accompanied by a concurring opinion that does not support the majority opinion, lower courts are less likely to comply with it (Corley 2010). Similarly, lower courts are less likely to follow plurality opinions—those in which a majority of the justices concur in the result but not in the reasoning (Corley 2009).

Accordingly, in addition to defining consensus on the basis of votes on the merits, we define it in terms of *opinion* consensus. Figure I.1 also reflects the proportion of cases during the study period that were decided with opinion unanimity, meaning that there was only one institutional opinion of the Court, with no dissents and no concurrences. On average, the Court reached opinion unanimity in one out of four cases, and while unanimity was not as prevalent in opinion writing as it was in votes on the merits, during a number of terms the Court issued a single opinion in one out of three cases. Yet again, the data on both opinion and voting unanimity shown in Figure I.1 belie conventional wisdom.

The book's second contribution is to *explain* the high level of consensus on the Court. We do this by constructing a model reflecting the variety of forces that concurrently influence the Court's decisions. According to the dominant model of Supreme Court decision making, the justices base their votes on their ideological attitudes and values (Segal and Spaeth 1993, 2002). There is little doubt that ideology substantially influences individual justices. But if the justices vote ideologically, why do liberals and conservatives ever agree, and why do they reach consensus and, indeed, unanimity, so frequently? Scholars currently do not possess a clear answer to this question, and consequently unanimous cases present an intriguing and perplexing puzzle. Are they simply outliers or are they those that the Court, in retrospect, should not have spent its valuable time on? Are these cases uninteresting, concerning relatively boring issues of law? Or is it possible that their frequency suggests that we still have much to learn about how the Supreme Court decides cases, especially as a collective body? In fact, Segal and Spaeth (1993, 2002) provided neither an analysis of nor an explanation for unanimous cases. However, according to one scholar, "If we exclude a large proportion of cases from our analysis, claiming that we cannot predict or explain them because of their unanimity, we are certainly missing a large part of the behavior of the Supreme Court. We are then left guessing what happened in those cases" (Benesh 2003, 124). Thus, we offer here the first comprehensive explanation for why justices who are often described as highly polarized reach the same legal conclusions so often.

Existing scholarship on the Court gives primary attention to the ways in which ideological, strategic, and legal considerations influence the choices made by justices. Political scientists devote considerable attention to the attitudinal model, which contends that "legal rules governing decision making (e.g. precedent, plain meaning) in the cases that come to the Court do not limit discretion. . . . [B]ecause the Supreme Court is the court of last resort, the justices . . . may freely implement their personal policy preferences" (Segal and Spaeth 2002, 111). Other scholars posit that the justices are influenced by strategic considerations (Epstein and Knight 1998; Maltzman, Spriggs, and Wahlbeck 2000). According to the strategic model, justices "take into account the effects of their choices on collective results when they vote on outcomes and write or support opinions. . . . Because of this motivation, the positions they take may differ from the positions they most prefer" (Baum 1997, 90). Proponents of the legal model (e.g., Bailey and Maltzman 2008; Richards and Kritzer 2002) assert that justices are heavily influenced by legal norms, which come from socialization in law school and the legal community, and therefore they use accepted tools of legal reasoning that include legal text, legislative intent, and precedent to make principled rather than results-oriented decisions. Hence, the process of legal reasoning can lead them away from their sincere policy preferences.

Most studies of the U.S. Supreme Court focus on determining which of these models best captures judicial decision making. We argue instead that consensus on the Court is a reflection of multiple, concurrently operating influences. In particular, it can be understood only by recognizing the multitude of factors that influence the justices in every single case. Rather than single out a specific group of factors as the primary explanation for consensus, we argue that various potential influences all operate in each case and, many times, in a complex, interactive fashion.

First and foremost, our theory of consensus highlights the important interaction between attitudes and law. There is considerable research showing that attitudes are the driving force behind the decisions of the Supreme Court (Hagle and Spaeth 1993; Howard and Segal 2004; Segal and Cover 1989; Segal et al. 1995). We support this view, but at the same time we recognize that legal considerations shape the Court's decisions both by directly affecting them and by enabling or constraining the extent to which attitudes operate in each case. Specifically, while attitudes are always in play, in some cases the justices' ability to vote their preferences is constrained by legal forces. Furthermore, a central benefit of our comprehensive theory of consensus is that it highlights how legal and attitudinal factors simultaneously influence the Court's decision making, and recognizes how the overall weight of each may vary from case to case.

We place a heavy emphasis on the interplay between attitudes and law, but we believe that strategic considerations also influence the Court's ability to achieve consensus. Additionally, we take into account institutional changes that we believe influence the degree of consensus that the Court is able to achieve, as well as a number of case-specific factors. Institutional developments—such as the external political environment and internal procedures—vary over time and can affect the way justices think about a case. In addition, not all cases are created equal, and we posit that variation among them contributes to whether the Court is able to reach agreement. The key to understanding consensus, then, is recognizing the multitude of diverse factors that together influence the justices. We propose that these forces stem from five broad categories—attitudinal, legal, strategic, institutional, and case-specific—and only by taking into account all of them can we truly understand why consensus occurs.

The book's third contribution is to test empirically whether the justices reach agreement when the legal answer is simply more obvious and clear. While a number of scholars propose that legal clarity explains consensus on the Supreme Court (e.g., Goldman 1969; Klein 1984; Pritchett 1941), this claim has never been empirically or systematically tested. For example, Pritchett (1941, 890) argued that unanimity results when "the facts and the law are so clear that no opportunity is allowed for the autobiographies of the justices to lead them to opposing conclusions." He then ignored unanimous decisions in his analysis of judicial behavior because he assumed that legal factors sufficiently explained them, and perhaps in part because measuring legal clarity is so difficult. We therefore present a mechanism for capturing the level of uncertainty and ambiguity facing the justices with regard to the strongest legal answer in each case, to determine whether Pritchett's assumption is correct. That is, instead of measuring law in terms of the influence of precedent, text and intent, or different canons of construction, we measure the level of legal certainty in each case to determine how law influences decision making. We then empirically test this measure and find that it helps us to understand the influence of legal factors on Supreme Court decision making as well as when the Court is most likely to reach consensus and unanimity.

The Importance of Understanding Consensus

Some of the most important Supreme Court decisions of the past one hundred years have been unanimous. This is no accident. Justices realize that consensual decisions on important and potentially divisive topics can carry more weight. Consider *United States v. Nixon* (1974), in which the

Court unanimously ordered President Richard Nixon to turn over tapes and other records relating to White House conversations that had been subpoenaed as part of a criminal investigation. According to an article in *Time* magazine (1974), "Definitely and unanimously, the court ended President Nixon's effort to withhold evidence from Special Prosecutor Leon Jaworski in the Watergate case. . . . The presence on the court of three conservative Nixon appointees . . . effectively pre-empted any charge that the President had been the victim of his liberal enemies. As if to emphasize the strictly legal, nonpolitical nature of its decision, the court did not once refer to the ongoing impeachment inquiry." The article noted that, during the discussion of the case, "Chief Justice Burger . . . suggest[ed] that the interests of the nation—and of the court—would best be served by a unanimous decision."

In *Brown v. Board of Education* (1954)—in which racial segregation in public schools was held to be unconstitutional—the Court also recognized the importance of a unified response. Chief Justice Earl Warren "wanted a single, unequivocating opinion that could leave no doubt that the Court had put Jim Crow to the sword" (Kluger 1977, 683). Scholars routinely suggest that the unanimity Warren secured helped insulate *Brown* against subsequent challenges. For example, Smith (2005, 118) argued: "*Brown's* core holding was never subjected to serious challenges. A unanimous Supreme Court decision saw to that." Motley (1979, 316) made a similar argument: "A divided Court might have rendered the decision unenforceable in many communities, or in any event in more communities than those in which resistance was actually encountered after the unanimous decision. The unanimity of the *Brown* decision was essential to its viability and added immeasurably to its ultimate acceptance by most Americans." The end result was a decision that irrevocably changed American society and for which to this day the Court, led by Chief Justice Warren, is credited with declaring segregation "inherently unequal" with a single, commanding voice.

Although many have noted the importance of unanimity in *Brown*, the following memo, which accompanied Chief Justice Burger's first draft of the majority opinion in *Swann v. Charlotte-Mecklenburg Board of Education* (1971), demonstrates that unanimity was also valued in subsequent cases involving racial segregation as an aid in the implementation process:

> I am sure it is not necessary to emphasize the importance of our attempting to reach an accommodation and a common position, and I would urge that we consult or exchange views by memorandum or both. Separate opinions, expressing divergent views or conclusions will, I hope, be deferred until we have exhausted all other

efforts to reach a common view. I am sure we must all agree that the problems of remedy are at least as difficult and important as the great Constitutional principle of *Brown*. (quoted in Epstein and Knight 1998, 99–106)

Studies of other countries note the importance of consensus among policy makers on the likelihood of the public accepting a government and its policies. Numerous studies of Japan highlight its "consensual governance" style (e.g., Haley 1992; Rohlen 1989; Samuels 1987) as well as the fact that this consensual approach is heavily supported by both the public and government bureaucrats (e.g., Aberbach et al. 1990; Richardson and Flanagan 1984). In a broad study of governmental legitimacy, Anderson and Guillory (1997) examined citizen support for eleven European democracies and found that support for government among political losers is higher when there is a greater amount of consensus in the decision making process itself. Alternatively, levels of support fall when government systems operate in a more purely majoritarian manner. Finally, social psychological studies of small-group decision making suggest that attempts to achieve consensus and unanimity can have important consequences for the decision makers themselves. Those seeking unanimity express a higher degree of satisfaction and more agreement with the group's ultimate decision (e.g., Miller 1989; Schweiger, Sandberg, and Ragan 1986).

Increased public support for consensual government decisions provides the additional benefit of allowing a government more freedom to craft policy proposals and potentially solve vexing social problems. Since the time of Rousseau and Locke, political philosophers have argued that people can remain free even though subject to the decisions of government. As long as those decisions reflect broad consensus, they necessarily reflect the desires of free individuals. Consensus thus legitimates the actions and policies of a democratic polity. In the realm of U.S. foreign policy, George (1980) argued that long-term support for a policy requires a national consensus on its legitimacy. The greater the degree of national consensus, the more freedom presidents possess to pursue their short- and long-term policy goals. Similarly, Mooney and Lee (2000) found that policy making on issues of morality is much more constrained when there is dissensus among the public as opposed to when there is consensus. Hence, increased consensus allows policy makers more freedom to determine policy content. Smoke (1994) also suggested that the existence of a national consensus can enable policy makers to make broad policy changes and ensure that these changes enjoy legitimacy and broad support.

Without consensus, policy makers must tread more carefully as to the size and scope of their proposals and must pay more attention to the possibility that their ideas will receive little support, be viewed as illegitimate, or both. Research on the U.S. Supreme Court in particular finds that nonconsensual decisions run the risk of implementation problems or even outright noncompliance (e.g., Johnson and Canon 1984; O'Brien 1996). For example, O'Brien (1996, 336), argued that "less agreement and more numerous and longer opinions invite uncertainty and confusion about the Court's rulings, interpretation of law, and policy-making," which, he said, leads to instability and confusion as to the rule of law itself. At his retirement, Justice Byron White urged his colleagues to think about how the Supreme Court's decisions influence lower courts: "I hope the Court's mandates will be clear, crisp, and leave those of us below with as little room as possible for disagreement about their meaning."[3]

Others find that nonunanimous decisions suffer a greater risk of being overruled by the Supreme Court in the future "because non-consensus lowers the credibility of an opinion and signals the possibility of future legal change" (Spriggs and Hansford 2001, 1104). For example, in *Payne v. Tennessee* (1991), concerning the admissibility of victim impact evidence during the sentencing phase of a death penalty case, Chief Justice Rehnquist explained the majority's decision to overturn the Court's previous decisions in *Booth v. Maryland* (1987) and *South Carolina v. Gathers* (1989) in part based on the following considerations: "*Booth* and *Gathers* were decided by the narrowest of margins, over spirited dissents challenging the basic underpinnings of those decisions. They have been questioned by members of the Court in later decisions, and have defied consistent application by the lower courts" (*Payne*, 828–830). Nonunanimous Supreme Court decisions are also in greater jeopardy of being overridden by Congress than are unanimous decisions (Eskridge 1991; Hettinger and Zorn 2005).

These realities suggest that it is important for us to understand the sources of consensus and how it is achieved (Smoke 1994). If consensually based governmental policies can increase support both for particular policies and for the government as a whole, understanding how governmental bodies arrive at consensual decisions—particularly unanimous ones—becomes imperative. Furthermore, previous research on the U.S. Supreme Court suggests that disagreement among the justices increases the likelihood of challenges to the Court's very authority. Thus, understanding how the justices reach unanimity and consensus is essential to understanding the Court's role in the political process and in preserving the rule of law.

Chapter Overview

The U.S. Supreme Court is currently entrenched in an era of dissensus. During the 1800s and early 1900s, it operated under a norm of consensus, but this norm broke down during the mid-twentieth century. How did this breakdown occur? In Chapter 1, we show how the Court transitioned from a collective body to a body composed of a collection of individuals. Specifically, we highlight a number of what Orren and Skowronek (2004) have termed "distinguishable events" that brought about "durable shifts" in the extent to which consensus could be achieved. We trace these trends by an extensive examination of the Supreme Court during the Roosevelt Court—the "critical juncture" or moment in time when we argue the Court shifted from consensus to dissensus (Pierson 2004). Our analysis is predicated primarily on an original investigation of the private papers of Justices William O. Douglas and Harlan Fiske Stone. We argue that various institutional changes instituted during the Roosevelt Court affected the Court's decision making processes and brought about and entrenched a "dissensus revolution" in which individual expression went from virtual nonexistence to the norm. Understanding how dissensus became entrenched illustrates just how difficult it has become for modern justices to agree on anything. However, as explained earlier, even in the modern era of dissensus, consensus still occurred quite frequently during the study period. Thus, in subsequent chapters we explore how, once started on the dissensus path, the justices were ever able to agree.

In Chapter 2, we explicate our comprehensive model of consensus on the U.S. Supreme Court, beginning with a review of the literature that demonstrates the importance of policy preferences, strategic considerations, and legal factors in judicial decision making. We discuss previous attempts to understand Court consensus and then propose our model; we also discuss the notion of legal certainty as a mechanism for understanding the influence of law on judicial decisions. Chapter 2 ends with a detailed explanation of how we operationalized each of our independent variables.

Chapter 3 begins our empirical examination of the factors that influence the Supreme Court's likelihood of achieving unanimity and consensus in an era of dissensus. We focus on votes on the merits and find that, in addition to particular strategic and case-specific factors, consensus and unanimity are shaped by attitudinal and legal considerations.

Whereas Chapter 3 defines consensus in terms of the justices' votes on the merits, Chapter 4 takes into account separate opinions and defines consensus in terms of *opinions*. Since a unanimous vote may obscure true disagreement among the justices, especially disagreement over legal doctrine, we investigate when the justices are less likely to feel the need to write separately. We therefore apply our theory of judicial decision making to the question of whether these same influences help to explain consensus in opinion writing. Again, we find that opinion consensus is largely a function of attitudinal and legal considerations as well as some strategic and case-specific factors.

Taken together, Chapters 3 and 4 provide strong support for our main argument, which is that consensus on the U.S. Supreme Court is a function of multiple, simultaneously operating factors that add to the story of how the justices reach agreement. First and foremost, we find a connection between attitudes and law: when the level of legal certainty facing the justices is high, attitudes are more constrained and consensus and unanimity are more likely. However, divisions are more likely when the level of legal certainty is low. Furthermore, consensus occurs more frequently in certain strategic contexts. In particular, unanimity on the merits is more likely when the chief justice authors the majority opinion, but opinion consensus is less likely when the Court declares a statute unconstitutional. Finally, case-specific factors matter: voting and opinion consensus are both more likely when the case concerns a non-civil-liberties or non-politically salient issue, and/or is decided in a liberal direction. Understanding consensus, then, necessitates taking into account the multitude of forces that operate on the Court in each case.

The findings presented in Chapters 3 and 4 necessarily raise an additional, important question: In an era of dissensus, when the Supreme Court's docket is almost entirely discretionary, why does the Court decide to hear so many cases that result in unanimous or highly consensual opinions? Chapter 5 explores why the Court grants certiorari to cases that are ultimately decided unanimously. We examine cert pool memos for all cases granted and decided during the 1986 term. Based on our exploration of the substantive conclusions reached by the memos' authors as to each case's certworthiness, we offer some initial findings and conclusions on the differences between ultimately unanimous cases and non-unanimous cases at the certiorari stage. Overall, our investigation suggests that unanimous cases appear to be those in which the justices believed it was important to clarify the law and issue a final, national ruling on an issue of great importance, and for which a single, unified answer could be reached.

Chapter 6 offers a review of our findings and an exploration of their broader implications. In particular, we highlight the need for studies of judicial decision making to take into account the totality of forces that influence judges, including attitudinal, legal, strategic, and case-specific factors. We also discuss what we have learned about unanimous opinions: they are not uninteresting, but rather involve important legal issues that the justices feel are necessary to decide and for which they could agree on a single legal answer. Thus, these cases speak to the role of the Court in clarifying the law and in reinforcing the rule of law across the nation.

The Roosevelt Court

The Critical Juncture from Consensus to Dissensus

The goal of this book is to explain consensus on the U.S. Supreme Court. A useful perspective from which to begin is to appreciate how the Court transitioned from a consensual to a dissensual body. We argue that this institutional transformation was the result of a series of internal and external changes to the judicial decision making process during the Roosevelt Court—a period roughly from 1937 to 1947 that was dominated by justices appointed by President Franklin D. Roosevelt. These developments—occurring both on the Court and in the broader political environment—fundamentally altered the dynamic among the justices and forever changed the way they decided cases. The end result was the replacement of collective expression—once the long-standing norm—with individual behavior. This chapter thus serves to highlight the central question investigated throughout the book: Given all of the institutional pressures that point toward dissensus, how are the justices ever able to agree? In other words, how do we explain the puzzle of unanimity?

Here we seek to explain why and how the modern era of dissensus began. To do so, we highlight what Pierson (2004, 55) termed a "conjuncture"—a moment in time when "discrete elements or dimensions of politics" collide to produce a new, and often unintended, effect. Specifically, we identify a number of institutional developments that dramatically altered the extent to which consensus could be achieved in the Court's decision making. We trace these trends by undertaking an extensive examination of the Roosevelt Court—the conjuncture, or moment in time, when its ability to achieve consensus changed.

Our investigation is based primarily on the private papers of Justices William O. Douglas and Harlan Fiske Stone, including memos sent between the justices, draft opinions, and other correspondence, which we use to determine the durable shifts in the Court's decision making processes during these years. Our analysis shows that various institutional changes instituted both before and during the Roosevelt Court affected the Court's decision making and brought about and entrenched a dissensus revolution in which individual expression went from virtual nonexistence to the norm.

While most scholars attribute the breakdown in the norm of consensus to Chief Justice Stone and his leadership style (e.g., Walker, Epstein, and Dixon 1988; cf. Haynie 1992), we break with them by highlighting the internal and external institutional developments that increased dissensus. More simply, to truly understand how the dissensus era arose we need to understand how the Court itself changed. By focusing merely on Stone's personal style, one might make the argument that another chief, with a different style, could return the Court to its previous levels of consensus. We argue instead that the institutional changes implemented during the Roosevelt Court so fundamentally changed the Court's operation that a return to the norm of consensus was virtually impossible.

Table 1.1 shows the important institutional developments—internal and external, cause and effect—that occurred during the Roosevelt Court era. As we detail next, once on the dissensus path, there remained only a "critical juncture" to fundamentally alter the institution (Pierson 2004, 134–135). That moment arrived with the conjuncture of the external intellectual force

TABLE 1.1

Institutional dissensus developments of the Roosevelt Court

Causes	Effects
External developments • Judges' Bill (1925): increased discretionary docket, growth in civil liberties cases • Influence of legal realism • Rapid personnel changes *Internal developments* • Expanded conference discussion • Circulation delays: breakdown of twenty-four-hour return of circulated opinions • Reargument of cases • Academic atmosphere	*Majority coalition behavior* • Decline of acquiescence • Court opinions departing from conference views • Proliferation of concurrences in the judgment only • Criticism of dissents by majority coalition members • Concurrences as "counter-dissents" *Minority coalition behavior* • Justices note every dissent • Dissents over small disagreements • Dissenters raise issues not mentioned in petitions • Circulated dissents praised by minority coalition members • Dissents criticize concurrences

of legal realism, the largely discretionary docket created by the Judiciary Act of 1925, popularly known as the "Judges' Bill," and the appointment of New Deal legal liberals, including the elevation of Stone to chief justice, who brought with them a more open, academic style. Under Stone, the justices developed new internal practices that undermined long-standing norms and ushered in the modern era of dissensus. Conference discussion was expanded, opinion writing and opinion circulation delays became common, and there were frequent calls to reargue contentious cases. In short, an academic atmosphere took hold.

External and internal developments on the Roosevelt Court had a dramatic, long-lasting effect on both majority and minority behavior. Justices writing majority opinions increasingly departed from the views of the Conference, the norm of acquiescence broke down, and more concurrences and dissents were issued than at any previous time in the Court's history. Furthermore, majority opinions and concurrences were used to criticize dissents. Dissenters expressed small disagreements and discussed issues not raised in petitions, all the while praising each other for not acquiescing to the majority. The basic character of the decision making process was completely transformed.

The Roosevelt Court justices did not initiate these changes out of whole cloth. Specifically, developments toward the end of the consensus era foreshadowed the coming dissensus revolution. We propose that the consensus era on the Supreme Court began at the institution's inception in 1789 and lasted into the Hughes Court, from 1931 to 1940. Interestingly, it began at the end of the eighteenth century in a decidedly individualistic manner, with the earliest justices issuing their opinions seriatim (i.e., individually in each case), and ended at the close of the nineteenth century with a resurgence of individual expression, presaging the dissensus era to come. However, it is the period in between that largely defines what we term the consensus era. From the Marshall Court to the end of the nineteenth century, Supreme Court decision making was dominated by the institutional norm of consensus, including a desire for unanimity and a distaste for dissent and individual expression. Decision making took place orally; the justices largely acquiesced and said nothing publicly if they disagreed with the majority; institutional opinions were often delivered by the chief justice and not circulated to the other members of the Court for input (as they are today); and the practice of circuit riding provided justices with a regular outlet for individual expression. As Epstein, Segal, and Spaeth (2001) showed in their examination of the docket books of Chief Justice Waite, justices commonly muted disagreements expressed at Conference and instead joined the majority opinion. As a result, between 1801 and 1940, the Court handed down unanimous decisions approximately 90 percent of the time, if not more often (Epstein et al. 2007).

At the end of the nineteenth century, however, a number of institutional developments occurred that placed the Court on a path toward increasing dissensus. During the Fuller Court (1888–1910), the courts of appeals were created and the Supreme Court gained limited discretionary review over its docket, thereby allowing it to choose more important, and often more difficult, cases to decide. Also, circuit riding, the outlet for individual expression, was abolished. Now draft opinions began to be circulated to each member of the Court, and for the first time the justices were able to thoughtfully critique a written opinion before it was issued. These institutional developments helped promote dissensus and presaged the coming, modern era of increased discretion over dockets, the influence of legal realism, and further changes to the decision making process.

Figure 1.1 compares indicators of dissensus across consensus-era Courts. Although the transition from the relatively consensual Fuller and White

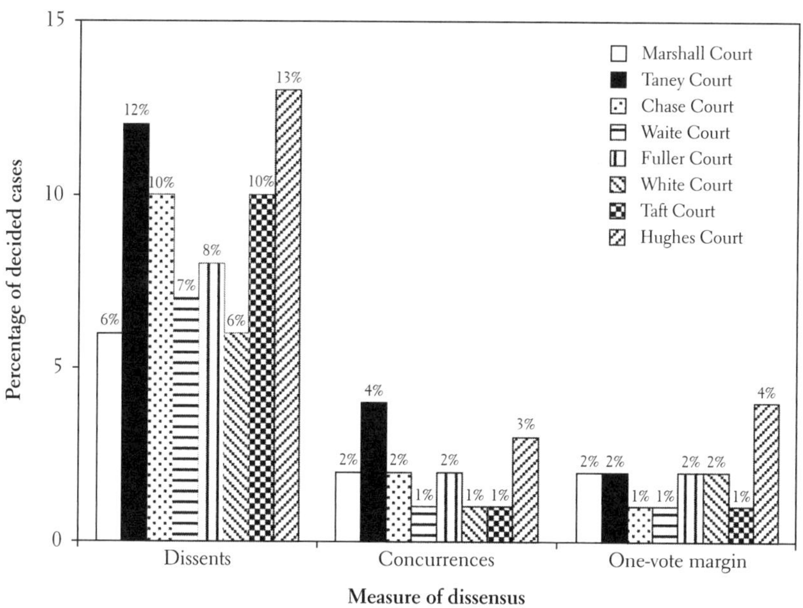

Figure 1.1. Measures of dissensus in consensus-era courts

SOURCE: Data from Lee Epstein, Jeffrey A. Segal, Harold Spaeth, and Thomas G. Walker, *The Supreme Court Compendium: Data, Decisions and Developments*, 4th ed. (Washington, DC: CQ Press, 2007).

Courts to the more divided Taft and Hughes Courts is evident from the percentages of dissents, concurrences, and cases decided by a one-vote margin, the levels of dissensus under Hughes were still similar to those under Taney. Thus, while dissensus was seemingly on the rise, there was no reason to believe that the Court would not soon return to more consensual levels. And yet, as we demonstrate, the justices of the Roosevelt Court so changed the way the Court functioned that even they appear relatively consensual compared to their successors.

Revisiting the Roosevelt Court

President Roosevelt made nine appointments to the Supreme Court, including the elevation of Stone to chief justice. Hugo Black, Stanley Reed, Felix Frankfurter, William O. Douglas, Frank Murphy, James Byrnes, Robert Jackson, and Wiley Rutledge joined Stone and the other holdovers to make up what C. Herman Pritchett (1948) termed "the Roosevelt Court." And while it is conventional to name Courts after their chiefs, we consider the justices who served with Stone to be members of the Roosevelt Court in this discussion, for it is this set of justices who transformed the Court from a largely consensual body into an institution where individual expression was common.

Figure 1.2 illustrates the dramatic sea change in nonconsensual behavior under Chief Justice Stone. While levels of dissensus increased during the Taft and Hughes Courts, there can be little doubt that the Roosevelt Court justices transformed the institution during Stone's tenure as chief (Caldeira and Zorn 1998; Halpern and Vines 1977; Mason 1956; Murphy 1964; Pritchett 1948; Walker, Epstein, and Dixon 1988). Nearly half of all Stone Court decisions had at least one dissent, nearly one in five contained a concurrence, and one in ten was decided by a single vote. No previous group of justices had ever come remotely close to these levels of public discord.

Figure 1.3 further shows that the dissensus trend ushered in by the justices of the Roosevelt Court was anything but an aberration. As new justices joined holdovers such as Black and Douglas, they adopted the dissensus norms begun by their predecessors. Dissent rates regularly reached 60 percent, concurrence rates continued to climb, to 40 percent, and cases decided by a one-vote margin reached 20 percent. Although the personal predilections of the holdovers certainly contributed to the growth of dissensus over time, a number of important institutional changes that occurred during the Roosevelt Court continued to be influential on future Courts and helped to entrench the norm of dissensus, which continues to this day.

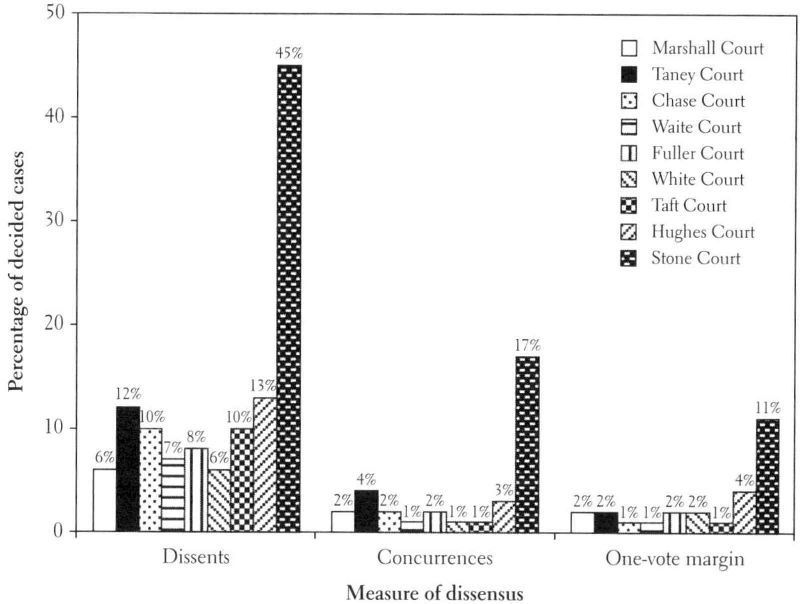

Figure 1.2. Comparing the Stone Court to its predecessors: Measures of dissensus
SOURCE: Data from Lee Epstein, Jeffrey A. Segal, Harold Spaeth, and Thomas G. Walker, *The Supreme Court Compendium: Data, Decisions and Developments*, 4th ed. (Washington, DC: CQ Press, 2007).

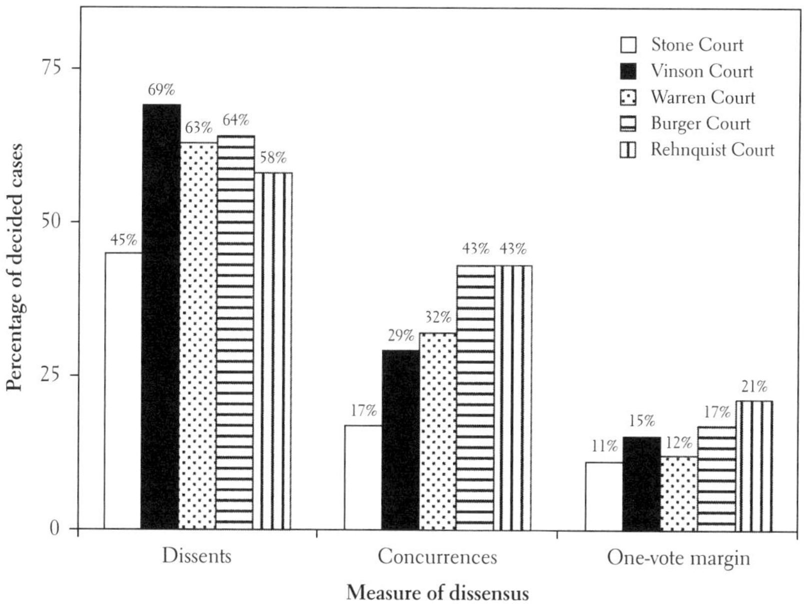

Figure 1.3. Comparing the Stone Court to its successors: Measures of dissensus
SOURCE: Data from Lee Epstein, Jeffrey A. Segal, Harold Spaeth, and Thomas G. Walker, *The Supreme Court Compendium: Data, Decisions and Developments*, 4th ed. (Washington, DC: CQ Press, 2007).

Once the justices of the Roosevelt Court set out on the dissensus path, their practices and behavior only increased the amount of divisiveness over time. Figure 1.4 shows that cases with dissents reached an all-time high of 52 percent in 1943, only to be topped at 60 percent in 1946. This upward trend continued until 80 percent of the decisions handed down in 1952 contained a dissent—a record that still stands. Dissents were common among Roosevelt Court justices in landmark cases. These included *Betts v. Brady* (1942), in which Black, Douglas, and Murphy disagreed with the majority opinion denying a right to counsel for indigent defendants; *West Virginia State Board of Education v. Barnette* (1943), in which Frankfurter, Reed, and Owen Roberts dissented from a ruling protecting students from being forced to salute the American flag and recite the Pledge of Allegiance in public schools; and *Korematsu v. United States* (1944), in which Roberts, Murphy, and Jackson opposed the Court's decision allowing the government to intern Japanese Americans during World War II.

Figure 1.4 also reveals an increase in the percentage of cases with a concurrence, which climbed to another record of 31 percent in 1946. Eventually, the justices issued concurrences in 57 percent of cases by the 1970 term—an as yet unsurpassed high-water mark. Even some of the landmark cases

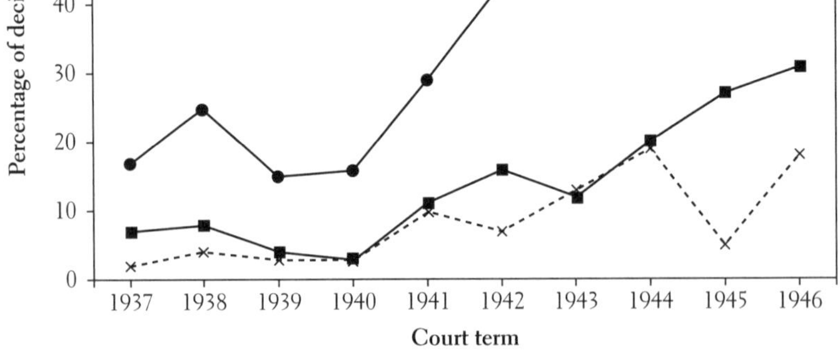

Figure 1.4. Measures of dissensus on the Roosevelt Court, 1937–1946
SOURCE: Data from Lee Epstein, Jeffrey A. Segal, Harold Spaeth, and Thomas G. Walker, *The Supreme Court Compendium: Data, Decisions and Developments*, 4th ed. (Washington, DC: CQ Press, 2007).

decided unanimously contained concurrences. For example, both Stone and Jackson concurred in *Skinner v. Oklahoma* (1942), which invalidated state criminal sterilization laws; and Douglas, Murphy, and Rutledge each issued separate concurrences in the World War II Japanese-American curfew case *Hirabayashi v. United States* (1943).

Finally, Figure 1.4 shows that the percentage of cases decided by a one-vote margin reached an apex of 19 percent in 1944. For example, both the Free Exercise tax-solicitation case *Murdock v. Pennsylvania* (1943) and the Commerce Clause insurance case *United States v. Southeastern Underwriters Assn.* (1944) were decided by a single vote.[1]

It is important to note that the Court's disagreements were not simply the product of a few justices. Figure 1.5 illustrates how each justice on the Roosevelt Court increased his level of dissenting votes over time. For example, Stone's dissents increased from 4 percent of cases in 1940 to 19 percent in 1944; Roberts's, from 19 percent in 1940 to 36 percent in his final year on the bench; Black's, from 9 percent in 1940 to 21 percent in 1946; Reed's, from 5 percent in 1940 to 12 percent in 1946; Frankfurter's, from 1 percent in 1940 to 23 percent by 1946; Douglas's, from 9 percent in 1940 to 21 percent in 1946;

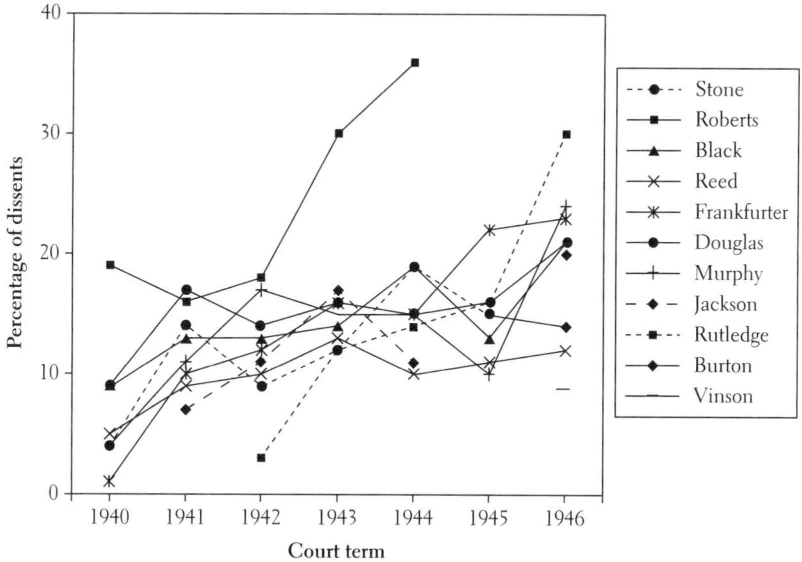

Figure 1.5. Dissenting behavior of the Roosevelt Court justices, 1940–1946
SOURCE: Data from Lee Epstein, Jeffrey A. Segal, Harold Spaeth, and Thomas G. Walker, *The Supreme Court Compendium: Data, Decisions and Developments*, 4th ed. (Washington, DC: CQ Press, 2007).

Jackson's, from 7 percent in 1941 to 20 percent in 1946; and Rutledge's, from only 3 percent in 1942 to a striking 30 percent in 1946. As the figure shows, the dissensus trend was plainly a collective enterprise.

Still, despite the unprecedented amount of dissensus occurring on the Roosevelt Court, the justices reached consensus half of the time and in a number of important cases. They spoke in a single voice in the "fighting words" case *Chaplinsky v. New Hampshire* (1942), the World War II "enemy combatant" case *Ex parte Quirin* (1942), and the Commerce Clause agricultural case *Wickard v. Filburn* (1942). These decisions illustrate that even on a fractured Court the justices could agree on some of the most controversial issues of the day.

It is plain from the data that the Court experienced then-unprecedented levels of disagreement while Stone was chief justice. However, the extent to which Stone was personally responsible for this discord continues to be debated; for this reason we discuss Stone's leadership and the personal and jurisprudential divisions among his colleagues. And, while we acknowledge that Stone's freewheeling style helped foster an environment in which conflict thrived, we illuminate a number of intra-institutional developments that further undermined the old-era norm of consensus, already threatened by the extra-institutional pressures of the discretionary docket, legal realism, and rapid personnel changes. Thus, the justices of the Roosevelt Court came together at a time when conditions for increased dissensus were ripe. We argue that it was ultimately these institutional developments, rather than simply the leadership style of Chief Justice Stone or personal feuds among the justices, that transformed the Court. Nevertheless, those latter factors certainly helped reinforce the institutional developments that entrenched dissensus over time.

External Developments: Discretionary Docket, Legal Realism, and Personnel Changes

Three important external developments were central to the breakdown of consensus during the Roosevelt Court: (1) congressional legislation that gave the justices a large measure of discretion over the cases they would decide, opening the door to more contentious issues; (2) the controversial intellectual ideas of legal realism—in particular the notion of law as indeterminate—that provided an environment for conflict to thrive; and (3) President Roosevelt's successful appointment of justices who were critical of their predecessors and therefore receptive to changing the institution both procedurally and substantively. In this section, we briefly address how each influenced the Court's decision making processes. Without these crucial developments, the justices would have had neither the incentive nor the opportunity to undermine consensual norms or to create internal procedures conducive to dissensus to the extent that they did.

Trifling Cases: The Judges' Bill of 1925

The Judges' Bill of 1925 eliminated the vast majority of mandatory appeals and allowed the Court to choose which certiorari petitions it would consider. This was perhaps the most important development of the Taft Court.[2] Relieving the justices of their burdensome mandatory docket allowed them to focus on the most significant, and usually most contentious, issues of the day, and the implications of this for the decline of consensual decision making cannot be overstated. In short, the justices no longer faced large numbers of relatively easy cases on which they could all agree. Consider the comments of Justice John H. Clarke in his 1922 resignation letter to President Wilson:

> Much more than ½ the cases are of no considerable importance whether considered from the point of view of the principles or of the property involved in them, but, nevertheless, a conscientious judge writing them must master details with the utmost care. My theory of writing opinions has always been that if clearly stated 9 cases out of 10 will decide themselves,—what the decision should be will emerge from the statement of the facts as certainly as the issues will. . . . I protested often, but in vain, that too many trifling cases were being written, that our strength should be conserved for better things. (quoted in Post 2001, 22–23)

Some have dismissed Clark's remarks as the product of personal melancholy over his sister's death; however, Justice George Sutherland made similar comments. In his Senate testimony in favor of the Act, Sutherland explained that "a very large proportion of the cases that come" to the Court "ought never to be there at all" and that the justices were burdened by "a large number of trifling cases" (Post 2001, 23).

The Judges' Bill greatly limited the types of cases granted a mandatory appeal to the Supreme Court.[3] With this reduction of its mandatory jurisdiction, the Court could focus more attention on deciding important constitutional and statutory questions, and spend less time on routine appeals cases.

Not surprisingly, the justices increasingly chose to adjudicate cases containing difficult and complex legal issues of national importance—namely, those involving civil rights and liberties. Cases involving freedom of speech, religious liberty, privacy, the rights of the accused, and race and sex discrimination not only became a permanent feature of the annual caseload but also divided the justices as never before. Indeed, even the New Deal liberal justices appointed by Franklin Roosevelt differed on these and other matters. The establishment of the Supreme Court's discretionary docket was thus a key external development that helped usher in a new era of dissensus.

The Lawmaking Function: Legal Realism

Distaste with the legal formalism and conservative decisions of pre–New Deal conservative courts led to the intellectual movement known as legal realism (e.g., Frank 1936; Llewellyn 1930, 1962; Pound 1908). The notion of indeterminacy in law can trace its roots back before legal realism to the sociological jurisprudence of progressives who sought to use law to achieve social change. For them, the law was no longer a fixed set of principles used to settle narrow disputes but was now part of an ongoing debate over larger social issues. Loosely based on notions of legal indeterminacy and the centrality of individual judges, legal realism was never a school of thought or coherent critique of law and judging, and certainly it was not instructive for future jurisprudence (see, e.g., Kalman 1996). The Roosevelt Court was populated by the first generation of jurists who came of age under its influence. As a result, legal realism's lack of coherence manifested itself in a Court that continually grappled with the nature of judging. For example, Justice Frankfurter wrote Black in 1939:

> I think one of the evil features, a very evil one, about all this assumption that judges only find the law and don't make it, often becomes the evil of a lack of candor. By covering up the lawmaking function of judges, we miseducate the people and fail to bring out into the open the real responsibility of judges for what they do.[4]

David O'Brien (1999, 102) similarly explained: "[A]s a result of their disagreements over the course of liberal legalism and constitutional interpretation, the New Deal justices were inclined to articulate their distinctive views in individual opinions."

The discretionary docket and the theoretical shift from legal determinacy to legal realism resulted in a number of distinct changes. The length of opinions increased, as did the number of citations to past cases, law review articles, and other authorities (Post 2001; Kagan et al. 1978). With lengthier opinions containing increasing amounts of information, the justices had more to disagree with when determining whether to join an opinion and more to respond to and comment on when writing separately. The level of dissensus rose dramatically as a result.

Poisoning the Well of Collegiality: Stone and His Associates

While President Franklin Roosevelt may have failed to "pack the Court," he was successful in appointing justices who supported the New Deal. Roosevelt made nine appointments in all: Senator Hugo Black of Alabama (1937), U.S. Solicitor General Stanley Reed (1938), Professor Felix Frankfurter of Harvard Law School (1939), Securities and Exchange Commissioner William O. Douglas (1939), U.S. Attorney General Frank Murphy (1940), Senator James Byrnes of South Carolina (1941), U.S. Attorney General Robert Jackson (1941), and Judge Wiley B. Rutledge of the U.S. Court of Appeals (1943); he also elevated Harlan Fiske Stone to chief justice in 1941.

Stone served as chief justice for only five years, having been an associate justice for the preceding sixteen terms. When he was rumored to be Taft's replacement years before, Taft said that it would be "a great mistake," as "Stone is not a leader," and "would have a good deal of difficulty in massing the Court" (quoted in Mason 1964, 66). Taft's characterization may very well have been apt. Stone's behavior prior to his elevation suggests that he was often more interested in individual expression than in collective action.

As an associate justice, Stone found himself on the losing side in a number of bitterly divided 5–4 decisions: *Olmstead v. United States* (1928), which upheld warrantless wiretaps as long as a dwelling is not physically entered; *Railroad Retirement Board v. Alton Railroad Co.* (1935), in which the Court invalidated the Railroad Pension Act of 1934 on Due Process and Commerce Clause grounds; and *Morehead v. New York ex rel. Tipaldo* (1936), which struck down a state minimum wage law for women and children.

Furthermore, Stone issued dissents even when strong majorities were against him, as in *Federal Trade Commission v. Eastman Kodak Co.* (1927), about which he wrote Justice Edward T. Sanford: "I voted the other way, and I find myself unable to agree with your opinion notwithstanding its excellent form. I will let you know at the Conference whether I care to do anything further with respect to it."[5] The Court's opinion limited the FTC's regulatory power, and Stone decided to issue a dissent, which Justice Louis Brandeis joined. Similarly, Stone was the lone dissenter in *Minersville School District v. Gobitis* (1940), a case upholding compulsory flag salutes in public schools. His position against the policy became law three years later, however, when the Court reversed course in *West Virginia State Board of Education v. Barnette* (1943).

Stone was not shy in expressing his individual views by way of joining or authoring concurring opinions. For example, in *Sorrells v. United States*

(1932), in which the Court recognized entrapment as a defense based on the defendant's predisposition to commit the crime, he wrote Chief Justice Hughes: "I am holding your opinion . . . until I can give it a little more deliberate examination. . . . I am not much concerned about the result, but I think I am troubled by the process by which it is reached."[6] Ultimately Stone, as well as Brandeis, joined the separate concurrence issued by Roberts that rejected predisposition in favor of an analysis of the conduct of law enforcement. In another example, he wrote Hughes during the 1938 term: "I return herewith my concurrence in your opinion in the Labor Board case. It is excellent as far as it goes, but I do not think it goes quite far enough in one respect. . . . If you prefer not to make any change, I will be quite content to state my point very briefly in a separate memorandum, at the same time concurring in all that you have written."[7]

Stone's penchant for individual expression did not go unnoticed by his colleagues. For example, Justice James McReynolds advised him in a 1930 note: "All of us get into a fog now and then. . . . Won't you 'Stop, Look, and Listen'? In my view we have one member [Louis Brandeis] who is consciously boring from within. Of course, you have no such purpose, but you may unconsciously aid his purpose. At least do think twice on a subject—three times indeed. If the Court is broken down, then there will be rejoicing in certain quarters. I cannot think the last 3 dissents which you have sent me will aid you, the law or the Court."[8] Stone defended his actions and revealed his preference for more exchange among the justices both in Conference and in opinion writing and circulation:

> I am sure you will give me credit for being sincere in the views which I express. If I did not hold them strongly and believe that very many thoughtful men, trained in the law, would agree with them, I should not take the trouble to write any dissent. . . . I think you will not misunderstand me when I add that I am profoundly convinced that during that time some very serious mistakes have been made by the Court, which would not have been made had it not been for the disposition of the majority to rush to conclusions without taking the trouble to listen to the views of the minority. If the majority overrules the settled decisions of the Court, if it insists on including in opinions, over the protests of the minority, what is not necessary to the decision . . . if it insists on putting out opinions which do not consider or deal with questions raised by the minority, it must, I think, be expected that the minority will give some expression to their views. Otherwise, their function is reduced to registering a vote which is not even published. What I have written in Nos. 281 and 282 is, I think you will agree, at least worthy of consideration, but I was not even given an opportunity to state my position at the Conference. If the Court is willing to put out

> its opinion without meeting that argument or referring to its own decisions . . . any consequence for such ill considered action should not, I think, be attributed to me or what I have written.[9]

Chief Justice Taft was also concerned about the increasing level of individual expression and wrote Stone in 1927:

> I am quite anxious, as I am sure we all are, that the continuity and weight of our opinions on important questions of law should not be broken any more than we can help by dissents. Of course there are some who have deep convictions on the subject of the law governing the relations between employer and employee, whether it involves interstate commerce or not, and I suppose it is to be expected that in their attitude of protest in the past they should find distinctions enabling them to continue their attitude in cases presenting what are substantially the same issues; but with respect to those Judges who have come into the Court since these decisions were rendered, I am sure it is not their purpose to depart from what has been declared to be accepted law. . . . I hope you will look into this matter with care, because 5 to 4 decisions of the Court, while they must sometimes occur, don't help the weight of its judgment.[10]

Stone replied: "I, of course, appreciate the importance of avoiding dissents which do not seem necessary, and I am sure that you know me well enough now to know that I am not disposed to be opinionated or over-cocky about the opinions which I do hold."[11]

Stone did acquiesce at times, but he continued to issue separate opinions and went further by encouraging his colleagues to dissent in cases in which he voted with the minority. For example, he wrote Justice Roberts concerning the inheritance tax case *Coolidge v. Long* (1930): "I hope you are going to write something in . . . the Massachusetts Tax Cases. I think the Court is making the mistake which it has made before, of holding that a state tax is unconstitutional. . . . With your familiarity with the similar system of taxation in Pennsylvania, you will, I am sure, be able to demonstrate that it is within the state power."[12]

By the time of Hughes's retirement, Stone was more than halfway into his second decade on the Court, and Hughes recommended him to President Roosevelt for elevation to chief justice (Danelski and Tulchin 1973). However, Stone did little to temper the judicial and personal divides that had been brewing among the justices; rather, he helped foster them through his open, academic style. As a result, the justices of the Roosevelt Court were frequently engaged in personal and jurisprudential skirmishes. As they joined the Court, President Roosevelt's appointees immediately began testing the landscape.

Felix Frankfurter was a longtime Harvard Law professor, and many felt he would be a leader on the Roosevelt Court. He explained to Stanley Reed how he viewed his role: "The fact is that I am an academic and I have no excuse for being on this Court unless I remain so" (Urofsky 1991, 47). Frankfurter was notorious for his long speeches in Conference, lengthy memoranda of all kinds, and unrelenting lobbying of his colleagues and their clerks. For example, he wrote Stone regarding the Contract Clause case *Municipal Investors Assn. v. Birmingham* (1942): "I have had a go with Reed's law clerk but not yet with him on the *Birmingham* case."[13] Additionally, his verbose style and disparaging comments led to deteriorating relationships with many of his colleagues, including William O. Douglas, who eventually stopped speaking to him (Ferren 2004, 277). One day in Conference, Douglas announced: "When I came into Conference I agreed in the conclusion that Felix has just announced. But he's talked me out of it" (Urofsky 1991, 48). Frankfurter biographer Melvin Urofsky (1991, 48) concluded: "We can see the disastrous effects of Frankfurter's personalization of issues in the disintegration of the Court during the war years . . . Frankfurter, of course, does not share the full blame. . . . There is no doubt, however, that Frankfurter's behavior poisoned the well of collegiality."

For his part, Douglas drew the ire of the other justices for his public profile. Roberts became disillusioned with him, as well as his other colleagues, over what he saw as unprecedented activism and public posturing, including a press leak in the energy rate regulation case *Federal Power Commission v. Hope Natural Gas* (1944). Douglas vehemently denied that he was the source of the leak, writing Stone: "The rumor now floating in these halls is that I 'leaked' the *Hope Natural Gas* story to Drew Pearson through Tom Corcoran. That is an outright, contemptible lie. There is not a grain of truth in it . . . I never breathed a word about any case pending before the Court to them or to anyone else, at that time or at any other time."[14]

Despite Douglas's denials, Roberts no longer lunched with the other justices, refused to join them in the robing room for the traditional handshake before taking the bench, stopped speaking to most of them, and limited his Conference contributions to terse statements of his vote (Ferren 2004; Newman 1994). When he retired at the close of the 1944 term, his colleagues could not agree on the customary farewell letter after Black balked at language in Stone's initial draft, and no letter was ever sent.

Robert Jackson's appointment created further personal problems—particularly with respect to his relationship with Hugo Black. When Jackson accepted President Truman's offer to be the chief Nazi prosecutor at the end of World War II, the other justices were displeased that they were not consulted, that Jackson was entering the political arena, and that they would have to increase their workloads to make up for his absence. But it was the case of *Jewell Ridge Coal Corp v. United Mine Workers of America* (1945) that led to the greatest acrimony. The Court held that mine workers could be compensated for time spent traveling to work sites while underground. The final decision was 5–4, with Black in the majority and Jackson in dissent. However, Jackson felt that Black should have recused himself in the case because the miners were represented by Black's former law partner and personal lawyer Crampton P. Harris, and he filed an opinion explaining his position. The strained relationship between the two never recovered.

Internal Developments: Conference Discussion, Opinion Writing, Circulation Delays, and Reargument

Already influenced by legal realism and with a now largely discretionary docket, the new justices of the Roosevelt Court decided to alter a number of long-standing procedures. The result was expanded Conference discussions, opinion writing and circulation delays, and an increase in reargument of cases. While it is theoretically possible that each of these practices could have fostered consensus, the justices of the Roosevelt Court instead exploited them for individual purposes. Though they may not have been fully aware of it at the time, the internal practices they developed undermined consensus and entrenched dissensus as successor justices joined their ranks. In this section, we detail how the internal changes made by Stone and his colleagues fundamentally transformed their ability, and that of future justices, to achieve consensus.

Free Speech for Everybody: Expanded Conference Discussion

Stone's ideal of how the Court should function was forged during his service under Chief Justice William Howard Taft. On the Taft Court, the justices exercised considerable freedom of expression during their private Conference discussions, particularly Justice Willis Van Devanter, who served as "task leader" because of what Taft recognized as "his power of statement and his immense memory."[15] Stone recalled Taft's collegial style: "When I first went on the Court in Taft's time the discussion was very free, although sometimes discursive. During the last of his service there was much more inclination to rush things through especially if he thought he had the support of certain members of the Court" (quoted in Mason 1964, 66–67).

Chief Justice Hughes, in contrast, ran the Conference in an efficient, almost autocratic fashion. He recounted case facts from his photographic memory and stated his opinion, and at times the justices simply voted for the outcome he suggested. When there was discussion, each justice stated his views in order of seniority. Hughes would then comment and call for a vote in reverse order. As a result, all discussion began and ended with him. Roberts recalled: "The Chief Justice was an intense man. When he had serious business to transact he allowed no consideration to interfere with his operations. He was so engrossed in the vital issues that he had not time for lightness and pleasantry" (quoted in Danelski 1960, 10).

Roosevelt's appointees who served with Hughes, including Stone, felt stifled and wished for Conference discussions entailing a more meaningful exchange. For example, after reading Stanley Reed's opinion in the tax case *Higgins v. Smith* (1939), Stone responded: "As I stated at the conference, I think I prefer to put the opinion on [a different] ground. . . . I think I shall probably adhere to that view but I will wait to see what happens at the conference."[16] Douglas (1980, 222–223) recalled Stone's frustration: "The manner in which Hughes conducted the Conference annoyed Stone. . . . Stone was, first, last and always, a professor who wanted to search out every point and unravel every skein. So he instituted the custom of having a rump conference at his house every Friday afternoon after the Court. He would preside as the de facto Chief Justice and discuss all the cases to be decided the next day. . . . This rump conference seemed to bring Stone satisfaction because he could express himself." Frankfurter, too, subtly sowed the seeds of dissatisfaction with the relatively brief Conferences. He wrote Stone in 1939: "I am sending this to you as a continuation of a discussion for which there was no adequate time in Conference."[17] Similarly, he wrote Stone later that same year: "The atmosphere Saturday afternoon was hardly conducive to a clarifying exchange of views."[18]

Once Stone succeeded Hughes, the Conference atmosphere changed immediately. As Frankfurter (1953, 902) recalled: "[Stone] was a very different personality from Hughes. . . . Stone was much more easy-going. The conference was more leisurely. The atmosphere was less taut, both in the courtroom and the conference room." After presiding over his first Conference, Stone wrote Frankfurter: "To tell the truth, yesterday was a happy day, because we succeeded in doing our job more completely than I had dared to hope earlier in the week. It was the more so because I am convinced that all this was accomplished without foreclosing desirable discussion or curtailing adequate consideration of the questions on which we had to pass."[19]

But if Conferences under Hughes were too businesslike, Stone's were criticized as too academic and freewheeling. Stone's dramatic expansion of Conference discussion not only failed to increase consensus but ultimately exasperated his colleagues. Even Frankfurter—long a proponent of increased deliberation—sought to limit individual sessions to improve the quality of exchange. He wrote Stone after the first Conference of the 1942 term:

> The easy-going, almost heedless way in which views on Constitutional issues touching the whole future direction of this country were floated Saturday afternoon leads me to put to you a conviction I formed in regard to Conferences not long after I came on the Court. It is that it would be conducive to the most fruitful results if we kept the Conferences as rigorously within the four hour schedule as we do our sessions in open Court. . . . The mind is called upon not only to think hard with the kind of responsibility which really takes it out of one, namely, the responsibility of decision, but to do all this in the interplay of nine personalities. Surely the law of diminishing returns sets in after four hours of that sort of intellectual tension. On more than one Saturday I have noted that the discussion after four-thirty gave evidence of fatigued minds and occasionally of frayed nerves.[20]

Frankfurter responded when his colleagues heard of his desire to change the Conference format:

> Some of you at least have understood me as suggesting we contract discussion at Conference. That is precisely not my view. . . . To decide cases with inadequate discussion is to disregard the conception of a Court. . . . My only point is that the discussion should be by fresh and not fatigued minds. The kind of intellectual effort that is implied by discussion among nine judges concerning such problems as come before us cannot, I believe as a psychological fact, be sustained best for more than four hours. My suggestion, therefore, is not that we should contract discussion but that our Conferences should be restricted to four hours as well as our sessions in open Court, that we should stop promptly at the end of four hours and begin anew at the second or even a third Conference.[21]

However, despite repeated attempts to reform Conference discussion, the problem only got worse. Douglas (1980, 222–223) explained:

> When Stone became Chief Justice, our Conference was never finished by four-thirty or five. We moved the starting time back, first to eleven and then to ten o'clock, but we still could not finish by six on Saturday. We would come back at ten o'clock on Monday and sit until five minutes before noon, and then go into Court for four hours to hear cases argued. We would again go into Conference at four and sit until five or six. Sometimes we still would be unfinished by the end of the day and have to go back into Conference at ten on Tuesday morning, and again at four in the afternoon on Tuesday. Once we even had Conference on Wednesday from ten to noon and from

four to six—to finish up the previous Saturday's Conference List. Under Stone we were, in other words, almost in continuous Conference. He believed in free speech for everybody, including himself.

A notable result of long Conferences was a rise in dissensus on the Court, as David Danelski (1960, 23) explained:

The unprecedented number of dissents and concurrences during Stone's Chief Justiceship can be only partly attributed to the displacing of the old tradition of loyalty to the Court's opinion. A major source of difficulty appears to have been the free-and-easy expression of views in conference. Whether the justices were sure of their grounds or not, they spoke up and many times took positions from which they could not easily retreat . . . [and thus] what began in conference frequently ended with elaborate justification as concurring or dissenting opinions in the United States Reports.

Inexcusable Delay: Opinion Writing

For most justices, opinion writing is a long and arduous process. At the close of the 1943 term, Stone wrote Frankfurter: "I am only beginning, now that opinion writing is over, to find out what is on my desk."[22] Try as they might, many of the justices of the Roosevelt Court were unable or unwilling to draft their opinions in a timely manner, thereby prolonging an already lengthy process. Increased time meant longer opinions with more arguments to disagree about and more time to find disagreement.

Because of these delays, Chief Justice Stone regularly struggled with opinion assignments—particularly as newly appointed justices were continually arriving. Wiley Rutledge had been on the Court for only a little over four months, but felt that he was not doing his fair share of the work. He wrote Stone at the end of the 1942 term:

You have been more than easy upon me in assignments and, frankly, I have something of a feeling that I have not done my full share here this spring, certainly not as much of the total load as I had hoped to be able to carry, and I am afraid that a very considerable part of this has fallen upon your own shoulders. That I regret. Nevertheless, I want you to know I appreciate your considerate understanding and also that I hope to be able to function more efficiently and effectively in the fall than I have up to now.[23]

Stone replied:

The matter of assignments is a most perplexing and difficult task with the Chief Justice. There are so many and competing angles which have to be recognized. I have long thought, though, that a new judge beginning the work of the Court should be put at his ease in taking on the work until he is thoroughly familiar with it. I have much hope that next year we will have the experience, which we have not had for some years, of a court working through the term without changes. It will be amazing how much better we can do our work and how much more easily we can carry it on under those conditions.[24]

Particularly because of the proliferation of separate opinions, opinion writing became so prolonged that Stone even proposed extending recess in order to concentrate on it.[25] As the justices took more time to craft lengthier opinions, their colleagues took more time to consider their positions. As a result, the relatively new process of opinion circulation changed.

Stewing over Their Worries: Opinion Circulation

Though the practice of formally circulating opinions had been in place since the Fuller Court, under Stone an important check on the norm dissolved. Prior to the Stone Court, comments were returned to the opinion author within twenty-four hours of circulation. Now, however, the divides in Conference carried over into circulation practices, with justices taking more time to respond to draft opinions. When their suggestions were not met, they were more likely to issue separate opinions than at any time in the Court's history. An academic atmosphere pervaded the Court, and delays became common to the point that justices pushed for cases to be reargued.

Stone outlined the Court's circulation practices in a memorandum to newly appointed Justices James Byrnes and Robert Jackson:

So far as may be, opinions are written during recess and considered and approved at the conference held at the end of the recess, and are handed down on the following Monday. When the opinion is prepared and printed the writer sends page proofs of the opinion, usually by messenger, to each member of the Court. The recipient is expected to examine the opinion promptly and if he agrees with it return it to the writer with his concurrence or approval endorsed on the back of the opinion, noting such suggestions as to change in form or phraseology as he thinks desirable. If his suggestions affect the substance or require extensive change of the opinion, he should send the suggestion in memorandum form or call on the writer of the opinion and explain fully his views. If he voted with the writer of the opinion but is unable to agree with the opinion, he should promptly notify the writer to that effect. Prompt examination and return of the opinions, where that can be done by reasonable effort, greatly facilitates the work of the Court and avoids the congestion in the printer's office which would ensue if all the opinions were returned late in the recess period.[26]

But even Stone had trouble sticking to twenty-four hours. Sometimes he would "hold" an opinion and reserve judgment in order to see what others might say. For example, after reading Frankfurter's opinion in *National Broadcasting Co. v. United States* (1943), in which the Court held that the Federal Communications Commission had the power to issue regulations concerning broadcast networks and their affiliates, Stone wrote: "I think you have done a very thorough-going job on these cases, and I shall accept your opinion unless someone is moved to write. In that case I shall reserve judgment until I see what he has to say."[27] Ultimately, he joined the majority despite a dissent from Justice Frank Murphy. Similarly, he wrote Robert H. Jackson after reading his majority opinion in the flag salute–pledge of allegiance case *West Virginia Board of Education v. Barnette* (1943), which overturned *Gobitis*: "You have done a good job, and I am holding your opinion to see what Brother Frankfurter has to say about it."[28] Frankfurter issued a dissent, but Stone stayed with the majority.

Occasionally, Stone would ask that an opinion be returned to him after the author had seen his comments on the draft, as in this letter to Douglas: "I am returning your opinion herewith, with my approval, but after you have looked it over I will be glad if you will return it to me so that I can see the force of anything that others may write."[29] At other times, he would ask to see a proposed majority opinion a second time, usually after the circulation of separate opinions, as when he wrote Chief Justice Hughes: "When I read the Black and Douglas dissent to your opinion . . . I wondered whether I had completely misread your opinion. It is for that reason that I sent for it."[30]

Circulation delays were by no means solely within Stone's purview. Jackson wrote Stone concerning the inheritance tax case *Utah v. Aldrich* (1942): "I have filed a dissenting opinion. If there is not need for haste in the matter, I would like to have it go over."[31] Stone noted: "Douglas agrees to let this wait." Similarly, Frankfurter wrote Stone in 1939: "Your jurisdictional analysis is powerful, but I am still struggling with doubts, and I would like to sleep on them, instead of either acquiescing with an inner restlessness or writing something that would be too superficial. I wonder, therefore, if you would mind letting me stew over my worries, and see whether they do not evaporate with a little more time or precipitate into something I could show you with self-respect. Would it bother you, therefore, if the opinion went over until next week?"[32]

Ultimately, Frankfurter grew frustrated with the old mechanics of circulating opinions—a process that fostered consensus—and proposed a new system, one that eventually led to greater dissensus. Prompted by the right-to-counsel case *Hawk v. Olson* (1945), he wrote Stone:

Reed's memorandum setting forth various changes in his *Hawk* opinion emphasizes the very unsatisfactory situation due to the practice of circulating to members of the Court only one copy of proposed opinions. If one is in agreement with an opinion, or agrees with proposed modifications, one naturally returns it. One may of course withhold it and send a separate note, indicating proposed changes. The latter is unsatisfactory and unduly time-taking both for the writer of an opinion and for its critic. But unless one holds on to the opinion subsequent changes, such as those proposed by Reed in his *Hawk* opinion, it cannot be appraised with the necessary care that is called for where every word, and even every nuance, may make a difference because if not meticulously considered may come to plague one in the future.

The short of it is that two copies of every opinion ought to be circulated so that one may be returned and the other withheld to await the event. It does seem almost funny that the Supreme Court of the United States should be denied this obvious means of doing its job competently because it may entail what surely cannot be more than a negligible few dollars for extra printing costs.[33]

In *Oklahoma Press Publishing Co. v. Walling* (1946), which applied the Fair Labor Standards Act to newspaper publishing and distribution, Justice Rutledge grew so frustrated by the delays and qualifiers from his colleagues that he sought to have the case reassigned:

After a second circulation, which was accompanied by a memorandum requesting justices in accord upon the result to give me the benefit of whatever suggestions they might have for revision of the opinion, the status of the case is (and has been for more than three weeks) as follows: Mr. Justice Reed has concurred in the opinion. The Chief Justice has asked me to rewrite the opinion, as I understand his request, without reference to or discussion of either private corporations or self-incrimination. Mr. Justice Black has indicated he has suggestions to make, whenever the case otherwise may be ready to go down. Mr. Justice Frankfurter has indicated he will have certain suggestions to make. I have not heard from Mr. Justice Douglas or Mr. Justice Burton. Mr. Justice Murphy voted in dissent.

In these circumstances, it seems obvious that I will not be able to write an opinion for the Court. I do not wish to be responsible for holding up the disposition of the case longer. Accordingly I now return the case to the Chief Justice and ask that he reassign it to some other justices for writing. To avoid any possible invidious personal implication, I desire to state, in advance of reassignment, that I shall either file a statement of my own views or concur in the result, on the final disposition of this case.[34]

But nearly two weeks later, after Stone had reassigned the case to himself, there seemed to be more consensus. Rutledge informed him: "Justice Burton has indicated his concurrence in the opinion. . . . Justice Douglas has indicated his agreement. . . . So have Justices Black and Frankfurter. Justice Reed has concurred."[35] Stone then suggested that Rutledge continue with his draft, and Rutledge agreed, further explaining: "If I created in your mind the notion that I was washing my hands of the case I am sorry, for that was not really my intention. At the time I circulated the original memorandum, in view of the situation which it set forth concerning the responses and lack of responses which I had received after two submissions, I thought that I could not satisfy a majority."[36] Stone replied: "I took the case very reluctantly and only because I thought you felt that you were at the end of your rope."[37] As it turned out, only Murphy issued a separate opinion—a dissent—from Rutledge's majority opinion. Still, the hand-wringing over this case demonstrates the difficulty the justices faced in achieving consensus, especially as certain justices pushed for increased opinion circulation of and input on final opinions.

The Quality of the Clearing: Rearguing Cases

The lengthier and more academic atmosphere in Conference and delays in opinion writing and circulation led to a further slowing down of the wheels of justice through calls for cases to be reargued. One would think that cases needing reargument would be those in which the justices felt the initial argument or the legal briefs were lacking. On the contrary—internal memoranda of the Stone Court reveal that the justices had little faith in better-quality arguments or briefs the second time around. Instead, they pushed for reargument to give themselves more time, and with that extra time disagreements flourished.

For example, during the debate over whether or not to schedule reargument in the landmark Commerce Clause case *Wickard v. Filburn* (1942), Frankfurter wrote Stone: "If the Act is to be sustained, it would be much healthier to have a decision so far-reaching in its practical application made after adequate argument and after the kind of reflection by members of the Court upon the issues that simply could not be achieved in these last hurried days of the term."[38] Jackson agreed: "The performance of the Court below and of the plaintiff's counsel gives little hope that they would much sharpen the real issue, and I am afraid that most of the Government men feel too sure of the Court to bother with enlightening it. So I would avoid the row with Black. . . . on the method and with such meager help as we will get from reargument settle down in the fall to deciding the merits."[39] Stone wrote his colleagues: "In this case Justice Reed takes no part. Justice Black and Justice Douglas are for prompt disposition of the case now, not reargument.

The other members of the Court, except myself, desire reargument. . . . I therefore am assuming that the case will be assigned for reargument."[40] The case eventually was reargued the following term, and the justices did reach agreement on the merits.

Reargument became a standard device used by subsequent justices. According to Hoekstra and Johnson (2003), it occurred in fifty-nine cases during the Vinson Court, in forty-seven during the Warren Court, and in sixty-six during the Burger Court. They concluded: "When the conference vote produces a minimum-winning coalition the case is more likely to be held over for reargument. We argue that the justices recognize this situation as one where the outcome is uncertain because of the instability of the coalition, and they therefore use reargument to obtain more information" (356).

Writing for a Law Review: Promoting an Academic Atmosphere

Expanded Conference discussion, opinion-drafting and circulation delays, and an increased number of rearguments were endemic to the larger academic atmosphere fostered by the justices of the Roosevelt Court. Rather than speedily resolving cases with minimal writing, they increasingly saw their function as thoroughly explicating the relevant legal issues by maximizing the written word. And no single justice had as great a hand in promoting academic values on the bench than former Harvard Law professor Felix Frankfurter.

A little over one month after being sworn in, Frankfurter explained to Stone why he was issuing a separate opinion in the death tax standing case *Texas v. Florida* (1939):

> If the Green case [the deceased against whose estate taxes were being levied] were the end of it—if there were no others in prospect—I would not care about it and hold my tongue. I don't want to be a Cassandra, but I will bet dollars to doughnuts that this is but the beginning of efforts to push us further and further into taking these . . . controversies. . . . You will, of course, tell me with complete freedom what you think about my draft. In many ways what I have cherished most since I have come on the Court is the feeling you have conveyed to me, that we ought to deal with one another's opinions as though they were writings in a law review.[41]

Once again, Frankfurter likened his new job as justice to that of his old as professor in this exchange over his majority opinion in the Native American tax case *Board of Comm'rs of Jackson County v. United States* (1939). Hugo Black circulated a separate concurring opinion, and Frankfurter wrote him a three-and-a-half-page memo on the nature of judging: "Just because we agree in the result . . . and because no immediately important public issue is involved by our different approaches in reaching the same legal result, it is at once interesting and profitable to discuss the underlying jurisprudential problem. And so I venture to make some observations on your opinion, I hope in the same spirit and for the same academic purpose as I would were I writing a piece as a professor in the *Harvard Law Review*."[42]

Despite Stone's attempt to quash Frankfurter's proposed concurrence in the utility rate case *Driscoll v. Edison Light & Power Co.* (1939), Frankfurter persisted:

> You know the weight I attach to your judgment, and how very deeply I weigh your counsel for intrinsic reasons as well as because of the garnered wisdom of your experience here. Naturally, your observations about my concurrence . . . made me pause and reconsider what already had received as much anxious thought as anything that has confronted me since I have come down here. These are, of course, matters of delicate judgment and ultimately of an abiding inner feeling. But after worrying about it and literally spending sleepless moments over it, I should be suppressing a deep conviction if I said nothing about Reed's opinion.[43]

The "deep convictions" of the Roosevelt Court justices had reshaped the Court from one in which institutional opinions were the norm into a body of law professors who saw their job as constructing individual law review articles.

Though Frankfurter was unquestionably its chief educator, it is plain that the Roosevelt Court's other justices viewed their roles in academic terms as well. Perpetual Conferences became intensive seminars in the law. Delays in opinion writing and circulation were increasingly common as justices became more thoughtful in responding to opinions. When one term did not allow enough time to fully explore the issues in a case, they pushed for reargument. This new conception of judging ultimately led to important changes in the Supreme Court's internal practices and forever changed the nature of decision making for subsequent Courts.

Institutional Effects: Dissensus in Majority and Minority Coalitions

In the previous sections we detailed how changes in a number of external and internal practices undermined Supreme Court consensus. Legal realism, a discretionary docket, and rapid personnel changes, coupled with expanded Conference discussion, opinion writing and circulation delays, case reargument, and an overall academic atmosphere created conditions for individual expression to flourish. But what form did this burgeoning dissensus take?

The personal and jurisprudential divides on the Roosevelt Court manifested themselves in numerous ways. In this section we highlight how the institutional developments previously discussed affected the behavior of both majority and minority coalitions. First, we detail how majority coalitions fractured in new ways. Specifically, the norm of acquiescence declined, majority opinions began departing from Conference views, and concurrences became common tools to express individual disagreement with majority and minority opinions. Second, minority coalitions increasingly formed and strengthened. Justices began to write dissents to express small disagreements, to address issues not raised in petitions, or to criticize concurrences. Furthermore, a feeling of solidarity among dissenting coalitions grew as minority coalition members praised circulated draft dissents. These practices became norms that served to entrench a culture of dissensus that lasts to this day.

Taking a Different View: Majority Coalition Behavior

Acquiescence was a common practice for most of the Court's history. Those who cast minority votes in Conference routinely chose to remain silent, or to acquiesce, rather than note or write a dissent. Acquiescence gave majority opinions the appearance of greater unanimity than they actually enjoyed. For example, when Stone expressed concerns over Oliver Wendell Holmes's opinion in the bond contract case *Leach v. Peirson* (1927), Holmes wrote him: "The only thing I can say in answer to your scruples . . . is that I don't share them. . . . I see it differently. All I can say is that I can't—and don't see anything to agree. The opinion is affirmed by all but Brandeis who says I shall not dissent."[44] In the end, Stone, like Brandeis, acquiesced. Stone also acquiesced in the Federal Employers' Liability Act case *Chesapeake & Ohio v. Leitch* (1928) after writing Holmes: "I have your opinion. . . . I voted the other way. . . . I don't think I care to note a dissent unless others do, but I will wait and see."[45] In another example from the 1944 term, Stone wrote Frankfurter: "I voted the other way in this case but I shall acquiesce in the decision unless some of my brethren see the light and point out that you cracked the law in order to satisfy your moral scruples. But if I do go along I beg of you to take out of the opinion . . . two references."[46]

Over time, the justices of the Roosevelt Court increasingly shunned acquiescence in favor of individual expression. The example of *Polish National Alliance v. Labor Board* (1944) illustrates the unwillingness of opinion writers to accommodate their colleagues, making acquiescence difficult for justices with concerns and ultimately resulting in separate opinions. What began as a seemingly simple unanimous *per curiam* opinion sustaining an unfair labor practice order devolved into dissensus in the form of a separate concurrence. Stone assigned the *per curiam* to Frankfurter, but Frankfurter was unable to incorporate the views of the Conference. He wrote Stone:

> I believe I am not behind any of my brethren in the desire to achieve the utmost of public expression that our resourcefulness can contrive in a situation involving such contrariety of views as that engendered by the insurance cases. And if that can be achieved by a *per cur* in the *Polish Alliance* case I am all for it. But I am sure nobody wants to be a party even to a *per cur* that does not accurately reflect the record. . . . Accordingly, I have drawn up and enclose herewith the *per cur* such as this record alone justifies.[47]

Stone replied:

> I, of course, agree with you fully about the case. . . . I am perfectly willing to join in a *per curiam*. . . . Unfortunately, Brother Black and his associates take a different view, with which you and I do not agree, but which nevertheless they wish to have stated in the *per curiam* as representing their position. . . . I do not object to the *per curiam* stating that that is the position of a given number of members of the Court, however much I disagree with it. Unless we are prepared to go that far, it seems to me we cannot avoid putting down all the opinions. In the present posture of the case I would prefer to have them go down, stated in shorthand fashion, than to have them elaborated.[48]

Stone's attempt to "save" the *per curiam* and prevent the Court from issuing separate opinions in the case failed. In the end, Frankfurter issued a majority opinion while Black issued a concurrence joined by Douglas and Murphy.

Majority opinion authors who did not faithfully follow the consensus achieved at Conference were taken to task by their colleagues and their recalcitrance served to bolster potential dissenting voices. For example, Douglas circulated an opinion for the Court in the search and seizure case *Davis v. United States* (1946); Stone's memorandum to the Conference stated: "The proposed opinion in the *Davis* case goes on a ground which, in its essentials, was not the ground on which the case was voted to be affirmed at Conference. And, unless my memory fails me, it was not a ground which was urged by any member of the Conference. (This is not to imply that a case should not be written on new ground.)."[49] In the end, Stone sided with the majority, but Frankfurter, Murphy, and Rutledge dissented.

A more complex issue arose in the all-white primary case *Smith v. Allwright* in 1944. Stone initially assigned the opinion to Frankfurter, but Jackson suggested "that the Court's decision, bound to arouse bitter resentment, will be much less apt to stir ugly reactions if the news that the white primary has been outlawed is broken to it, if possible, by a Southerner who has been a Democrat and is not a member of one of the minorities which stir prejudices kindred to those against Negros."[50] The chief justice subsequently reassigned the case to Reed. In response, Frankfurter lobbied Reed to change his opinion, suggested that Stone write a separate opinion, and ultimately had Reed note at the bottom of the majority opinion: "Mr. Justice Frankfurter concurs in the result." Frankfurter wrote Stone: "I tried hard to make Reed give the *Allwright* opinion the form and atmosphere of aggressive candor so as to avoid a needless grievance on the score of how we are doing what we are doing. But Reed had his own notions of appeasement which are bound to fail as is all appeasement not rooted in reason. Something like this I feel should be said. Of course it would be best of all if you said it. If you do, I shall eagerly suppress this."[51] Ultimately, the Court failed to reach unanimity, with Roberts issuing a dissent along with Frankfurter's concurring notation. As Frankfurter's behavior demonstrates, concurring in the judgment only further undermined consensus.

Consensus was undermined as well by members of the majority coalition criticizing both circulated dissents and attempts by majority opinion authors to address dissenters' concerns. For example, when Douglas circulated a proposed dissent to Jackson's majority opinion upholding an Interstate Commerce Commission ruling on the Motor Carrier Act of 1935 in *Gregg Cartage & Storage Co. v. United States* (1942), Stone advised Jackson: "While I think all that you say in the new material added to the opinion in this case is true . . . still I have some doubts whether you should accept it. . . . I am inclined to think that you should stand your ground. I am only making this by way of suggestion. I should not care to say anything further unless someone else did."[52] In the end, Douglas dissented and was joined by Black and Byrnes.

The rise in dissents also led to a new form and level of importance for concurrences: responding to the dissent. Thus, the 1943 term marked a turning point in the development of dissensus. For the first time justices issued concurring opinions for the sole purpose of critiquing a dissent. Frankfurter was the first target. In two cases handed down in the middle of the term—the patent case *Mercoid Corporation v. Mid-Continent Investment Co.* (1944) and the rate-fixing case *Federal Power Commission v. Hope Natural*

Gas (1944)—he dissented from the respective majority opinions written by Douglas. Frankfurter's critiques were harsh. He wrote Stone about Douglas's *Mercoid* opinion:

> From what I have circulated you will know that I am the opposite of happy over his perfectly gratuitous treatment of 'contributory infringement.' Nor am I happy over his treatment of *res judicata*. . . . Am I wrong in finding at present a too eager tendency not merely to bring the law in conformity to our present needs but gloatingly to show up the unwisdom, if not injustice, of our predecessors? If such an attitude is good for society then I wholly misconceive the notion and the function of Law.[53]

In each case, Black and Murphy issued concurring opinions that sharply chastised Frankfurter for relying on his own "preconceived views on 'morals' and 'ethics'" in the former case and for advancing a "patently . . . wholly gratuitous assertion as to Constitutional law" in the latter. These "counter-dissents," as Judge John Ferren (2004) termed them, further institutionalized dissensus. And while the disagreements on the Court had a basis in law, they were almost certainly exacerbated by personal discord.

Going Too Far: Minority Coalition Behavior

Minority coalition behavior was also transformed during the Roosevelt Court. But, unlike the fracturing of majority coalitions, minority coalitions became stronger and more common. An increased number of dissenting votes and opinions was the most obvious effect of the institutional changes that occurred, yet there were several other outgrowths that reflected the dissensus revolution in which the justices were engaged.

The institutional norm of dissenting once in an issue area but acquiescing in subsequent cases—a practice that Louis Brandeis said even the "great dissenter" Oliver Wendell Holmes routinely followed during his years on the bench—disappeared as new justices such as Hugo Black and William O. Douglas consistently noted every dissent. Stone himself issued more separate opinions as chief justice than he had as a member of the Hughes Court (O'Brien 1999). Indeed, Stone dissented more often than any chief before or since, and his colleagues were not shy in urging him to do so. For example, Frankfurter wrote him following the Conference vote in *Schneiderman v. United States* (1943), in which the Court overturned the government's decision to denaturalize a citizen for membership in the Communist Party: "Your exposition of *Schneiderman* was masterly. You must lay it out in your dissent with all the powerful detail with which you stated the case to us. The requirement of being 'attached to the principles of the Constitution of the United States' carries an historic meaning not lessened by time, to which you will, I know, give magisterial illumination and authority in your dissent."[54]

Willingness to dissent over relatively small disagreements with a majority opinion was another way in which consensus was undermined. For example, in *United States v. Classic* (1941), Douglas, joined by Black and Murphy, issued a dissent even though he agreed with the central holding of Stone's majority opinion that Congress's power to regulate federal elections includes primaries. The Court upheld the federal government's use of the Enforcement Act of 1870 to prosecute corrupt primary election officials, but the dissenters saw this as too broad an interpretation of a statute that was enacted prior to the existence of primaries and therefore should, in their minds, be limited to general elections. Douglas (1980, 330) wrote: "So I agree with most of the views expressed in the opinion of the Court. And it is with diffidence that I dissent from the result there reached."

Dissenters were also increasingly willing to raise issues not brought up by the parties to the case. This controversial tactic is illustrated in the following exchange over *Medo Photo Supply Corp. v. Labor Board* (1944), in which the Court upheld the board's unfair labor practices ruling. Rutledge had written Stone to let him know he had decided to dissent, arguing "that this case simply goes too far."[55] Stone replied:

> Your proposed dissent in this case seems to me to take up questions which were not raised by the petition for certiorari and which certainly I had not thought that the Court was deciding. . . . It is not the habit of the Court to decide questions not raised by the petition for certiorari, and no action was taken by the conference authorizing a different course. The writer of a dissent is of course a free-lance and he can go as far afield as he likes. But it is not usual for one to dissent on a ground not raised by the petition or decided by the Court, and which he has not asked the conference to consider. A dissent under such circumstances places the majority in the false attitude of deciding against a proposition which they have never been asked to decide either by the petitioner or the dissenter.[56]

Finally, dissenting opinions began incorporating criticisms of concurring opinions. For example, in *Korematsu v. United States* (1944), upholding the internment of Japanese Americans during World War II, Roberts informed his colleagues: "I shall add a paragraph to my dissenting opinion, on page 6, as follows: Concurring opinions filed in the case seem to attribute to me the view that the petitioner was convicted of disobeying an order to go to an Assembly Center, or of disobeying an order to immure himself in a Relocation

Center. . . . I have yet to hear any answer to the proposition that the petitioner was at the same time subject to two conflicting orders."[57]

Both majority and minority coalitions were greatly affected by the external and internal developments detailed in previous sections. Institutional changes such as the discretionary docket and expanded Conference discussion led to a number of divisive consequences: the breakdown of the norm of acquiescence, the departure of Court opinions from Conference views, and the use of concurrences to express disagreement with both majority and dissenting coalitions. Minority coalitions also became increasingly common and were bolstered by justices who noted every dissent and disagreement over small issues, including those not raised in the petitions. Finally, dissenting justices praised each other, thereby solidifying their formal opposition rather than acquiescing or working for consensus. These discordant practices became behavioral norms for future justices as they joined the Roosevelt Court holdovers who continued them.

Danger in Dissent: Contemporaneous Reactions

Contemporary writers noted from the start of the Roosevelt Court the unprecedented levels of dissensus, and they sensed a fundamental shift in the Court's internal decision making practices. The press covered the internal rifts and asked the Court to make changes. For their part, the justices many times reacted defensively and expressed little desire to modify their behavior. For example, on January 6, 1944, the *New York Herald Tribune* published a critique by an anonymous "Member of the Bar of the Supreme Court" entitled the "Danger in Dissent":

> On Jan. 3, the Supreme Court of the United States handed down thirteen opinions in twenty-one cases. In four of these the court was unanimous; in nine there were dissents as follows: three 5 to 4, two 6 to 3, one 5 to 3, one 7 to 2, two 8 to 1. The justices who dissented and the number of their dissents were Murphy 5, Black, Reed and Frankfurter 4 each, Roberts 3, Douglas 2, Stone . . . C. J. 1, Rutledge 1.
>
> It is not to be expected that the justices will always agree, but there seems to be a growing tendency to disagree; and if this is not checked the effect on the public will be unfortunate, making for doubt and uncertainty and a lack of respect and a loss of confidence in the court. . . .
>
> A court of last resort, whether in a state or in the Federal system, exists for the purpose not merely of determining the rights of the parties but in order to settle the law, so that the whole body of citizens may know what it is and what it will continue to be. The turnabout of the Supreme Court in the case of Jehovah's Witnesses is a glaring instance of uncertainty. Two justices reversed themselves within three years.

One would think that in cases involving the Bill of Rights a judge would know his own mind in 1940 as well as in 1943. . . .

One of the least desirable practices that has grown up in the Supreme Court in recent years is the concurring opinion in which a justice who agrees with the decision but is dissatisfied with the language of the opinion or its implications insists on expressing himself in his own words.

In this last batch of decisions two of the justices have indulged themselves in concurring opinions criticizing the approach and attitude if not the character of one of their colleagues. This breach of judicial propriety is in violation of the high traditions and the dignity of the court.

The Supreme Court is not a mere judicial tribunal of nine men; it is a co-ordinate branch of our government charged with grave responsibilities and endowed with great authority and power. Personal differences should be confined within the council chamber and not proclaimed from the bench.[58]

The editors of the newspaper noted that the letter was written by "a lawyer of distinction, for whose judgment the *Herald Tribune* has the greatest respect." They continued: "The present court is a relatively new body. It is dealing with new concepts of government. Therefore, it was to be expected that some time would elapse before it shook down into a workable team. Unfortunately, the record appears to show that this goal is as far from realization as ever, if not farther than ever. In the interests of the people, who must know the law to abide by it, one may hope that this trend will be reversed—and speedily."[59] Stone circulated the articles to the other justices with a note:

Attached is a clipping from a recent *New York Herald Tribune*, which comes to me from an anonymous sender. I do not know who the writers are, but they are evidently friends of the Court as an institution. Their articles seem well intentioned and merit our prayerful consideration.

I do not find myself in full accord with them, but I desire to make only the following comments. The right of dissent is an important one and has proved to be such in the history of the Supreme Court. I do not think it is the appropriate function of a Chief Justice to attempt to dissuade members of the Court from dissenting in individual cases. Nevertheless I feel free to say that there is considerable scope for judicial self-restraint in the matter of dissent, lest its usefulness and effectiveness be impaired by its abuse. It is not necessary to play every fly speck in the music, not every difference of opinion calls for a dissent, and there are many cases where the settlement of a rule is more important than that it be settled one way rather than another, or that the different modes of settlement be emphasized. Dissent is of little worth unless it is read. The more numerous the dissents, the more trivial the matters with which they deal, the less likely are any to be read, and the more the public is likely to

> gain the impression that we are obsessed with trivialities rather than the larger issues which the Court is called on the decide.
>
> It is one of the oldest and, until recently, one of the most honored traditions of the Court that its opinion be written by a single judge. It is for this reason that the writing of the opinion is assigned to a particular judge only after conference, so conducted that he may be fully informed as to the individual views of the justices. It is for this reason that any member of the Court is entitled to ask the writer of the Court's opinion to modify it, and that both should seek some accommodation of their diverse views before separate concurring opinions are written. Adherence to this practice has tended to give coherence to the work of the Court, to make the effect of its decisions readily ascertainable and understood, and to command the respect of the public, which may readily be lost by over-emphasis of differences of opinions which do no produce differences in result.[60]

Frankfurter wrote Stone not long after: "If you have not already seen them, these four articles in *The New York Law Journal* may interest you. They are evidently written by one—I wonder who he is?—who either had knowledge or informed himself before writing about the tradition of expressing differences of opinion on this Court. What a lot of ignorant tosh has been appearing lately on this subject!"[61] Stone replied: "As is pretty well known, I do not believe in dissenting just for the sake of dissenting, or overruling just for the sake of overruling. But there are occasions which call for both lines of effort, and no doubt I shall do my share in the future as I have in the past."[62]

In November 1944, the *Associated Press* even went so far as to informally ask the justices to issue off-the-record comments on their opinions. Frankfurter asked Graham Claytor, former clerk to Associate Justice Louis Brandeis, what he thought Brandeis's response would have been and then circulated Claytor's reply to the other justices. Claytor wrote: "[Brandeis] would not have expected a responsible news agency so far to forget the Court's judicial function as to ask it to interpret for the papers its own decisions. Such an attitude indicates a state of mind which has come to look upon the Court not as a tribunal but rather as a colorful source of sensational if complex news stories."[63]

Conclusion

The Roosevelt Court era ended with Stone's death on April 22, 1946; perhaps fittingly, he suffered a stroke on the bench and died later that night. According to C. Herman Pritchett (1954, 1), Stone's "ineptness in the exacting role of Chief Justice was, to some extent at least, a contributing factor in the disintegration of the Court which occurred between 1941 and 1946." Although we contend that the extent to which Stone was responsible for the breakdown of consensus is debatable, it is more than plausible to conclude that the era of dissensus began during his tenure. And while Stone's leadership style almost certainly exacerbated discord, it was the institutional changes—both internal and external—that conclusively ushered in the new dissensus era.

Outside the Court, three factors laid the foundation for individual expression: legislation allowing the justices discretion over their dockets, the influence of legal realism, and the appointment of justices who were critical of traditional jurisprudential philosophy. Changes in the Court's internal practices—expanded Conference discussions, opinion writing and circulation delays, reargument of cases, and an overall academic atmosphere—built on this foundation. Divisions occurred in both majority and minority coalitions. Majorities fractured as the norm of acquiescence eroded, Court opinions increasingly departed from Conference views, and concurrences, used as tools to disagree with both the majority and minority coalitions, exploded. Additionally, justices who disagreed with the majority began noting every dissent, even over small disputes and issues not raised in petitions, and took aim at concurrences.

In the years after Stone's death, the justices continued to disagree at record levels, and further institutional changes made it increasingly difficult, if not impossible, to return to the high degree of consensus achieved prior to Stone's chief justiceship. For example, the increased use of law clerks; justices and their staffs working daily in their own building; opinion assignment equalization; and Conference voting changes were hallmarks of the Warren Court. The end of notation and the formalization of dissent assignments occurred during the Burger Court. And increased bureaucratization, in the form of rapid opinion circulation with majority opinion assignment penalties, as well as a shrunken docket and shortened Conference deliberations, were features of the Rehnquist Court. The end result is a modern Court marked by high levels of dissensus.

This chapter explored why the Supreme Court changed from a consensual body into one composed of individuals willing to express even minor disagreements. Understanding how dissensus developed is a necessary component of understanding how consensus occurs. A number of institutional developments instituted during the Roosevelt Court era resulted in the breakdown of consensus. A puzzling facet of the dissensus revolution, however, is how frequently consensus, and unanimity in particular, still occur. Therefore, we now investigate why, given all of these institutional pressures against consensus, the Court renders so many unanimous decisions in every term. In Chapter 2, we explicate our comprehensive theory of consensus. In subsequent chapters, we test our theory to ascertain the forces that enable the Court to overcome the institutional barriers highlighted in this chapter and successfully achieve unanimity.

Closing the Jaws of the Decision Making Vise

A Theory and Model of Consensus

On June 1, 1981, the U.S. Supreme Court handed down a unanimous decision in *Little v. Streater.* Gloria Streater identified Walter Little to the Connecticut Department of Social Services as the father of her recently born child. Social Services then brought a paternity suit against Little to establish his liability for child support. Little, who was incarcerated, requested that blood tests be conducted, but under Connecticut law at the time, the person asking for such tests was also responsible for their cost. Little argued that he was indigent and could not afford to pay. The trial court authorized the tests but denied Little's request that the state pay for them. As a result, the tests were never conducted.

At trial it was determined that Little was the father of Streater's child, and he was ordered to pay support. This ruling in part stemmed from the fact that, under Connecticut law, if a mother was consistent in her accusations as to the identity of the father, her testimony was considered *prima facie* evidence and the burden of proving nonpaternity fell to the father. However, the father's testimony alone was not enough to dispute the charges.[1] Little sued, alleging that he had been denied his Due Process rights under the Fourteenth Amendment.

The Court, in a single opinion authored by Chief Justice Burger, ruled unanimously that the existing Connecticut law both placed an indigent defendant "at a distinct disadvantage in that his testimony alone is insufficient to overcome the plaintiff's *prima facie* case" (*Streater,* 12) and effectively denied him the ability to refute the claims brought against him by requiring that he bear the cost of the blood tests in violation of the Due Process Clause. The Court emphasized that in this situation the cost of the necessary tests essentially foreclosed Little's ability to defend against allegations of paternity.

Why were the justices able to reach complete agreement in this case? Certainly the question was not a trivial one nor was this a group of justices who always agreed. For example, these same justices split 5–4 in another family law case, *Moore v. City of East Cleveland* (1977), over the question of whether a local housing ordinance that limits who can live together, including relatives, deprived a grandmother who lived with her grandsons of her Fourteenth Amendment Due Process rights. In *Moore*, the Court's decision resulted in six separate opinions, including one regular concurrence, one special concurrence, and three dissents. Perhaps most notably, Chief Justice Burger dissented, arguing that the lawsuit should have been barred since all administrative avenues for recourse had not been pursued even though the ordinance was being challenged on constitutional grounds.

How did the same justices who disagreed on so many levels in *Moore* achieve complete consensus in *Streater*? As discussed in the introduction, we currently possess few answers to this puzzle of unanimity, yet there exists a substantial literature on the topic of judicial behavior in general. We therefore offer a comprehensive theory of consensus on the U.S. Supreme Court to explain this phenomenon. In this chapter, we explicate both our theory of consensus as well as how we propose to empirically test it in the subsequent chapters. We begin by providing an overview of existing research on Supreme Court decision making, which currently proposes three major influences on justices' decisions: attitudes, strategy, and law. We then briefly summarize previous attempts to understand unanimous decision making before introducing our theory, which suggests that consensus is a function of multiple, simultaneously operating legal, attitudinal, strategic, institutional, and case-specific factors. We end the chapter by detailing the variables used to measure these factors.

We also propose a novel way to empirically capture legal considerations and their influence on judicial decision making in general and consensual decision making in particular. Specifically, we offer the concept of *legal certainty*. Simply put, in those cases where the level of legal certainty regarding the strongest legal answer is high, the likelihood of consensus and even unanimity is greatest. Alternatively, when there is considerable ambiguity and uncertainty as to the strongest legal answer, the law's influence is reduced and other forces, such as attitudes, exert more influence and can lead to more divided opinions. Although measuring law has proved no easy task, our conceptualization of legal certainty provides a new way to gauge this operationally difficult concept.

Conventional Wisdom about Judicial Behavior: Theories of Supreme Court Decision Making

The goal of this book is to explain how the Court reaches consensus. To understand consensus, we must first explore the range of potential factors that may influence the justices' decisions. In this section we discuss the dominant theories of judicial decision making—attitudinal, strategic, and legal—which scholars generally pit against each other in an attempt to identify the one driving force. We argue instead that a more integrated approach is necessary to understand why the justices agree.

The Attitudinal Model

The attitudinal model holds that judges base their decisions on their ideological attitudes and values. Its roots stem from the legal realist movement of the early twentieth century. Legal realists challenged the formalist idea that law, as expressed in judicial precedents and the text of statutes, determines the outcomes of particular cases. They argued that extralegal factors influence judicial decisions since, at least most of the time, existing law does not demand only one result (e.g., Frank 1936; Llewellyn 1930, 1962; Pound 1908). Although legal scholars then turned to the normative question of how judges *should* decide cases (e.g., Bickel 1986; Dworkin 1978; Ely 1980), political scientists began empirically examining how judges *actually* decide cases.

An early attitudinal pioneer was C. Herman Pritchett.[2] Pritchett's seminal 1941 article argued that scholars of the Supreme Court should study only those cases in which justices publicly air their dissents. Most notably for our purposes, Pritchett dismissed unanimous cases as relatively uninteresting because "presumably the facts and the law are so clear that no opportunity is allowed for the autobiographies of the justices to lead them to opposing conclusions" (1941, 890). He then posited that divisions among the justices reflect differences in their "conscious and unconscious preferences and prejudices," and he encouraged scholars to turn their attention to the information revealed by nonunanimous decisions (ibid., 890). In *The Roosevelt Court,* Pritchett analyzed nonunanimous decisions between 1937 and 1947, specifically examining voting blocs as well as dissents and concurrences. He interpreted the Court's policies in terms of liberalism and conservatism, and concluded that the justices' decisions were "motivated by their own preferences" (1948, xiii).

Inspired by Pritchett's work, judicial scholars began viewing Supreme Court decision making through a behavioralist lens. Glendon Schubert first suggested that case stimuli and the justices' values could be ideologically scaled. He found that political and economic liberalism explained the majority of the justices' votes (Schubert 1965). More recently, Segal and Spaeth (2002, 86) argued that "the attitudinal model holds that the Supreme Court decides disputes in light of the facts of the case vis-à-vis the ideological attitudes and values of the justices. Simply put, Rehnquist [voted] the way he [did] because he [was] extremely conservative; Marshall voted the way he did because he was extremely liberal." Segal and Spaeth tested this proposition on all Supreme Court search-and-seizure cases from the 1962 through 1998 terms; they found that, by combining facts and attitudes in a multivariate analysis, their model correctly predicted 71 percent of the justices' votes.

Overall, the attitudinal model proposes the relatively straightforward notion that the justices' votes are primarily driven by their personal policy preferences in conjunction with the particular facts of the case being decided. They are aided by some important structural conditions: life tenure, a seat at the apex of the federal judicial hierarchy, and the attendant shielding from political pressure applied by the other branches of government or the public. Thus, the justices, as relatively unfettered political actors, are free to vote their sincere policy preferences on the cases they hear.

The Strategic Model

The strategic account of judicial decision making, like the attitudinal model, begins with the premise that the justices wish to see their personal policy preferences enacted into law. However, unlike attitudinalists, proponents of the strategic model do not believe that the justices are unconstrained actors. "Rather, justices are strategic actors who realize their ability to achieve their goals depends on a consideration of the preference of other actors, the choices they expect others to make, and the institutional context in which they act" (Epstein and Knight 1998, 10).

In his classic book, *The Elements of Judicial Strategy* (1964), Walter F. Murphy introduced the concept of strategic judicial behavior, a key feature of which is the idea that institutions and their structural design matter. According to Maltzman, Spriggs, and Wahlbeck (2000, 13), the "strategic explanation places rational political actors back into their institutional context." Whereas the attitudinal model recognizes how institutional features may increase the justices' freedom, the strategic model maintains that these rules and norms may also constrain the justices and limit their available choices.

For instance, the Court requires that, in order for an opinion to be considered binding precedent, its author must persuade a majority of the justices to join it. Thus, "[majority opinion] authors recognize that they are not necessarily free to express their most preferred positions in the opinion, but that they must consider the views of other justices too. If they fail to accommodate the views of their colleagues, their opinions may not carry the imprimatur of the Court. This rule may therefore prompt a justice to accommodate a justice in either the first or subsequent drafts of the majority opinion" (Maltzman, Spriggs, and Wahlbeck 1999, 47).

Institutional rules external to the Court may also influence judicial decision making. One example is the ability of Congress to overturn the Court's statutory decisions, which means that the justices must take into account the preferences of Congress. Otherwise, "Congress could replace [the justices'] most preferred position with their least" (Epstein and Knight 1998, 15). As a result, when its ideal policy is not immune from congressional reversal, the Court may strategically alter its preferred policy in favor of one that Congress cannot reverse.

However, empirical support for this separation-of-powers (SOP) model is mixed (Bergara, Richman, and Spiller 2003; Eskridge 1991; Gely and Spiller 1990; Segal 1997). Scholars have more successfully applied it to constitutional decisions, arguing that the Court responds to the preferences of sitting elected officials when evaluating a statute's constitutionality (e.g., Bergara, Richman, and Spiller 2003; Harvey and Friedman 2006; Lindquist and Solberg 2007; Spiller and Gely 1992; cf. Sala and Spriggs 2004). They suggested that the Court may act strategically by anticipating the preferences and reactions of the elected branches. Epstein, Knight, and Martin (2001, 585) gave the following description of the Court's strategic motivations in the context of judicial review:

> [G]iven the institutional constraints imposed on the Court, the Justices cannot effectuate their own policy and institutional goals without taking account of the goals and likely actions of the members of the other branches. When they are attentive to external actors, Justices find that the best way to have a long-term effect on the nature and content of the law is to adapt their decisions to the preferences of these others. In this sense, the resolution of the 'countermajoritarian difficulty' results in an important effect of the separation of powers system: a strategic incentive to anticipate and then react to the preferences of elected officials.

The strategic model thus argues that understanding judicial decision making requires considering the specific court's institutional rules and structure, both of which may expand or contract a judge's ability to vote her personal preferences. In reference to the Supreme Court, while institutional features such as life tenure free the justices, other features and rules simultaneously constrain the justices, potentially leading them to vote in a strategic—rather than an ideologically sincere—manner. Strategic justices therefore vote not only based on their preferences and the specific case facts but also in light of the contemporaneous environment. Understanding the justices' votes therefore requires acknowledging the multitude of internal and external factors that may influence them.

The Legal Model

To what extent does law influence Supreme Court decision making? The classic legal model suggests that there is some logical form of reasoning internal to law (Cross 1997). Its proponents argue that the decisions of the justices are substantially influenced by legal considerations. In other words, "judges want only to interpret the law as well as possible" (Baum 2006, 5) and "legal analysis . . . can and should be free from contaminating political or ideological elements" (Kronman 1993, 250). Although there is some debate regarding how to define the legal model, the use of reasoned judgment based on text and precedent remain key parts of legal decision making (Cross 1997).

Still, empirically measuring law and its impact on judges' decisions can be difficult. Part of the problem is that scholars can explain judicial decisions on multiple grounds. For example, Gibson (1991) argued that variations in voting show that judges "have enormous discretion when they make their decisions. The text of constitutions, statutes and precedents does not *command* the votes of the judges. Since there is no 'true' or 'objective' meaning to constitutional phrases like 'due process of law,' judges *cannot* merely follow the law" (258; italics in original). Bailey and Maltzman (2008) showed how Justice Clarence Thomas's dissent in *Lawrence v. Texas* (2003) can be explained either as a reflection of his legal views—namely, his discomfort with unenumerated rights—or as an expression of his political and moral opposition to gay rights. In other words, distinguishing the legal and political components of a judicial decision is inevitably difficult, in part because law and politics are so closely intertwined. As Whittington (2000) noted, part of the problem is "the difficulty of regarding them as either separate spheres or trying to collapse one category into another" (631).

The entanglement of law and politics also means that quantitatively distinguishing political and legal motivations can be difficult. It is perhaps not surprising that many of the studies that highlight the influence of legal forces are either qualitative (e.g., Epstein and Kobylka 1992) or historical institutional (e.g., Gillman 1993, 1996; Graber 1991) in nature. As Baum (1994, 4) explained, quantitative examinations of legal influences may fail due to "the difficulty of developing systematic tests for the impact of such considerations of law." In their attempt to highlight the role of law, Bailey and Maltzman (2008, 381) similarly demonstrated how "legal factors can easily get hidden or, in statistical terms, be hard to identify." Moreover, variations in how scholars conceive of and measure law and its potential influences have led to widely differing answers as to the degree to which legal factors guide the justices.

Until recently, the most persuasive arguments for the importance of legal influences have generally come from interpretive qualitative studies. For example, Epstein and Kobylka (1992) analyzed the Supreme Court's death penalty and abortion decisions, finding that in the early stages of doctrinal development, the justices were substantially influenced by the legal arguments under consideration. Similarly, scholars such as Gillman (1993, 1996) showed that Supreme Court decisions in Due Process and Commerce Clause cases in the late nineteenth and early twentieth centuries are best explained as reflecting core jurisprudential norms, while Graber (1991) highlighted how modern Free Speech doctrine reflects a concerted attempt to reconcile political preferences with the available legal alternatives. Finally, Perry's (1991) work on agenda setting showed that certiorari decisions reflect strong legal influences that mitigate purely ideological or strategic calculations.

Political scientists engaged in quantitative studies often focus on discerning the influence of precedent on Supreme Court justices. The importance of precedent in the American legal system is well documented (e.g., Easterbrook 1982; Posner 1992; Rasmusen 1994), and empirically measuring its influence is, for all intents and purposes, relatively straightforward. Yet the results from these studies are mixed. Early studies found support for the legal model, conceptualizing it as the degree to which Supreme Court justices are constrained by precedent. For example, Segal (1984, 900) assessed Search-and-Seizure doctrine and found that "the legal model was quite satisfactory" in predicting outcomes. George and Epstein (1992) analyzed Death Penalty doctrine and similarly concluded that legal factors work in conjunction with extralegal factors: the former having the greatest impact in the early stages of an issue's life and the latter becoming more influential as the issue evolves.

Taking a different approach to the influence of law, Segal and Spaeth (1996, 1999) tested whether a dissenting justice in a major case changes his vote to support that precedent in a later case—in other words, whether justices feel bound by the Court's established precedents even when they initially voice disagreement with a particular precedent. They found that justices voted in conformity with precedent only 9 percent of the time and concluded that "in the realm of *stare decisis*, minority will does not defer to majority rule" (1999, 315). These findings in part reflect the consequences of the dissensus revolution explored in Chapter 1. However, in response to this study other political scientists retested their models, finding that in a substantial number of cases justices whose policy preferences conflicted with the policy contained in precedents later joined opinions reaffirming those precedents, which suggests that these justices felt bound by existing precedent regardless of their personal beliefs (e.g., Brenner and Stier 1996; Songer and Lindquist 1996). Additionally, Wahlbeck (1997) found some support for the influence of precedent in his examination of changes in the Court's Search-and-Seizure policy.

Continuing to muddy the debate beyond precedent, other studies have found little or no impact for the influence of text and intent (e.g., Howard and Segal 2004) or different canons of construction (e.g., Brudney and Ditslear 2005) on judicial decision making. However, a narrow focus on law as either precedent or text may overlook other legal influences. As Feldman (2005, 96) argued, the influence of law in judicial decision making "cannot be reduced to a single approach or to some simple and mechanical formula." Or, as stated more bluntly by Dworkin (1978, 15), law is not "a set of timeless rules stocked in some conceptual warehouse awaiting discovery by judges." Thus, measuring law as a set of carefully drawn parameters may either incorrectly reduce legal interpretation to a mechanical process that is potentially "overly simplistic and misleading," or conceal other potential ways in which legal forces may guide judicial behavior (Feldman 2005, 99). According to Gillman (2001, 468), the "most notable complaint has been that behavioralists are forced by the conventions of their positivist methodology to conceptualize legal interpretation in fairly formalistic terms (so that clear predictions about behavior can be tested), and this leads [critics] to believe that behavioralists test only those versions of legalist arguments that are least persuasive and most easily falsified."

On the other hand, using such a mechanism to empirically measure law may also obscure precisely *how* legal forces influence judicial decision making. Legal scholars assert that political scientists tend to suppress the role of law in judicial decision making while overstating the role of politics (e.g., Tamanaha 2010). In particular, they acknowledge that judging comprises both legal and political elements, viewing law as a guidepost that judges are obligated to follow rather than, in the view of many political scientists, as a constraint that must be slipped if necessary (ibid.). Consider Cross's (1997, 326) argument: "The ropes [of law] may be tight or loose, possibly knotted with skill and redundancy. These ropes will strive to bind thousands of judges, each of whom possesses different levels of escape skills. If we try to contain judges with law, it is imperative to understand which brand of rope and which type of knot are most effective and inescapable." In contrast, Tamanaha argued that law should be viewed as a guide instead of a hindrance or obstacle to "sincere" judicial decision making. For Tamanaha, conceptualizing legal factors as restrictions on "sincere" judicial behavior pits law and attitudes against one another, rather than examining how both forces can simultaneously influence judges' decisions. Dworkin (1986, 255) similarly argued that judges develop "thresholds" of acceptable legal positions that "will eliminate interpretations that some judges would otherwise prefer, so the brute facts of legal history will in this way limit the role any judge's personal convictions of justice can play in his decisions." In sum, these scholars suggest that law's influence on judicial decision making is not static but rather fluid, dynamic, and likely intertwined with other, concurrently operating forces.

Recently, a number of political science scholars have advocated a more nuanced and dynamic version of the legal model that captures the impact of both law and personal policy preferences on judges' decisions (e.g., Bailey and Maltzman 2008; Bartels 2009; Lax 2007; Lindquist and Klein 2006; Richards and Kritzer 2002). For example, Bailey and Maltzman (2008), Lax (2007), Bartels (2009), and Richards and Kritzer (2002) argued that law works to constrain judicial discretion; they differed, however, as to when and how it does so. Lax (2007) presented a formal model of legal rule making on collegial courts, arguing for a case-space model that recognizes how multiple judges "take the law seriously" when aggregating their preferences to create a set of rules, even when ultimately deciding based on their personal preferences. This model reveals how a majority rule is both created and reinforced by institutional structures that undercut the ability of justices to engage in logrolling. In the end, Lax's formal treatment of judicial decision making warns against trivializing the role of law in the pursuit of demonstrating the influence of attitudes, strategy, and institutions.

Richards and Kritzer (2002) offered perhaps the first systematic and dynamic empirical analysis of how legal forces may affect decision making on the Supreme Court. They argued that legal influences can be seen through the study of "jurisprudential regimes" that structure the justices' decision calculi. Jurisprudential regimes reflect the Court's internal decision structures for specific issue areas which are then applied in future cases. Rather than identifying the precise rule created by past precedents, jurisprudential regimes identify the relevant case factors and level of scrutiny that the justices determine should guide them in future cases. In other words, for Equal Protection cases, the critical question is what parameters the Court designs for when to invoke strict scrutiny as opposed to rational basis, because the level of scrutiny necessarily impacts the likelihood of the Court upholding the governmental policy or action. Importantly, Richards and Kritzer acknowledged that these legal structures also reflect the justices' policy values and goals, and ultimately concluded that the use of jurisprudential regimes reveals how legal forces, as distinct from ideological forces, influence judicial decision making.

Bailey and Maltzman (2008) took a different approach and focused on three important legal doctrines—*stare decisis*, judicial restraint, and a strong preference for First Amendment Free Speech protections—arguing that both legal and ideological forces are salient and allow us to "identify the cases where these factors are particularly likely to be considered by a justice" (371). Bailey and Maltzman engaged in a justice-level analysis to assess the degree to which these core legal doctrines influence each justice's votes. They concluded that "[the] justices are not simply life-tenured policy maximizers" (382) but rather are influenced by important legal considerations when deciding cases.

Bartels (2009) argued for moving away from so-called hybrid models that show the independent effects of legal and ideological considerations; he proposed instead that legal rules act to constrain the degree to which the justices' ideological preferences can operate in a specific case. Bartels built on Richards and Kritzer's idea of jurisprudential regimes to investigate whether these doctrinal structures influence not only the Court's decisions but also the operation of the justices' personal policy preferences. Specifically, he assessed how applying different levels of scrutiny to regulations concerning free expression affects the degree to which ideological voting occurs. Bartels found that certain legal rules, such as the requirement to assess certain laws under strict scrutiny, constrain ideological discretion. However, other rules, such as those governing the Court's evaluation of laws under rational basis, permit ideological considerations to predominate.

Finally, instead of conceptualizing law as an external constraint, Lindquist and Klein (2006, 136) asked "whether the justices are influenced by a desire to make legally sound decisions through what they see as proper methods."

Specifically, they examined the impact of attitudinal and jurisprudential factors on Supreme Court cases that involve circuit conflict, finding that jurisprudential considerations—as well as attitudinal concerns—affect how the justices arrive at their decisions.

All of these studies advance our knowledge of judicial decision making, in no small part because they offer ways to empirically assess the complex and nuanced effects of legal factors. More recent studies have shifted from viewing law as a mechanistic tool to viewing it as a dynamic force. Also they have moved beyond the old notion of measuring legal influence by identifying static doctrines and discerning whether justices apply them strictly in future cases to the new idea of capturing how legal texts, rules, norms, structures and/or regimes affect the choices available to the justices. These studies suggest not that law is comprised of readily identifiable checklists that must be followed but rather that it is varied and vibrant, and best conceptualized as a set of forces influencing, and perhaps constraining, judicial choice and behavior.

The preceding overview of the major judicial decision making theories highlights their differences and similarities. Sophisticated models grounded in one theoretical tradition routinely take into account the assumptions and empirical findings of the others. However, they often do so only to pit each against the others in a quest to determine the predominant explanation for judicial behavior. In contrast, as will be discussed more expansively later in this chapter, we offer a comprehensive theory of Supreme Court decision making which accounts for how attitudes and law operate simultaneously on justices as they strategically interact with each other, and with actors outside the Court, to achieve shared goals within the larger political environment. We submit that such a model offers the most compelling explanation of how the Court is able to achieve consensus.

We now provide a brief overview of previous attempts to explain unanimity and consensus on the Supreme Court before turning to an explication of our theory of judicial decision making.

Behavior That Deviates: Existing Explanations for the Decision to Agree

The United States Supreme Court makes decisions as a collective body, but it is also composed of nine separate and equal justices who operate in the context of institutional rules and norms. Inquiry into how the Court arrives at its decisions is therefore necessarily a question of how the individual justices vote, how they interact to reach a collective decision, and under what conditions they conduct their work. While the current models of judicial behavior detailed in the preceding section address these important questions, they do not offer a compelling answer to the puzzle of unanimity. Instead, contemporary research focuses on explaining why the justices disagree. Nevertheless, "students of judging can learn as much from behavior that deviates in some way from our theoretical expectations as from behavior that accords with them" (Edelman, Klein, and Lindquist 2008, 821). In this section we discuss existing studies of Supreme Court unanimity.

Studies of Court unanimity have focused primarily on the question of whether unanimous decisions increase the legitimacy and authority of Court decisions (Gerber and Park 1997; Moorhead 1952; O'Brien 1999; Ulmer 1986; Walker, Epstein, and Dixon 1988). According to Judge Learned Hand (1958, 72), a nonunanimous decision "cancels the impact of monolithic solidarity on which the authority of a bench of judges so largely depends." Numerous studies also empirically analyzed the breakdown in the "norm of consensus" (Caldeira and Zorn 1998; Epstein, Segal, and Spaeth 2001; Haynie 1992; Lanier 2003; O'Brien 1999; Walker, Epstein, and Dixon 1988); they sought to determine why and when the modern era of dissensus on the Court began. As detailed in Chapter 1, we break from these previous studies by arguing, based on an historical institutional assessment of the justices' papers, that the breakdown in the norm of consensus is attributable to internal and external institutional changes that were implemented during the Roosevelt Court era.

Why the Supreme Court decides some cases unanimously is a question that has, comparatively, garnered relatively little attention. A debate arose in the 1960s between Joel Grossman and Sheldon Goldman over the role of attitudes and judges' backgrounds in achieving unanimity. Grossman (1967) argued that attitudinal factors influence even unanimous votes while Goldman (1969) gave weight to Pritchett's theory by suggesting that "objective" case situations offer little room for attitudes to sway the justices' voting decisions in unanimous cases. Goldman specifically proposed that in certain cases law is unclear and ambiguous and, as a consequence, the justices vote their attitudes. In other cases, law is clear, and so the decision is unanimous. Klein (1984, 112) agreed: "It may well be that in the numerous cases where the Supreme Court justices agree, their agreement may be explained by the presence of a very clear precedent."

Brenner and Arrington (1987) proposed extending the psychometric model of Supreme Court voting—which suggests that justices' votes reflect their attitudes on the issue in the case as well as case stimuli (Schubert 1961)—to unanimous decisions. In their study they examined all civil liberties and economic cases decided during the 1946–1952 and 1958–1983 terms, relying on a relatively simple yet effective methodology that compared the ideological direction of split versus unanimous decisions and then further analyzed whether the Court voted to affirm or reverse the lower court. They found that liberal outcomes dominated unanimously decided cases, and that there was an ideological bias in case selection, and therefore concluded that attitudes play a part in influencing even unanimous outcomes. They did not, however, systematically test for alternative explanations, nor did they offer a prediction as to the magnitude of the effect of ideology relative to other influences.

More recently, Hensley and Johnson (1998) attempted to explain unanimity, highlighting the "troubling" lack of knowledge in this area given that "[unanimous] decisions constitute a sizable portion of judicial decisions" (387). They examined all cases decided by the Rehnquist Court from the 1986 through 1990 terms and offered five explanations for unanimity: (1) cases where less time elapses between oral argument and the decision date; (2) routine or less important cases; (3) cases with a liberal ideological orientation; (4) cases involving federal action; and (5) cases without civil liberties issues (396). While they found support for each, all of their findings and conclusions were based only on descriptive and bivariate analyses.

Finally, a group of recent studies (Edelman, Klein, and Lindquist 2008, 2012; Roy and Songer 2010; Songer and Siripurapu 2009) focused on whether the attitudinal model explains unanimous decision making. The attitudinal explanation is that the lower court decision represents an "extreme" position on the ideological scale, and all nine justices are either more liberal or more conservative than the position of the lower court case. In other words, "the Supreme Court will only unanimously reverse a liberal decision on the court below when the most liberal justice on the Supreme Court prefers an outcome more conservative than that adopted by the lower court" and vice versa (Songer and Siripurapu 2009, 69–70). All of these studies concluded that attitudes do not adequately explain how the justices achieve unanimity and they subsequently posited that legal or jurisprudential concerns must therefore drive unanimous decisions. However, these studies did not provide direct support for the influence of legal factors.

In sum, we have little guidance as to how to understand unanimous decision making by the Supreme Court. The literature on unanimity provides, at best, an incomplete picture of why the Court reaches consensus. We therefore take up the task suggested by Epstein, Segal, and Spaeth (2001) and Hensley and Johnson (1998)—to determine what drives decision making in unanimous cases—by offering the first theoretically rigorous and comprehensive assessment of unanimity on the U.S. Supreme Court. We do so by focusing on the institution of the Court itself. We are not interested in how individual justices arrive at their votes but rather how the Court as a whole works as a single entity to render a decision. The fact that the justices must arrive at a collective decision—that a precedential ruling of the Court requires an opinion representing a majority of the justices—is an important component of explaining consensus.

A Comprehensive Model of Consensus

The crux of our theory is that consensus on the Supreme Court can only be understood by recognizing the multitude of factors that influence the justices in every single case, many times in a complex, interactive fashion. Law, attitudes, strategy, institutional imperatives, and case-specific factors all play an important role. In this section we explain each component of our theory and the specific variables used to construct our model of consensus. We draw from the existing literature, but we also present some novel mechanisms for measuring the concepts included in our model. Given our focus on unanimity and consensus, we operationalize our variables in the way that best helps us capture how consensus is achieved. As a result, some of our measures are variations of those used in other studies of judicial decision making where the focus was not on consensus but rather, for example, on the creation of minimum-winning coalitions.

Our desire to assess the influence of law on the Court leads us to create a number of measures designed to capture the nonideological components of the concept in question. For example, as explained in more detail later, we attempt to identify lower court cases containing dissent based on ideological as opposed to nonideological grounds. By separating out nonideological dissents, we can better assess when consensus is likely to occur as well as how it is influenced by ideological and nonideological considerations.

We begin with a detailed discussion of how we seek to improve on previous attempts to capture the influence of law through our measure of legal certainty. We pay particular attention to the interplay between legal certainty and attitudes before discussing how we operationalize these influences as well as strategic, institutional, and case-specific factors. Table 2.1 provides a summary of how each variable was coded; Table 2.2 reports summary statistics for each variable.

TABLE 2.1

Variable descriptions

Variable	Variable coding scheme
Legal considerations	
Level of Legal Certainty	Additive index based on five discrete variables, each coded dichotomously. The final index ranges from 0, the lowest level of legal certainty, to 5, the highest level of legal certainty.
Attitudinal	
Ideological Polarization	Absolute value of the distance between the median justice's Martin-Quinn score and the most extreme justice's Martin-Quinn score. Determined based on the justices who heard each case.
Extreme Lower Court Decision	Using the Judicial Common Space (JCS) scores, coded a lower court decision as 1 if any member of the lower court panel had a JCS score that was more liberal or conservative than the JCS score of the most ideological Supreme Court justice who heard the case, and 0 otherwise.
Reversed Lower Court Decision	Coded 1 if the lower court decision was reversed, and 0 if the lower court decision was affirmed.
Extreme Lower Court Decision × Reversed	An interaction variable composed of *Extreme Lower Court Decision* and *Reversed Lower Court Decision*. Coded 1 if the Supreme Court voted to reverse an extreme lower court decision, and 0 otherwise.
Strategic considerations	
Chief Justice Writes Opinion	Coded 1 if the chief justice authored the majority opinion, and 0 otherwise.
Median Justice Writes Opinion	Coded 1 if the median justice (in terms of all the justices who heard each case) authored the majority opinion, and 0 otherwise.
Altered Precedent	Coded 1 if the Supreme Court altered previous precedent, and 0 otherwise.
Declared Statute Unconstitutional	Coded 1 if the Supreme Court decision struck down a federal statute as unconstitutional, and 0 otherwise.
SG Party	Coded 1 if the solicitor general is either the petitioner or respondent, and 0 otherwise.
Institutional context	
Addition of Syllabus	Coded 1 if the case was decided after 1971 (when the syllabus was added to all published decisions), and 0 otherwise.
Formalization of Dissent Assignment	Coded 1 if the case was decided after 1975 (when dissent assignments became formalized), and 0 otherwise.
Docket Size	Measured as the number of cases granted and decided every term.
Number of Law Clerks	Measured as the total number of law clerks working for all of the justices each term.
Chief Justice	We created dummy variables for each chief justice, and excluded the dummy variable for Chief Justice Warren as the baseline for comparison.
Case factors	
Issue Area	We created dummy variables reflecting whether the case involved a civil rights and liberties, governmental power, or economic activity issue, and we excluded civil liberties cases as the baseline for comparison.

(*continued*)

TABLE 2.1 *(continued)*

Variable	Variable coding scheme
Political Salience	Coded 1 if the case decision was discussed on the front page of the *New York Times*, and 0 otherwise.
Liberal Decision	Coded 1 if the case was decided in a liberal direction, and 0 if it was decided in a conservative direction.
Time Left until End of Term	Reflects the number of days between the date when oral arguments for each case were held and July 1, the end of the Supreme Court's term.

TABLE 2.2

Descriptive statistics for independent variables

Variable	Mean	Standard deviation	Minimum	Maximum
Legal considerations				
Level of Legal Certainty	3.303	1.006	0	5
Attitudinal				
Ideological Polarization	4.700	1.093	1.089	7.669
Extreme Lower Court Decision	0.101	0.302	0	1
Reversed Lower Court Decision	0.627	0.484	0	1
Extreme Lower Court Decision × Reversed	0.062	0.242	0	1
Strategic considerations				
Chief Justice Writes Opinion	0.102	0.303	0	1
Median Justice Writes Opinion	0.075	0.263	0	1
Altered Precedent	0.018	0.131	0	1
Declared Statute Unconstitutional	0.023	0.151	0	1
SG Party	0.399	0.490	0	1
Institutional context				
Addition of Syllabus	0.686	0.464	0	1
Formalization of Dissent Assignment	0.595	0.491	0	1
Docket Size	120.352	26.224	74	155
Number of Law Clerks	30.290	7.225	17	39
Rehnquist Court	0.361	0.480	0	1
Burger Court	0.373	0.484	0	1
Case factors				
Governmental Powers Issue	0.227	0.419	0	1
Economic Issue	0.290	0.454	0	1
Political Salience	0.129	0.335	0	1
Liberal Decision	0.495	0.500	0	1
Time Left until End of Term	166.680	69.098	3	629[a]

[a]We calculated this number as the end date of the term in which the case was decided minus the oral argument date. The maximum number reflects cases that were carried over but not reargued the following term.

Law and Legal Certainty

While we view attitudes as the driving force behind the decisions of the Supreme Court, we also submit that attitudes may be constrained by legal forces. Specifically, we suggest that legal considerations may constrain or enable ideological voting. As Baum (1997, 66) argued, "[t]he easy case gives precedence to legal considerations, because judges are directed to the result that has greater legal support. From the perspective of motivated reasoning, judges are unlikely to reach a decision consistent with their policy preferences when they would have great difficulty justifying it in legal terms." It is difficult to imagine the Court agreeing to hear a case that is "easy"; however, as Kerr (2009) noted, "[e]ven in hard cases, there is usually one side that emerges as slightly stronger than the other." Furthermore, according to Murphy (1964, 1), "[t]here may be more certainty in law, even constitutional law, than the Legal Realists were once willing to admit."

Consider, for example, the corporate tax case *Commissioner of Internal Revenue v. National Alfalfa Dehydrating and Milling Co.* (1974), which resulted in a unanimous decision after Chief Justice Burger circulated the following memorandum:

> I have now read the Tax Court opinion in this case which, I confess, I had not previously done. I had relied on the CA [Court of Appeals] opinion which takes the 'practical' approach and produces a plausible result. The Tax Court opinion, however, makes out a strong case for a result that will be easier to administer and will likely produce uniformity and probably fewer appeals. I therefore now vote to reverse.[3]

Hence, the law itself—whether we mean precedent, legal texts, or original intent—often guides or dictates the answer to the legal question at hand.

Ronald Dworkin (1978) offered the most extreme perspective. His "right answer thesis" maintains that there are objective legal truths and right answers to even the hardest legal questions. Tamanaha (2006, 242) proposed a less radical approach: "Legal rules allow for more than one legally plausible outcome, though usually one outcome can be ranked as more legally compelling or defensible than the others." Collins's (2009) "legal persuasion" model extended this idea by arguing that justices need to be persuaded as to the correct legal answer, and amicus curiae play a central role in helping them arrive at "what they believe to be the legally correct decisions" (83).

We theorize instead that dissensus is more likely in cases where the level of legal certainty is low. In such cases there exists no clear legal answer, there are equally plausible answers on both sides, and the constraining power of law is consequently minimized. Thus, in these cases a low level of legal certainty presents an opportunity for the justices to vote according to their personal policy preferences. As Baum (1997, 65) noted: "[T]he ambiguity that typically exists in application of legal rules to a case gives judges great freedom to reach the result they prefer on policy grounds, whether or not they recognize that they are doing so." Similarly, Tamanaha (2010, 192) argued that when ambiguity over law exists, the justices possess "greater leeway for choice" and that the result of multiple plausible choices is an increased likelihood of divisions on the Court.

We do not know the exact point at which there exists enough legal uncertainty for the constraining power of law to be mitigated. But when a case contains "appreciable legal ambiguity," judicial discretion is relatively unfettered and justices can freely rely on their attitudes when deciding cases (Kerr 2009). In other words, "a very hard case gives judges free rein to justify whatever decision best accords with their policy views" (Baum 1997, 66). Importantly, since the level of legal certainty can vary greatly across cases, our theory of legal certainty helps to explain how law influences judicial decision making.

In contrast to previous work, we focus on determining whether or not the information available to the justices suggests that there exists a high level of certainty as to the strongest legal answer. Our conceptualization of legal certainty views the clarity of law as a type of continuum. We propose, similar to Bartels (2009), that when the level of legal certainty is high, and thus the level of certainty about the strongest legal answer is greatest, the justices are constrained from voting their attitudes. Alternatively, when more ambiguity as to the strongest legal answer exists, there is nothing to restrain the justices' attitudes from influencing their votes. In that situation, the justices have a "greater leeway for choice" (Tamanaha 2010, 192) and divisions among them become more likely. More specifically, our conceptualization suggests that unanimity and consensus result in cases where the level of legal certainty is great. However, when uncertainty exists as to which legal answer is strongest, dissensus is much more likely because this uncertainty enhances the justices' ideological discretion.

We analogize the interaction between attitudes and law to that of an object moving through the jaws of a vise. If the jaws are sufficiently tight, the object does not fit through or does so only such that the vise subsequently shapes it. However, when the jaws are open the object passes through unimpeded and in its original form. In terms of judicial decision making, we view the object as the justices' attitudes and the vise as the law. As shown in Figure 2.1, when legal forces act as a strong constraint, and thus the jaws

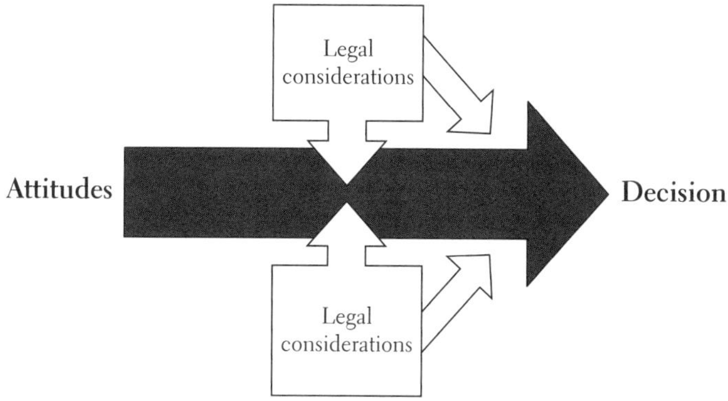

Figure 2.1. Constrained court

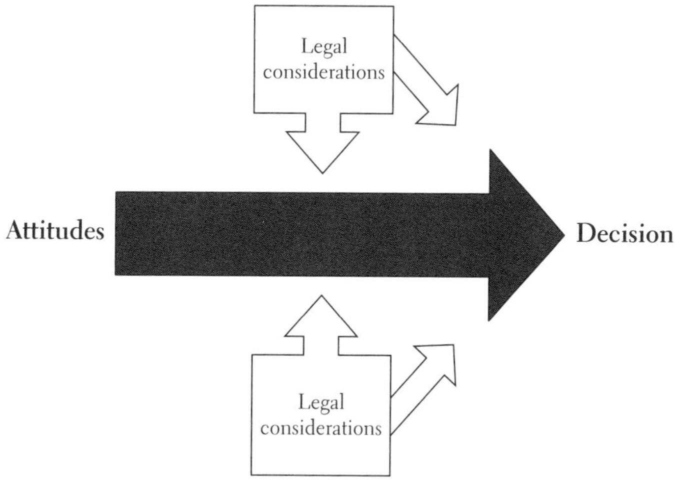

Figure 2.2. Unconstrained court

are relatively shut, the justices' attitudes cannot easily pass through the vise to influence the decision without hindrance. Such a situation represents a case where law is relatively clear and the justices are more certain about the strongest legal answer. If the justices are constrained from voting according to their policy preferences, they are more likely to achieve consensus.

Figure 2.2 represents a Court in which these same considerations enhance the justices' ability to decide the case according to their policy preferences. In this situation, the jaws of the vise are open and attitudes consequently dominate; law is ambiguous and strong arguments can be made on both sides.

According to Baum (1997, 65), legal ambiguity "gives [justices] great freedom to reach the result they prefer on policy grounds." If they base their decisions on their personal policy preferences, we expect the decision to be neither unanimous nor highly consensual. Moreover, we agree with Kritzer (2010) that "if attitudes are strong enough, they might push through jaws that are fairly narrow or tightly closed." Our model of consensus thus recognizes the importance of attitudes and law, as well as the complex way in which the two forces interact.

Our conceptualization of legal certainty offers a mechanism for understanding the importance of a force as nebulous as law in consensual decision making. "The region of legal uncertainty is where judges render decisions with the least legal guidance, and where judges' particular mix of legal and social views has the most leeway and impact" (Tamanaha 2010, 190). Thus, we maintain that ideology matters but that its influence is greater or lesser depending on the level of legal certainty a case entails. The notion of legal certainty we employ in many ways dates back to Pritchett's initial postulation as to the explanation for unanimity, but we expand on his idea in a number of important respects. First, we recognize that law is not a solitary influence on the justices but rather one of many operating in each case, and we recognize how these differing forces work in tandem and how their magnitudes may vary on a case-by-case basis. Second, we propose a way to empirically test these ideas: an index that captures the level of legal certainty that each case presents to the justices, which we describe in more detail later. Our notion of legal certainty thus allows scholars to determine whether law—as well as other potential factors—influences judicial decision making.

Our conceptualization of legal certainty also builds on prior studies of the legal model in a number of significant ways. First, we examine the influence of law on judicial decision making from an entirely different vantage point, that of consensus. In other words, our main question is fundamentally distinct from those proposed in earlier studies: we are interested in explaining unanimity and consensus on the Court, and so our focus is on creating a measure of legal considerations that aids in this enterprise. As we discuss later, our focus on consensus leads us to conceptualize law in a manner that captures how legal considerations may promote agreement.

Second, each of these prior studies examined the effect of legal considerations on each justice's vote. Our interest in consensus directs us instead to an institutional-level analysis to better understand how various factors influence the Court's collective decisions. Also, our measure of legal forces necessarily focuses on information available to the Court as a whole, rather than individual-level influences. Third, our notion of legal certainty moves beyond studies of single-issue areas and specific rule sets to offer a mechanism for capturing the influence of legal factors in all cases across all issue areas, thus facilitating systematic examination of judicial behavior.

To apply our theory of legal certainty, we ask: Given all of the information presented to the justices, how certain or uncertain is the legal answer to the question presented in a particular case? Our measure of legal certainty attempts to capture the dynamic influence of legal forces on judicial decision making, while at the same time utilizing variables that reflect the information the justices possess during the decision making process. In other words, our intent is to determine, on the basis of the information available to the justices while deciding the case, whether certain indicators exist that point to a higher or lower level of legal certainty regarding the strongest legal answer. Importantly, this means that our conceptualization of legal certainty is not based on factors that can only be determined *post hoc*, such as whether the decision was subsequently discussed on the front page of the *New York Times* or whether the decision ultimately declared a state or federal law unconstitutional. Instead, we focus on factors available *a priori* that suggest that a particular legal answer is stronger and more plausible than all others.

It is admittedly difficult to determine *a priori* whether a case is legally easy or difficult. Rather than identify a single measure that reflects the case's difficulty, we create an index to determine when more or less certainty as to the strongest legal answer exists. This index is constructed from five discrete measures, each of which indicates the degree of legal certainty facing the justices in each case. We do not claim that each variable's effect on consensus is entirely due to law. As discussed previously, it is very difficult to disentangle the influence of law from the influence of policy preferences. However, by taking all of these measures together and controlling for alternative explanations, the index isolates the degree of legal certainty in each case.

As will become apparent, we also do not attempt to directly measure law but instead rely on variables that credibly indicate cases in which the level of legal certainty is more likely to be higher or lower. In other words, we depart from studies such as Richards and Kritzer (2002), Bailey and Maltzman (2008), and Bartels (2009) by not delineating legal structures and their subsequent effects but rather identifying factors that suggest whether clarity in law exists. Our index thus seeks to capture an elusive and nebulous concept, law, with a group of credible yet imperfect measures. We now discuss our Legal Certainty Index and its five component parts.

We used five discrete variables, each coded dichotomously, to capture the facets of every case that might suggest a higher or lower level of legal certainty; each variable was coded such that 1 signals a higher level. We then simply added these five variables to create our index, scaled from 0 to 5, with 0 reflecting the lowest possible level of legal certainty and 5 representing the highest. Our goal was to identify variables that tap into this idea of legal clarity and operationalize them accordingly. We recognize, however, that some of them may capture attitudinal considerations as well. The following variables were used to create our Legal Certainty Index.

Legally Noncomplex Cases

We suggest that legally complex cases with multiple disputed legal questions or issues lead to less certainty and more ambiguity for the justices. In cases involving a high level of legal complexity, the range of possible outcomes expands and agreement must be reached across a multitude of issues. The more legal issues there are, the more difficult it is for the justices to arrive at one clear legal answer. As a result, more legal complexity in the case means that there is more legal uncertainty, which leads to a greater likelihood of dissensus (Wahlbeck, Spriggs, and Maltzman 1999). Conversely, in *Legally Noncomplex Cases*, which address only a few legal questions or issues, the range of potential legal answers is limited and consensus on the strongest legal answer is more likely.

An alternative argument is that "[c]ases with multiple issues will make the activation of traditional left-right cleavages more difficult, because justices might have preferences in two different directions on each of the separate issues present in the case" (Bartels 2011, 148). This may be true, but we suggest that complex cases also carry a substantial element of legal difficulty, especially if there are conflicting legal rules or jurisprudential regimes (e.g., Maltzman, Spriggs, and Wahlbeck 2000). Thus, although this particular variable does not disentangle law and attitudes, it does capture an element of legal certainty. Using data available through the *United States Supreme Court Judicial Database, 1953–2006 Terms* (Spaeth 2007; hereafter, the Spaeth dataset), we counted the total number of legal issues and laws that each case addressed. We then coded all cases addressing two or fewer legal issues and laws as 1, and all cases addressing more than two legal issues and laws as 0.

Lack of Amicus Participation in the Case

We argue that the presence of amicus curiae briefs expands the scope of conflict by bringing new issues to the justices' attention. Amici allow outside parties to influence a particular case by presenting their arguments to the

Court. They also serve the crucial function of highlighting alternative legal issues and arguments. "By introducing or expanding on issues the direct litigants were able to raise only in abbreviated form, amici make it difficult for the Justices to determine the correct application of the law in each case" (Collins 2008, 152). More amici, and thus additional points or legal arguments for the justices to consider, lead to increased legal uncertainty. Conversely, a *Lack of Amicus Participation* limits the number of legal arguments the justices must consider and thus limits their potential options as to the strongest legal answer.

Some scholars have used the number of amicus briefs filed in a case as a proxy for salience (e.g., Hettinger, Lindquist, and Martinek 2004; Maltzman, Spriggs, and Wahlbeck 2000; Wahlbeck, Spriggs, and Maltzman 1999). However, as Collins (2008) discussed in detail, there are many problems with this, including the fact that the number of amicus briefs filed is often weighted toward civil liberties and rights cases. Furthermore, Collins (ibid.) found that the justices' voting patterns are more variable in cases with many amicus briefs but less variable in salient cases.[4] This finding indicates that the justices' responses to amici do not mimic their reactions to variations in case salience, leading to the conclusion "that amicus briefs are an unsuitable measure of a case's broad significance" (ibid., 149). However, we recognize that this variable may also capture case salience, especially given that the information the briefs provide may relate to policy as well as law. Accordingly, in the models we present in Chapters 3 and 4, we separately control for political salience and issue area in an effort to isolate the impact of amicus briefs on legal certainty. We count the number of briefs filed in each case (ibid.).[5] We then code this variable 1 for one or no amicus briefs, and 0 for more than one.

Lack of Legal Conflict

It is our contention that dissensus on the Court is more likely when different lower courts hear similar cases and reach differing conclusions. Conversely, consensus is more likely if various lower courts all arrive at the same legal answer. The existence of a conflict between lower courts suggests that at least two different views exist about the strongest answer; thus, it is likely to be more difficult for the Supreme Court to reach a consensual decision. Specifically, the presence of a lower court conflict "indicates that an issue is of sufficient importance that it has arisen in different places, and *the disposition is not obvious*" (Perry 1991, 249; italics added). Furthermore, "[j]ustices may be less motivated by ideological considerations and more concerned to ensure uniformity in federal law" when there is a lower court conflict (Edelman, Klein, and Lindquist 2008, 836).

However, the fact that the case involves a conflict does not necessarily mean that the lower courts disagree about the law; rather, the disagreement may be ideologically driven. In particular, if a case raises an "important" and thus highly salient issue, it is more likely that this issue is one about which the lower court judges care deeply and so is more likely to activate their ideological predispositions. Conflicts in such cases do not reflect a thorny legal issue but rather highlight ideological splits among the circuits. On the other hand, a circuit split in a nonimportant and thus nonsalient case suggests that the disagreement is more likely a legal one. In other words, the Court attempts in these latter cases to resolve a lower court conflict that reflects a dispute over the correct legal answer rather than an ideological quarrel.

To distinguish conflict cases that are more likely to arise from a legal versus an ideological dispute, we focus on whether they involve an important or significant question. If the issue is an important one, it is more likely that the lower court judges are deciding the case according to their ideology, meaning that they disagree but their disagreement is not a *legal* one. We therefore hypothesize that when a case lacks a conflict altogether, or involves a conflict over an important issue (meaning that the dispute more likely reflects ideological rather than legal disagreements), the level of certainty should be higher and consensus should be easier to achieve. Accordingly, we code all cases that lack a conflict or involve an important conflict as 1; all those that involve a conflict in the lower court over a relatively "unimportant" question we code as 0. We name this variable *Lack of Legal Conflict*.[6]

Because the Spaeth dataset does not take into account the reason for granting review in appeals, we cannot discern which appeals cases present conflicts. We therefore exclude them from our data and limit our analyses to cases in which the Court granted certiorari. However, given that cert cases are those that the Court voluntarily decides to hear, presumably because they are important and difficult and thus less likely to result in unanimous or highly consensual decisions, whereas appeals cases are those that the Court is required to hear if properly filed, assessing only cert cases should present a tougher test of our theory of consensus than if appeals cases were also included in our analyses.

Lack of Legal Dissensus in the Lower Court

We believe that a *Lack of Legal Dissensus in the Last Lower Court* that heard the case suggests a high level of certainty as to the strongest legal answer, while the presence of dissensus indicates increased uncertainty and ambiguity as to the legal answer. When judges on lower courts disagree on the answer to the legal question at hand, there is an increased likelihood that this disagreement stems in part from dissension over the strongest legal answer (Edelman, Klein, and Lindquist 2008).[7]

In general, the dissent rate on courts of appeals is extremely low (Goldman 1975; Hettinger, Lindquist, and Martinek 2006), and so the fact that one judge disagrees with the majority opinion generally indicates that reasonable people can disagree about the legal answer (Edelman, Klein, and Lindquist 2008). However, not all disagreements are equal: some reflect ideological or partisan disputes while others represent a conflict over the most persuasive application of law. We therefore focus our attention on instances when a lower court judge disagrees, whether in dissent or concurrence, for apparently nonideological reasons. When a lower court judge offers an alternative legal viewpoint, thereby suggesting that the strongest legal answer is in dispute, we expect consensus on the Court to be less likely.

To capture nonideological dissensus—and thus instances of *legal* disagreement—we created a novel measure of lower court dissensus that attempts to identify nonideological divisions on the court immediately below the Supreme Court. Although the Spaeth dataset contains a variable denoting whether there was dissent in the lower court, we created a wholly new one, for three reasons. First, Spaeth's variable does not take into account concurring opinions. Since concurrences may reflect disagreement over the correct legal reasoning, excluding them may obscure real conflicts in the lower court over the correct application of law; this is particularly true for courts of appeals decisions, in which true dissent is relatively rare (Songer 1982). Second, Spaeth's variable reflects simply whether the Supreme Court notes in the majority opinion that there was a dissent in the lower court. Thus it misses the many times when a lower court judge dissents but the Court in its opinion declines to mention it. Third, Spaeth's variable does not distinguish between primarily ideological and nonideological—or legally based—dissent. Again, not all dissent is equal: on the one hand, it may reflect personal policy differences between the judges; on the other hand, it may reflect real disagreements about the correct legal reasoning. We are therefore interested in isolating disagreement among lower court judges that is likely driven by legal as opposed to attitudinal or ideological disputes.

To address these three concerns, we collected data about each lower court opinion to create a new variable, *Lack of Legal Dissensus in the Lower Court*. As discussed later in more detail, in the section describing the "extreme lower court" variable, cases appealed from state courts were excluded from our analysis, and so our data include only those appealed from federal courts. We therefore determined, based on the following steps, whether there was dissensus on the lower federal court where the appeal originated. First, we read each opinion of the lower federal court and identified whether it was unanimous or contained a dissent, a concurrence, or both. We included both concurrences and dissents since disagreements, especially in the courts of appeals, may manifest themselves in concurring opinions (Songer 1982). Second, we determined which judges heard each case and whether each one voted with the majority in all respects, concurred, or dissented. Third, we determined the party of the appointing president for each judge on the lower court as a proxy for judicial ideology.[8]

The fourth and final step was to determine whether the dissensus in the case could be considered nonideological—or legal—in nature. Since our index is scaled from low to high legal certainty, cases with no dissensus or ideological dissensus were coded 1, and cases with nonideological/legal dissensus were coded 0. For three-judge panels, if the dissenting judge was of the opposite party from that of the two judges in the majority coalition, this variable was coded 1 given the likelihood that the dissensus was ideological. Alternatively, if the dissenting judge was of the same party as that of one of the judges in the majority coalition, this variable was coded 0 since the disagreement could not be considered purely ideological. For en banc circuit court panels, if the majority coalition was composed entirely of members of one party and all of the dissenters were members of the opposite party, this variable was coded 1 since it suggests that the dissent reflected attitudinal factors. However, if either the majority or the dissenting coalition was ideologically incongruent, this variable was coded 0 since, again, the disagreement cannot be considered purely ideological. Similarly, if the panel itself was ideologically congruent and there was a dissent, this variable was coded 0 as the dissent was more likely legal in nature. In all instances, if the case contained a concurrence, this variable was also coded 0 because the concurring opinion writers agreed with the result reached by the majority but not with the legal reasoning; the disagreement, accordingly, was not based on purely ideological considerations. Lower court cases in which there was neither a dissent nor a concurrence were coded 1.

Statutory Interpretation

We argue that the degree of difficulty facing the justices in agreeing on the strongest legal answer may depend on the nature of the legal provision at issue. Specifically, if the case involves statutory interpretation rather than a question of constitutional law, agreement on the legal answer should be less difficult. The language of statutes is generally more detailed and less ambiguous than the language of the Constitution, which makes it easier for judges to determine legislative intent and plain meaning when interpreting them (Kritzer, Pickerill, and Richards 1998). For this reason, we hypothesize that the Court is more likely to reach consensus when the case involves statutory rather than constitutional interpretation.

There may be some constitutional cases that are legally easier than statutory cases, but generally we expect them to be legally harder. It can also be argued that such cases raise issues about which the justices possess strong personal feelings, and so they may be more likely than statutory cases to create ideological divides. While this argument has merit, it seems to us overly simplistic. Some constitutional issues may address salient topics, but not all engender the same level of interest and intensity. Similarly, many statutory cases may raise issues of equal (or even more) interest to the justices. However, we control for issue area and for case salience in our model estimations, which should illuminate if the difference between statutory and constitutional cases is mainly due to salience. To test this difference, the variable *Statutory Issue* was coded 1 if the case decided a statutory issue and 0 otherwise.

We combined the five variables just described to create a single Legal Certainty Index. This index ranges from 0 to 5, with 0 representing the lowest level of legal certainty and 5 reflecting the highest level of legal certainty. The variables work together to reflect the level of legal certainty facing the justices as they attempt to apply the law to the case before them. Our measures are admittedly imperfect, but we have strived to isolate the influence of legal considerations from other, particularly ideological, factors in constructing them. We also control for other factors, such as issue area and political salience, to further isolate the influence of law. Further, by combining the five variables into a single index we are better able to capture the influence of law than if we were to include each variable separately in our models.[9] The use of an index allows us to integrate the different aspects of legal certainty into one distinct, yet multifaceted, notion, while also recognizing that legal certainty is best conceptualized as existing along a continuum.

We expect that when the level of legal certainty is high (i.e., the case's score on the Legal Certainty Index is high), the law works to constrain the operation of attitudes and so the likelihood of unanimity or consensus increases. Conversely, as legal uncertainty and ambiguity increase (and thus the case's index score drops), the opportunity for attitudes to dominate increases, which means that the likelihood of the Court reaching a unanimous or highly consensual decision decreases.

In Chapters 3 and 4, we test the influence of legal forces in two distinct ways. Our conceptualization of legal certainty suggests that law influences judicial decision making on two levels: legal certainty exerts both a direct effect and an indirect effect on the justices' ability to achieve consensus. We therefore test for both the potential direct and indirect influence of law on the Court's decisions in the next two empirical chapters. To test the direct effect of law on consensus, we include in each model our Legal Certainty Index as an independent variable. Doing so tells us whether the level of legal certainty, controlling for other potential forces, directly and independently influences the achievement of unanimity and high levels of consensus.

However, our notion of legal certainty also suggests that law may exert an indirect force on the justices by constraining the ability of their attitudes and preferences to operate freely. Thus, we posit that when the level of legal certainty is high, the justices' ability to vote their attitudes is constrained, which in turn decreases the likelihood of reaching a consensual decision; alternatively, when the level of legal certainty is low and so the constraints imposed by law are lessened, the justices' attitudes predominate. To indirectly test the influence of law, and particularly its constraining force on attitudes, we reestimate the models of consensus presented in Chapters 3 and 4 but without the Legal Certainty Index as an independent variable and on a split sample. Specifically, we use the same variables minus the Legal Certainty Index first on the sample of cases in which legal certainty is high (i.e., a score of 4 or 5) and then on the sample of cases in which legal certainty is low (i.e., a score of 0, 1, 2, or 3). The results of these models reflect the influence that the level of legal certainty has, if any, on the operation of judicial attitudes as they relate to the achievement of consensus.

Attitudes

Attitudinal influences exert a potent force on Supreme Court decision making. As stated previously, the attitudinal model proposes that judicial outcomes reflect a combination of legal facts and the policy preferences of individual justices. Specifically, each case presents the Court with two competing policy alternatives, which, like the justices themselves, can be located in an ideological space. Based on the relative distance between a justice and each alternative, that justice votes for the alternative that is closest to his or her ideal point. The attitudinal explanation for unanimity is thus that the lower court decision represents an "extreme" position on the ideological scale, and all nine justices are either more conservative or more liberal than the lower court decision. In other words, "the Supreme Court will only unanimously reverse a liberal decision on the court below when the most liberal justice on the Supreme Court prefers an outcome more conservative than that adopted by the lower court" (Songer and Siripurapu 2009, 69) and vice versa. We utilize the variables described in the following sections to capture attitudinal influences on the likelihood of achieving unanimity and consensus.

Degree of Ideological Polarization

Since we seek to explain the collective votes of the Court, we utilize a collective measure to assess the effect of justice ideology on case outcomes: the degree of *Ideological Polarization* among the justices who participated in each case, measured as the absolute value of the distance between the median justice's Martin-Quinn score and the most extreme justice's Martin-Quinn score (Martin and Quinn 2002).[10] A smaller distance score suggests the justices are relatively ideologically compatible, while a larger one suggests more ideological polarization. We employ the absolute distance between the median and most extreme justices, rather than, for example, the standard deviation of the justices' Martin-Quinn scores, because of our interest in unanimity. The standard deviation measure reveals how compatible the majority of the justices are; it is particularly useful for questions concerning the formation of minimum-winning coalitions. However, we seek to explain those occasions when *all* of the justices are able to agree, including those located at opposing ideological poles. Thus, we are concerned not with the distance between the justices centered around the median but rather with the degree of polarization between the extremes. A more accurate measure of this concept of polarization would be the absolute value of the distance between the two most extreme justices, as a unanimous decision necessitates that the two most ideologically polarized justices join forces. However, the distance between the median and most extreme justice is a more conservative test of the influence of ideological polarization on consensus. All else being equal, we expect that the more ideologically compatible the justices are, the more likely that unanimity or a high degree of consensus will be achieved; the more ideologically polarized the justices, the more unlikely consensus becomes (Hurwitz and Lanier 2004; cf. Walker, Epstein, and Dixon 1988).

Reversing Extreme Lower Court Decisions

As stated previously, the attitudinal explanation for unanimous decisions on the Supreme Court is that the lower court decision likely represents an "extreme" position on the ideological scale and all nine justices are either more liberal or more conservative than that decision. Stated simply, the attitudinal model predicts that unanimity should occur only if the lower court decision is outside the range of views of the entirety of the Court. For this reason, we create an interaction term, *Reversal × Extreme Lower Court Decision*. The first constituent term, *Extreme Lower Court Decision*, captures whether the lower court decision can be considered "extreme" by comparing the ideology of each member of the lower court panel with the ideology of each justice who participates in the case. We use the Judicial Common Space scores, which provide preference estimates for Supreme Court justices that are directly comparable to preference measures of federal appeals and district court judges (Epstein et al. 2007); however, these scores do not allow comparisons between the justices and state court judges.[11]

An alternative measure of judicial ideology uses the party of the appointing official as a proxy: federal judges are given the same partisan identification as that of the president who nominated them, and state judges are given the same partisan identification as that of the governor in office at the time of their appointment. We believe there are two problems with this measure. First, since most state judges are not selected through a gubernatorial appointment process, a measure based on the incumbent governor is a particularly weak proxy for judicial ideology (e.g., Brace, Langer, and Hall 2000). Second, a simple partisan measure has only two values, Republican and Democrat, and thus does not account for potential variations in ideological preferences even among co-partisans. Given that we wish to identify lower court panels that are ideologically "extreme" in order to test the hypothesis offered by the attitudinal model concerning consensus on the Court, we need a measure that places each judge along an ideological continuum and allows for comparison even among judges of the same partisan allegiance. As a result, since there are no existing ideological preference measures for state court judges that are directly comparable to those for Supreme Court justices, state court cases are excluded from our analyses. Although we do not believe that there is much difference between state and federal cases when it comes to understanding consensus, we do recognize the possibility that the Court may treat these cases distinctly and therefore our understanding of consensus may be limited.

Some studies (e.g., Roy and Songer 2010) have examined the distance between the median of the appeals court panel and that of the Supreme

Court. However, our interest is not in examining how ideological distance influences Court voting outcomes but rather in determining whether a lower court decision can possibly be considered "extreme" and thus a candidate for a unanimous decision based on the reasoning presented by the attitudinal model. Using the Judicial Common Space scores, we identify the most ideologically extreme justices and judges for each case. Then, to provide the fairest test of the attitudinal explanation for unanimous decisions, we coded the case as "extreme" if any member of the lower court panel (regardless of the panel vote) was more extreme than the most ideologically extreme Supreme Court justice who heard the case.

The second constituent term, *Reversal*, reflects whether the justices voted to reverse the lower court. Using the Spaeth dataset, we coded this variable 1 if the Court reversed the lower court, and 0 otherwise.[12] We then interact this variable with the *Extreme Lower Court Decision* variable as the attitudinal explanation for unanimity does not anticipate unanimous affirmances. We expect that the Court is more likely to reach a unanimous or highly consensual decision when it reverses an extreme lower court decision.

Strategy

Our model puts a heavy emphasis on the interaction between attitudes and law, but we theorize that strategic considerations also influence the Court's ability to achieve consensus. According to proponents of the strategic model, "justices are strategic actors who realize that their ability to achieve their goals depends on a consideration of the preferences of other actors, the choices they expect others to make, and the institutional context in which they act" (Epstein and Knight 1998, 10). The strategic model thus suggests that the justices vote unanimously in certain cases, such as those in which they are concerned with maintaining the legitimacy of the Court. Additionally, although the justices prefer to see their personal policy preferences reflected in law, they must take into account other actors, such as Congress and the president, and therefore sometimes do not vote sincerely. Finally, the justices may take into account the institution in which they work and their role within it. To test for the influence of such strategic considerations, we utilize the following variables.

Altered Precedent/Law Declared Unconstitutional

The literature is mixed on the relationship between unanimity and the reversal of precedent or the overturning of statutes. On the one hand, scholars argue that when the Court overturns existing precedent or declares a federal, state, or municipal law unconstitutional, it is behaving as an "activist" Court (Keck 2004; Pickerill 2004). Because they are directly invalidating the actions of other political actors—and in some cases the will of the people—the justices often discuss the propriety of speaking with one institutional voice in an attempt to enhance the decision's legitimacy. Chief Justice Earl Warren's attempts to secure a unanimous decision in *Brown v. Board of Education* (1954)—which both reversed existing precedent and struck down multiple state and federal laws—are well known; the justices on his Court recognized the desirability of unanimity as well. Associate Justice Harold H. Burton wrote to Warren: "Today I believe has been a great day for America and the Court. . . . To you goes the credit for the character of the opinions which produced the all important unanimity. Congratulations."[13]

On the other hand, since exercising judicial review and overruling prior precedent are actions the Court does not take lightly, unanimity may be harder to achieve. Edelman, Klein and Lindquist (2012, 140) argued that overruling precedent is a "dramatic doctrinal step [that is more likely] in cases where justices feel especially strongly about the policy issues involved." As a result, justices may be more likely to vote ideologically—and thus more divisively—when overruling precedent than when upholding it. Similarly, Sala and Spriggs (2004) found that, contrary to their expectations, decisions by the Court to strike down statutes are best predicted by an attitudinal rather than separation-of-powers model. For these reasons, we control for whether the Court overturned an existing precedent or struck down a statute as unconstitutional, but we do not make a prediction as to the direction of the effect such an action may have on the justices' ability to render a unanimous decision.

Solicitor General

The solicitor general (SG) is typically selected by the attorney general, nominated by the president, and confirmed by the Senate. The SG represents the interests of the executive branch before the Supreme Court, arguing all cases in which the federal government is a litigant. The high success rate of the SG before the Court is well documented. The Court is more likely to grant certiorari in cases in which the SG files an amicus brief that supports review (Caldeira and Wright 1988; Provine 1980), and it generally agrees with the SG's position on the merits (Epstein et al. 2007; Johnson 2003; McGuire 1998). Explanations for this high success rate include institutional deference (Yates

2002), strategic litigation decisions (Zorn 2002), and the quality of the SG's legal arguments (Lindquist and Klein 2006; McGuire 1998). Research also demonstrates that the SG appears to reflect the ideological views of the appointing president (Meinhold and Shull 1998; Salokar 1992; Segal 1988).

We propose that the Court acts strategically when the SG represents either of the parties (and consequently acts as a representative of the president) and specifically predict that the SG is not only more likely to succeed on the merits but to succeed big, meaning that the vote is unanimous. We include a variable, *SG Party*, denoting whether the SG represents either the petitioner or the respondent, coded 1 if the SG represents one of the parties and 0 otherwise.

Majority Opinion Writer: Chief Justice and Median Justice

We include two variables that take into account the potential influence of the majority opinion writer on discouraging either concurrences or dissents: *Chief Justice Writes Opinion* and *Median Justice Writes Opinion*. According to Maltzman and Wahlbeck (1996, 581), vote switching is "not the norm on the Court, but neither is it rare," and other scholars have shown that final votes are many times driven by the ultimate content of the opinion (e.g., Bonneau et al. 2007; Maltzman and Wahlbeck 1996). We first test for whether the chief justice wrote the majority opinion. We propose that one way chief justices may leverage their institutional role to encourage consensus is by strategically utilizing their power of self-assignment. By self-assigning the majority opinion, chiefs can ensure that the opinion written after a unanimous conference vote commands a unanimous Court, thereby increasing the opinion's policy impact (Epstein and Knight 1998; Wahlbeck 2006). Slotnick's (1978) analysis of self-assignment found that chiefs are both more likely to assign themselves unanimous opinions and less likely to author opinions in highly divided cases. Furthermore, Johnson, Spriggs, and Wahlbeck (2005) argued that Chief Justice Burger would strategically vote at conference to gain the power of opinion assignment. In addition to assignment strategy, chiefs can also work to author an opinion that guards against other justices defecting. Thus, we expect that if the chief justice authors the opinion, there is a greater likelihood of the Court reaching a unanimous decision or a decision with a high level of consensus.

Second, whether the median justice wrote the majority opinion may influence consensus. Although existing scholarship has done much to explain the extent to which the median justice influences the content of the majority opinion (Bonneau et al. 2007; Lax 2007; Westerland 2003), there has been relatively little analysis of his or her ability to aid consensus. According to Maltzman, Spriggs, and Wahlbeck (2000), a moderate justice may be more likely to keep other justices from defecting if the majority is fragile (see also Wahlbeck 2006). Brenner and Spaeth (1988), however, found that during the Warren Court a marginal justice of a minimum-winning coalition was no more likely than any other to maintain the original coalition. In addition, Maltzman, Spriggs, and Wahlbeck (2000) discovered that opinion authors who are ideologically distant from the majority coalition are more likely to accommodate, suggesting that if the median justice is the majority opinion writer, she or he may be less likely to accommodate. On the other hand, justices may be more likely to find an opinion acceptable if its author is ideologically close to them (Maltzman, Spriggs, and Wahlbeck 2000). Given the conflicting theories regarding the median justice, we do not have a clear prediction concerning his or her influence on consensus, but we control for whether the median justice is the opinion writer.

Institutional Context

A focus on the structure of the Supreme Court, as well as on institutional changes that have taken place over time, may also provide some insight into how the Court achieves unanimity. Put simply, structure matters: procedural rules and structural design can have important consequences for an institution's outputs. For example, key structural differences between the U.S. House and Senate produce distinct policy outputs. Lazarus and Steigerwalt (2009) found, for example, that differential term lengths result in important differences in how each chamber distributes earmarks. Similarly, the Court's structure likely influences the decisions it renders. Both the attitudinal and the strategic models take into account the institutional context within which the Court operates. The attitudinal model's characterization of justices as unfettered political actors is premised on the existence of three major institutional components: the justices' life tenure, seat at the apex of the federal judicial hierarchy, and relative independence from political and public accountability. The strategic model is similarly based on the notion that institutional design influences the justices' actions. For example, the need for majority agreement to announce a decision of the Court, the possibility of justices writing separately, and the potential for external backlash by the other branches of government are all presumed to greatly influence the Court's inner workings and how the justices interact as well as vote. During the period under study (1953–2004), the Court underwent a number of important institutional changes that may have influenced the degree of consensus that it can achieve. We therefore include the following variables in order to determine whether major institutional changes help to account for consensual behavior:

Chief Justice

Chief justices possess unique powers compared to the other justices, and we hypothesize that different chiefs use these prerogatives differently. Specifically, the chief can be both a task and a social leader among his colleagues (Danelski 1960). Formally, the chief circulates the initial "discuss list" of petitions to be officially considered by the Court, speaks and votes first in Conference deliberations, and assigns opinions among himself and the other justices who agree with him in a given case (Danelski 1960; Murphy 1964; Rohde and Spaeth 1976; Segal and Spaeth 1993, 2002; Slotnick 1978; Ulmer 1970). The chief can also use his position to either encourage consensus or foster dissent (Danelski 1980; Walker, Epstein, and Dixon 1988). Caldeira and Zorn (1998) found that each chief justice promoted different consensual norms, and this variation caused the number of concurrences and dissents to shift over time as different chief justices took the helm. Thus, the ability of the Court to achieve consensus and unanimity may be directly influenced by whether the current chief justice believes that these are worthwhile goals (Rosen 2007a).

By all accounts, Chief Justice Warren was both an effective task leader and an effective social leader. Of his selection, Justice Sherman Minton commented: "The President could not have appointed a finer person to work with than Chief Justice Warren, who is a good solid lawyer and is coming along rapidly."[14] Warren rearranged the Court's calendar, shifting Conference days from Saturday to Friday. Conferences became orderly and succinct, in sharp contrast to Chief Justice Stone's freewheeling and never-ending Conferences. Warren also continued the practice, begun at the end of Chief Justice Vinson's tenure, of assigning opinions equally. Douglas (1980, 228) summed up Warren's style: "Most of the time Warren was polite, considerate and friendly, handling the Conference with consummate skill. He had no monopoly on stubbornness. But when he felt strongly on an issue—obscenity or flag burning—he held forth at length."

If Warren was respected by his colleagues, Chief Justice Burger was not. Over time, Burger's colleagues began to resent what they saw as disingenuous and even manipulative behavior. For example, Burger backdated documents to make it appear that he had completed his work more quickly than he actually had. Also, he routinely denied that law clerks drafted his opinions, even though the practice was common among all of the justices. However, it was in Conference and coalition formation where his colleagues felt he regularly crossed the line. According to Powell's biographer and former clerk John C. Jeffries, Jr. (1994, 532–533):

> Burger often came to Conference without a thorough knowledge of the cases. He would wander around the general subject and end up reserving his vote until the others had spoken. Over the years, his long-winded monologues and puffed-up pronouncements became repetitive and maddeningly predictable. Brennan said that Burger would "drive us all crazy—including Lewis—with the same law-and-order speech in every damn criminal case." According to another Justice, once others began to speak, Burger would frequently "interject his own comments and views . . . which might or might not be relevant."

Burger would also switch his vote post-Conference in order to control opinion assignment and to influence outcomes. For example, as detailed by Woodward and Armstrong in *The Brethren* (1979, 66), after one of his clerks asked him why he was assigning a majority opinion to himself after voting in the minority in Conference, he told the clerk, "That was a tentative vote." But according to Dennis J. Hutchinson, former clerk to Justices White and Douglas (1998, 357), Burger's misassignments were "a function more often of blunder than of design, although there were cases of both."

In addition to vote switching, Burger found other ways to influence assignments when he was in the minority. For example, he wrote Blackmun, Powell, and Rehnquist:

> I am remiss in not having discussed one aspect of the assigning process with those who came on the Court after my arrival. Harry is aware, since he served with Hugo, that traditionally assignments by anyone other than the Chief Justice were made by the Senior Justice of the Majority in coordination with the Chief Justice. While Hugo was here I made up a tentative list and then he and I conferred. This sometimes led me to alter my assignment of a case because there would be special reasons why a particular Justice should get an assignment that was Hugo's responsibility. This coordination worked very well, but it has not been followed since the end of the 1970 Term.
>
> This week I was, as my memo this date to the Conference shows, unaware that, for example, Bill Brennan had assigned . . . *NLRB v. Boeing Co.* to Bill Rehnquist, as was his right, since Douglas and I voted in the minority. In working out the assignments Saturday I got . . . [*Boeing*] and . . . (*Booster Lodge*) reversed in my mind and assigned both to Thurgood, thinking (erroneously) that since one case is likely

to be a brief p.c. [*per curiam*], the two should go together. My error, I repeat, was to confuse the "tail" case with the "dog" case. Had Bill Brennan coordinated with me or even informed me, I would have avoided my own mechanical error and a total of four re-assignments would have been avoided. . . .

The net of all this is that there seems to be a lack of willingness to coordinate my task with the (happily rare) assignments by Bill Douglas and Bill Brennan. It would, therefore, help me if each of you—when given an assignment before I have the entire assignment list ready—would request the assigner to inform me at or before the time of the assignment to you. I should have discussed this with you in January of 1972, but I would appreciate your cooperation from April 1973 forward![15]

Rehnquist served as an associate justice under Burger for fifteen terms before succeeding him as chief, and, given his experiences with Burger's machinations, it is not surprising that Rehnquist would behave differently from his predecessor. While he brought order and civility to the Court, it also appears that, like his predecessors, Rehnquist had little if any interest in using his new position to promote unanimity. He conducted himself as chief exactly as he had as a longtime associate: an individual justice with his own views who was not afraid to dissent. There is little evidence that he sought to promote consensus.

Rehnquist endeavored to spend as little time as possible in Conference. Former clerk Courtney Elwood explained that this was part of Rehnquist's overall goal to promote congenial relations among the justices and to minimize discord: "The Chief Justice believed that the Supreme Court works best when its members get along. . . . For instance, he kept the conferences short. It was not that he was not interested in the ideas or arguments of his colleagues. Rather, he understood that the more they dwelt over disagreement, the more acrimonious things would become" (quoted in "Supreme Court Bar Published Memorials to William H. Rehnquist" 2007, 5).

Shortening Conferences promoted more harmonious relationships among the justices, but it also made the post-Conference coalition formation process even more crucial. Justice Harry Blackmun commented on Rehnquist's leadership: "He gets through the agenda in a hurry and cuts down [on the] interchange between the justices and always says, well, that can come out in the writing" (quoted in O'Brien 2005, 200).

As in Conference deliberation, Rehnquist virtually ignored unanimity in the opinion writing and coalition formation processes. Instead, he continually stressed the need for the opinion writer to gain a majority only (Rehnquist 1987, 302). When asked about Rehnquist's concern for unanimity, Chief Justice Roberts recalled of his time as Rehnquist's clerk: "I don't remember [promoting unanimity] as a feature that Rehnquist stressed much" (quoted in Rosen 2007a). In the end, Rehnquist was willing to sacrifice consensus building—and the discord he felt would necessarily follow—for a generally harmonious working environment.

This brief discussion of the similarities and differences among the recent chief justices with regard to task and social leadership suggests that it is useful to test whether it matters who the chief justice is when it comes to consensus. We created dummy variables for each chief justice, and we use Chief Justice Warren as the baseline for comparison.

Addition of Syllabus

Consensual norms abruptly disappeared at the start of the Burger Court, including reluctance to be the sole dissenter (a practice known as "acquiescence"), and willingness to dissent without issuing an opinion (a practice known as "notation"). The average number of dissents without opinion went from 15 under Stone, 26 under Vinson, and 11.5 under Warren to a minuscule 1.5 under Burger (Cook 1995). A 1974 memo from Rehnquist to Burger regarding the criminal procedure case *Eaton v. City of Tulsa* (1974) illustrates how, as a new associate justice, Rehnquist found acquiescence distasteful: "I have pondered rather carefully your thought that when one disagrees with the majority in a case such as this, it may be best to say nothing and not highlight what one considers to be the failings of the majority opinion. I did follow the counsel in *Little*, 404 U.S. 553 (1972), when I joined your concurring opinion, but now that case is being cited as authority for the result the Court reaches here. Since Bill Brennan's opinion does go into some detail, I think it best to fight the matter out on the merits. I am going to circulate a dissent."[16]

Ultimately, Burger and Blackmun joined Rehnquist's dissent from the Court's *per curiam* opinion, and future justices continued the practice of publicizing their own dissents. For example, Rehnquist (198, 302) wrote after he was elevated to chief: "In the past it was a common practice for justices who disagreed with the opinion of the Court simply to note their dissent from the opinion without more ado, but this practice is very rare today." Twenty years later, Justice Stevens said, "I don't believe in suppressing dissent. If you disagree you should say so. . . . I just feel I have an obligation to expose my views to the public" (quoted in Rosen 2007b).

What led to the death of acquiescence and notation? We argue that it was the Burger Court's decision in 1971 to include at the start of every opinion a syllabus specifying each justice's vote. For example the syllabus for the abortion case *Roe v. Wade* (1973) delineates:

> BLACKMUN, J., delivered the opinion of the Court, in which BURGER, C. J., and DOUGLAS, BRENNAN, STEWART, MARSHALL, and POWELL, JJ., joined. BURGER, C. J., post, p. 207, DOUGLAS, J., post, p. 209, and STEWART, J., post, p. 167, filed concurring opinions. WHITE, J., filed a dissenting opinion, in which REHNQUIST, J., joined, post, p. 221. REHNQUIST, J., filed a dissenting opinion, post, p. 171. (*Roe*, 114)

Prior to this change, coalitions had to be inferred. For example, in the Free Speech case *Tinker v. Des Moines* (1969) only five justices are referenced: "MR. JUSTICE FORTAS delivered the opinion of the Court" (*Tinker*, 504), "MR. JUSTICE STEWART, concurring" (ibid., 514), "MR. JUSTICE WHITE, concurring" (ibid., 515), "MR. JUSTICE BLACK, dissenting" (ibid., 515), and "MR. JUSTICE HARLAN, dissenting" (ibid., 526). We must assume that Chief Justice Warren and Justices Douglas, Brennan, and Marshall agreed with the majority opinion, as it is unstated.

The addition of a syllabus now made each justice publicly responsible for his or her votes. In the past, the norm of acquiescence may have allowed for more ambiguity in how the justices felt about their stance in certain cases. Express public accountability, however, removed this cover, and may help explain why acquiescence and notation disappeared and individual expression continued to escalate. As a result, we include the variable *Addition of Syllabus* to measure changes associated with the end of acquiescence and notation as well as the inclusion of the syllabus. Decisions during or after 1971 are coded 1; those prior to 1971 are coded 0.

Formalization of Dissent Assignment

We posit that the practice of formally assigning dissents also helped undermine consensus. In 1953, Justice Frankfurter explained that only majority opinions were formally assigned; "as for dissents and concurrences—that's for each member to choose for himself" (1953, 904). Yet dissent assignment practices slowly changed from the volunteerism described by Frankfurter to collegial cooperation and finally to senior responsibility (Cook 1995). Justice Hugo Black, the senior liberal justice, made some attempts during the Stone Court to assign dissents, as did some subsequent senior justices including Frankfurter. However, the practice was not institutionalized until Justice William Brennan took the initiative at the start of the Burger Court. Following Black's departure, Brennan gingerly prodded his senior colleague,

William O. Douglas, to formally assign dissents. After Douglas's departure in 1975, Brennan assigned the opinion in every case where he was in the minority, circulating an assignment memorandum to his colleagues on the day of or before the Chief's majority opinion assignments were circulated. One of his goals in both circulating dissent assignment memos and selecting opinion writers was to solidify the minority coalition, thereby significantly undermining the ability of the majority coalition and the chief justice to achieve greater consensus (Cook 1995; Wood and Gansle 1997).

Subsequent senior dissenters followed Brennan's practice, and when Rehnquist became Chief he accepted the norm, writing matter-of-factly: "The senior justice among those who disagreed with the result reached by the majority at conference usually undertakes to assign the preparation of the dissenting opinion in the case if there is to be one" (Rehnquist 1987, 302). Still, this practice is not always as cut-and-dry as majority opinion assignment often is. This memo from Justice Harry Blackmun to Justices John Paul Stevens and Sandra Day O'Connor concerning the abortion protest case *Bray v. Alexandria Clinic* (1993) provides an example of ultimate senior responsibility with a healthy dose of collegial cooperation: "Dear John and Sandra: The three of us are in dissent in this case. It may well be that more than one of us will write in dissent. In line with our telephone conversations of this morning, John has agreed to undertake the initial writing and to coordinate with Sandra as the case develops. Whether I shall also write remains to be seen."[17] Volunteerism also occurred but within the norm of senior assignment, such as when Justice Lewis Powell wrote Brennan: "As you are the senior in dissent in this case, I write to say that I will be happy to draft a dissent for the four of us if you wish. . . . I merely want you to know of my availability" (quoted in Cook 1995, 22).

Just as controlling majority opinion assignment provides an incentive for chief justices to vote with the majority, formalizing dissent assignment provides an incentive for senior justices to vote against the majority. And while dissents (or the threat of dissent) can serve the purpose of exacting changes from the majority opinion and may ultimately be withdrawn, by expending resources to formally draft and circulate dissents, justices have an incentive to issue them. Hence, we include the variable *Formalization of Dissent Assignment*, coding decisions handed down during or after 1975 as 1 and those before 1975 as 0.

Docket Size

The Judges' Bill of 1925 relieved the justices of their burdensome mandatory docket and allowed them to focus on the most significant, and sometimes most contentious, issues of the day. Its implications for consensual decision making cannot be overstated: the justices were no longer faced with numerous relatively easy cases on which they could all agree, and with almost total discretion they began hearing those that were more controversial. Cases involving civil liberties and rights issues such as Freedom of Speech, Privacy, and the rights of the accused not only became a permanent feature of the Court's annual caseload but also divided the justices as never before. Indeed, as detailed in Chapter 1, even the New Deal liberal justices of the Roosevelt Court differed on these and other matters. The discretionary docket, in short, helped usher in a new era of dissensus.

Yet the discretionary docket of the modern Court has not been stable over time. Specifically, the Rehnquist Court dramatically decreased the number of cases it chose to decide. When Rehnquist took over as chief in 1986, the Court was deciding roughly 150 cases per term—a number that was relatively stable throughout Rehnquist's tenure as an associate on the Burger Court. Yet ten years later, the Court was only deciding half as many cases, which it continues to do under Chief Justice Roberts. Some studies suggest various reasons for this development, among them new justices hesitant to grant review (Cordray and Cordray 2001; O'Brien 1997), "Olympian" justices only interested in granting landmark cases (Hellman 1996), and the rise of law clerks and the development of the cert pool (Perry 1991; Starr 2006; Ward and Weiden 2006). Regardless of the impetus for the declining number of cases, we code for *Docket Size*, and posit that the shrinking docket allows for greater resources to be devoted to cultivating individual expression, thereby undermining consensus.

Number of Law Clerks

A number of scholars have concluded that law clerks influence the justices' decisions to issue separate opinions (Best 2002; O'Brien 2005; Posner 1996; Ward and Weiden 2006). In 1947, the number of clerks assigned to each justice went from one to two. When Fred M. Vinson joined the Court as chief justice, he immediately added a third clerk to his staff, prompting Judge Learned Hand to dub him "Vinson Incorporated" (Ward and Weiden 2006, 370). According to Ward and Weiden (ibid.), a former clerk thought that "Vinson Limited" was more appropriate. Most of Vinson's colleagues moved to two clerks each to help them deal with the growing number of petitions they had to consider each year. Yet, the role of clerks was not confined to the agenda setting process: they also prepared bench memoranda for their justices to use during oral arguments and occasionally drafted lengthy memoranda on a particular issue or point of law. Indeed, within the Court their stature had never been higher. As clerks demonstrated high levels of competence during the cert process and in drafting memoranda, the justices felt more comfortable allowing them to draft opinions, sometimes rarely or occasionally, as with Black and Douglas, and sometimes regularly, as with Vinson, Frankfurter, Frank Murphy, and Harold Burton.

Starting at the end of Vinson's tenure and fully realized under Warren, the opinion writing process transformed dramatically and with it the role of clerks. Douglas (1963) recalled:

> Hughes had a custom of never assigning an opinion to a man who already had an opinion that was unwritten. He made his assignments to those who had nothing to do. As a result, those who turned out work like Stone and Black and myself . . . each of us got more than a ninth of the load. And I think Stone continued that practice and I think Vinson did. . . . When Earl Warren came on as Chief Justice he instituted a different system. He decided that every member of the Court should pull the same size oar and row as hard as anybody else. And so he has roughly allotted the opinions one-ninth to each judge and he has tried to level it out so if a judge gets a big, complicated case the next time around he gets a simple case. He's tried to even out the workload.

Vinson's new method of assigning opinions equally was followed by subsequent chief justices and had an important long-term effect. Justices who were accustomed to writing very few opinions were suddenly expected to greatly increase their output, and they quickly turned to their clerks for help. Clerks for justices who wrote their own opinions relatively quickly, like Black and Douglas, were unaffected, while clerks for more methodical writers, like Frankfurter and Stanley Reed, found themselves writing virtually all of their justice's opinions. Data compiled by Palmer and Brenner (1988) illustrate this effect. After Vinson began equalizing opinion assignments, the Court's slowest opinion writers actually finished more quickly. Frankfurter went from 104 days to 77, Burton from 99 days to 73, and Vinson from 99 days to 75.

The number of clerks assigned to each justice continued to grow over time. Congress increased the allotment to three in 1970 and then to four in 1974. And while clerk increases were prompted by the steady rise in the number of cases petitioned to the Court, clerks were by this time drafting nearly all of the opinions for nearly all of the justices, a practice that continues. For this reason, we include the variable *Total Number of Law Clerks Each Term* and hypothesize that their increasing number and responsibilities further dissensus.

Case-Specific Factors

Lastly, we take into account a number of case-specific factors. Not all cases are created equal, and we posit that variation among important case characteristics contributes to whether the Court is able reach agreement. We assess the influence of four case factors shown in the literature to significantly affect judicial decision making: issue area, case salience, whether the decision is in a liberal direction, and time pressures associated with the end of term.

Issue Area

We explore whether certain cases, because of the issues they deal with, are more likely to result in divided decisions. Ideological preferences on civil liberties may be more defined and deeply held than those on other issue areas. Hurwitz and Lanier (2004) and Hensley and Johnson (1998) found that civil liberties cases are less likely to be decided unanimously than other types of cases. Additionally, Unah and Hancock (2006) and Bartels (2010) found that issue salience intensifies the impact of ideology on case outcomes. Thus, we expect that cases involving civil rights and liberties are least likely to be decided unanimously or consensually. We created dummy variables for whether the case concerns a *Civil Liberties and Rights Issue*, an *Economic Activity Issue*, or a *Governmental Powers Issue*, and we exclude civil liberties cases as the baseline for comparison.

Case Salience

We also test for the possibility that cases with a high degree of salience to external political actors and the public are salient to the justices as well and therefore more likely to expose divisions among them. As Grossman and Wells (1989, 59) argued, "[T]hese are the kinds of cases least likely to be decided unanimously. There is no a priori reason to expect . . . justices to be united on politically contentious issues that divide the country." Thus, *Salient Cases*—specifically those covered on the front page of the *New York Times* the day after the decision is announced (Epstein and Segal 2000)—should be less likely to result in unanimous or highly consensual decisions. Salient cases are coded 1, and nonsalient cases are coded 0.

Liberal Decision

We also control for whether the decision was in a liberal direction (*Liberal Decision*). Brenner and Arrington (1987) examined all civil liberties and economic cases decided during the 1946–1952 and 1958–1983 terms. They compared the ideological direction of split versus unanimous decisions and found that liberal outcomes dominate unanimously decided cases. To explain this finding, they suggested that "liberalism in the period under investigation was either a more complete or a more strongly held ideology" (83). Similarly, Hensley and Johnson (1998) found that 48 percent of all liberal decisions during the 1986–1990 terms were unanimous, a surprising result given that the Rehnquist Court consisted of a majority of conservative justices. They suggested a legal or strategic perspective to account for the liberalism found in these cases, specifically positing that the Rehnquist Court justices may have simply been upholding liberal precedent from previous Court eras or that the Court was serving goals that produced liberal rulings, such as increasing the Court's power. Given these findings, we coded liberal decisions as 1, and 0 otherwise.

Time to End of Term

In Chapter 4 we assess when and why the justices are able to reach agreement not only on the outcome of the case but also in terms of the legal reasoning presented in the opinion they issue, what we term "opinion consensus." With regard to opinion consensus, we control for the practical constraint of time on the production of separate opinions. End-of-term pressures are routinely discussed by the justices and their clerks. For example, David Kendall, who clerked in 1971, wrote Rehnquist:

> As a keen observer and avid timer of the judicial circulations of the Court this Term, it is my pleasure to notify you that your opinion for the Court in . . . *United States v. Allegheny-Ludlum Steel Corp.* has been nominated for the Parnelli Jones Memorial Award for the most supersonic opinion of the year. Our records indicate that this opinion, utilizing a normal unmodified type of judicial review, picked up three "joins" on its first day in circulation, four on its second, and picked up the final "join" on its third day out. Your opinion is thus in an excellent position to qualify for the Pole Position this Term. . . . All clerks with vacations scheduled for early in July are keenly grateful to you for your speed and persuasiveness in this case. Sincerely, David Kendall on behalf of the "End of the Term in OT 71" Committee of 31 "Say hey, we won't stay."[18]

Similarly, Chief Justice Rehnquist wrote his colleagues on June 2, 1994:

> As I write, there are four uncirculated majority opinions and 32 circulated majority opinions which have not been brought down—making a total of 36. Tomorrow let us establish target dates for each of the 32 circulated opinions, with a view that it may be possible to recess early in the week on Monday, June 27th. This would mean three more Friday conferences after tomorrow: June 10, June 17th, and June 24th.

It would mean that we could bring cases down on Monday, June 13th, and on a later date that same week if the cases were available; on Monday June 20th, and on one or two additional days in that week if the cases were available; and on Monday, June 27th, Tuesday, June 28th, and, if necessary, Wednesday, June 29th.[19]

Because justices are keenly aware of time pressures associated with the end of term, we hypothesize that time constraints affect separate opinion writing. Specifically, the amount of time a justice can devote to writing a separate opinion may affect whether he or she does so. Authoring a separate opinion is time-consuming, and justices may decide against writing a separate opinion, especially a concurrence, when their caseload is heavy. This workload pressure intensifies as the Court's term draws to a close. Wahlbeck, Spriggs, and Maltzman (1999) found that justices are less willing to write concurring opinions as the end of the Court's term approaches. We similarly expect to see more opinion consensus when the Court's workload is high and time is short; alternatively, the more days there are between the date of oral argument and the end of term, the more separate opinions and thus the less consensus we expect to see.[20] We measure the *Time Left until End of Term* by counting the number of days between the date of oral argument for each case and July 1st, when the Court's term traditionally ends.

Conclusion

In this chapter we present our theory of consensus and explicate how we propose to measure the central concepts that comprise our model. We argue that the key to understanding consensus is recognizing the diverse set of factors that work together to affect the justices in each case. Broadly, these forces are attitudinal, legal, strategic, institutional, and case-specific; we suggest each operates simultaneously to influence whether the Court is able to achieve consensus. In addition, we offer a mechanism for capturing law—our Legal Certainty Index—in an effort to test for its effects on judicial decision making and the achievement of consensus. Although our measure of legal certainty may be imperfect, we argue that it offers an important and useful step in moving toward a comprehensive understanding of how the Court successfully reaches consensus.

We now turn to an empirical examination of the Supreme Court's decisions between 1953 and 2004. Our goal is to determine the forces that explain how the Court reaches unanimous or highly consensual decisions. In Chapter 3, we examine consensus in terms of votes on the merits. In Chapter 4, we investigate consensus in opinion writing.

A Function of Design

Consensus in Votes on the Merits

On December 15, 2003, the United States Supreme Court handed down a unanimous decision in the case of *Maryland v. Pringle*. Joseph Pringle was a passenger in the front seat of a car stopped for speeding at 3:00 A.M.; another passenger was in the backseat. When the driver opened the car's glove box to retrieve the vehicle registration, the officer observed a large amount of money within. The officer, after checking for outstanding violations, issued the driver an oral warning. The officer then asked the driver whether there were any weapons or narcotics in the vehicle. The driver said no and then consented to a search of the car. The search revealed $763 in the glove compartment and five plastic baggies of cocaine behind the backseat armrest. All three occupants of the car were then arrested for possession of cocaine. At trial, Pringle argued that there was no probable cause to believe that he specifically was guilty of possession.[1] The Supreme Court unanimously disagreed, and, in a single opinion written by Chief Justice Rehnquist, held that it was reasonable for the officer to assume that all three occupants of the car were collectively engaged in the crime at hand.

Why did each of the justices reach the same decision? The same nine justices split 5–4 that same term on a number of other decisions involving the Fourth Amendment, including *Hiibel v. Sixth Judicial District Court of Nevada* (2004). In this case, the Court divided sharply over the question of whether Nevada's "stop and identify" statute, which made it a crime to refuse to identify oneself when stopped by a police officer, was constitutional under the Fourth and Fifth Amendments. The majority upheld the statute, arguing that in the course of a legitimate "*Terry* Stop," a state may require a suspect to disclose his or her name. Why did the same justices who were able to reach agreement in *Pringle* divide so sharply in *Hiibel*? In other words, how do we explain the puzzle of ideologically divided justices successfully achieving consensus?

In this chapter, we begin our empirical investigation of consensus on the Supreme Court. Our purpose is to determine why the justices are able to agree in some cases but disagree in others. In Chapter 1 our investigation of the historical shift from the "norm of consensus" to the modern era of dissensus—which we maintain irrevocably began during the Roosevelt Court era—pinpoints the many ways in which dissensus is not unexpected. However, the reality is that consensus is also relatively frequent. The question we do not yet have a good answer to is why—why does a Court with a largely discretionary docket loaded with contentious issues still reach agreement so often?

To address this important question, we return to our comprehensive theory of consensus as laid out in Chapter 2. This theory is predicated on the notion that multiple, simultaneously operating forces help explain consensus on the Supreme Court. While most studies of decision making attempt to discern which broad theory best explains how the justices arrive at their decisions, we argue that an exploration of how these theories operate in concert is necessary. We further argue that ideological and legal forces influence the justices in a complex, interactive fashion. In some cases attitudes may predominate; in others legal forces restrict the justices' ability to vote solely based on their personal preferences. In particular, as the level of legal certainty as to the strongest legal answer increases, the likelihood of consensus increases. However, when legal certainty is low, dissensus generally results.

In Chapter 2, we explicate our method of capturing this notion of legal certainty as well as the numerous other forces that we believe work concurrently to influence consensus on the Court. In this chapter and the next, we empirically test our theory on cases decided by the Court from 1953 to 2004. Our findings suggest that a multitude of different forces, including the level of legal certainty in the case, influence whether the Court is able to achieve unanimity or a high degree of consensus. Thus, understanding consensus necessitates the recognition of numerous factors—including legal forces—that influence the Court's decisions.

Examining Consensus and Unanimity

In this chapter we examine in a variety of ways the degree to which the Court's final vote on the merits was consensual in the period under study. In Chapter 4, we look beyond the vote to actual opinions, as disagreement over the correct legal answer can be obscured by looking only at the votes themselves. For example, even if the vote in the case was 9–0 and thus unanimous, some of the justices may have written separate concurrences, suggesting a low degree of what we term *opinion consensus*. This second set of analyses allows us to assess how the Court is able to achieve consensus not only as to the outcome of the case but also as to the strongest legal reasoning.

To conduct the analyses here and in Chapter 4, we focus on all cases appealed from a lower federal court that were granted certiorari, orally argued, and decided by the Court during the 1953–2004 terms,[2] using the Spaeth dataset. Our dataset contains cases decided under Chief Justices Warren, Burger, and Rehnquist. Since our interest is in explaining unanimous decisions (and thus the collective outcome of the Court), our unit of analysis is the individual case. It is here also that we depart from earlier studies that almost exclusively examined individual justices' votes. Assessing the justices' votes helps us particularly to understand dissensus; however, understanding consensus necessitates that we focus on the *Court's* decision to determine why a disparate group of justices can reach the same legal answer.

We utilize two distinct dependent variables to fully assess how the Court arrives at a consensual decision on the merits. The first dependent variable is whether the final vote in each case was *Unanimous*. Unanimous decisions include all instances where no justice dissented, regardless of the number of justices who participated in the case. These are coded 1, and all other decisions are coded 0. In our data, 40 percent of the decisions were unanimous.

Our second dependent variable is whether the final vote in each case was *Unanimous or Highly Consensual*. Here we are interested in exploring decisions in which a relatively high degree of consensus was achieved even if the final vote was not unanimous, as compared to decisions with greater dissensus. We consider the vote to be highly consensual if only one justice dissented. Our dependent variable is thus coded 1 if the vote was unanimous or included a single dissenting vote and 0 otherwise. In our data, approximately 51 percent of cases were decided with one dissent or complete unanimity; if we separate the two categories, 11 percent of cases were decided with a single dissenting vote.

Figure 3.1 displays the percentage of cases decided unanimously and/or highly consensually under Chief Justices Warren, Burger, and Rehnquist. Although there is little difference between Warren and Burger when it comes to the percentage of unanimous decisions handed down during their tenures, the justices who served under Rehnquist were more consensual. Specifically, 37 percent of the cases during Warren's tenure were decided unanimously, as were 38 percent during Burger's and 44 percent during Rehnquist's. These

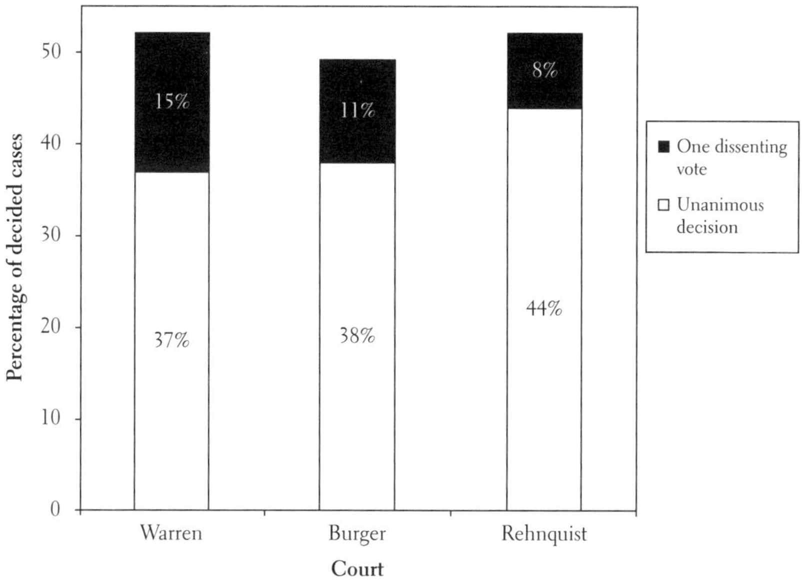

Figure 3.1. Comparison of the Warren, Burger, and Rehnquist Courts: Percentage of unanimous and highly consensual decisions

findings suggest that unanimity seems to be increasing, even as conventional wisdom suggests that the Court is growing increasingly polarized.

Alternatively, highly consensual decisions—those with a single dissenting vote—were most frequent under Warren, at 15 percent. Under Burger, approximately 11 percent resulted in a sole dissent, while only 8 percent were similarly decided under Rehnquist. Notably, when unanimous decisions are coupled with highly consensual decisions, the percentages across Courts are relatively stable, at approximately half of all decisions: 52 percent under Warren, 49 percent under Burger, and 52 percent under Rehnquist. Thus, the reality is that the Court between 1953 and 2004 achieved a high degree of consensus in approximately half of all cases, though we do see some slight variation in whether the justices were able to temper all dissent; again, unanimity was most likely during the more recent Rehnquist tenure. In the following analyses, we seek to explain how the justices reach unanimous as well as highly consensual decisions.

Exploring Unanimous Decisions

We begin by exploring what unanimous cases, as opposed to their more divided counterparts, look like. Given the independent variables explicated in Chapter 2, what differences do we find between unanimous and non-unanimous cases? In this section, we assess the data in an exploratory fashion and then turn, in the subsequent section, to a more rigorous, multivariate analysis of the factors that predict the likelihood of the Supreme Court handing down a unanimous decision on the merits.

What does a unanimously decided case, or a highly consensual case, look like? Unanimous decisions generally address issues that are less controversial overall than others. Perhaps not surprisingly, cases concerning civil liberties are the least likely to be decided unanimously: although 32.2 percent of these cases were unanimous, 44.3 percent of economic cases and 48.8 percent of governmental powers cases were unanimous (see Table 3.1). Similarly, 41.9 percent of civil liberties cases were unanimous or highly consensual compared with 56.2 percent of economic cases and 61.9 percent of governmental powers cases. Additionally, only 25 percent of salient cases were unanimous compared to 41.8 percent of nonsalient cases; 34.2 percent of salient cases were unanimous or highly consensual compared with 53.2 percent of nonsalient cases.

Our initial exploration reveals that unanimous and highly consensual cases reflect at least some strategic calculations. We posit that the identity of the opinion writer may influence the likelihood of unanimity. Most notably, the descriptive analysis reveals that decisions authored by the chief justice were overwhelmingly unanimous: of the 396 decisions authored by the chief justice between 1953 and 2004, 169 (42.7 percent) were decided unanimously and 53.5 percent were unanimous or highly consensual. Alternatively, 39.3 percent of the decisions written by associate justices were unanimous and 50.4 percent were unanimous or highly consensual. Thus, it does appear that chief justices have a slight advantage and can use their power of self-assignment to ensure consensus on the Court. Consensus is not necessarily the outcome, however, when the median justice authors the opinion. In our data, 34.5 percent of the 290 opinions authored by the median justice were in cases decided by a unanimous vote while 41.7 percent were unanimous or highly consensual.

We also expected that unanimity would be more likely when the solicitor general (SG) was a party to the case. Our initial results are in line with our expectations: of the 1,543 cases in which the SG participated, a unanimous

TABLE 3.1
Bivariate predictors of unanimous or highly consensual decisions

Independent variable	Percentage of unanimous decisions	Percentage of unanimous decisions or highly consensual decisions
Civil Liberties and Rights Issue	32.2	41.9
Economic Issue	44.3	56.2
Governmental Powers Issue	48.8	61.9
Chief Justice Majority Opinion Author	42.7	53.5
Associate Justice Majority Opinion Author	39.3	50.4
Median Justice Majority Opinion Author	34.5	41.7
Solicitor General Party to Case	40.2	51.4
Solicitor General Not a Party to Case	39.3	50.3
Salient Case	25.0	34.2
Nonsalient Case	41.8	53.2
Altered Precedent	33.8	41.2
No Alteration of Precedent	39.8	50.9
Declared Statute Unconstitutional	30.0	37.8
No Declaration of Unconstitutionality	39.9	51.0
Before Addition of Syllabus	36.5	51.2
After Addition of Syllabus	41.1	50.5
Before Formalization of Dissent Assignment	36.5	50.6
After Formalization of Dissent Assignment	41.8	50.8
Larger Docket Size	37.0	47.7
Smaller Docket Size	44.1	53.3
Smaller Number of Law Clerks	36.7	51.2
Larger Number of Law Clerks	44.8	54.4
Ideologically Compatible Justices	43.2	54.0
Ideologically Polarized Justices	34.5	49.5
Reversed an "Extreme" Lower Court Panel	38.8	54.2
Reversed a "Nonextreme" Lower Court Panel	41.0	52.2
High Level of Legal Certainty	40.8	53.1
Low Level of Legal Certainty	38.5	48.5

decision was achieved 40.2 percent of the time compared to 39.3 percent of cases in which he did not participate. Thus, it does appear that the SG has a slight advantage.

Our initial examination of the data with regard to the justices overturning past precedents or declaring laws unconstitutional shows that, of the sixty-eight times precedents were altered between 1953 and 2004, a unanimous decision occurred in 33.8 percent of these cases compared with 39.8 percent when the Court was not altering precedent. In regard to declarations of unconstitutionality, the data show that the Court struck down a statute ninety times between 1953 and 2004 and in twenty-seven cases (30 percent) the Court's decision was unanimous. When the Court was not striking down a statute, it achieved unanimity 39.9 percent of the time.

Thus, we find that some strategic considerations influence the likelihood of unanimity: it is more likely when the chief justice authors the majority opinion and when the SG is a party to the case. These exploratory findings suggest both that chiefs can utilize their unique powers to increase agreement and that the justices undertake some strategic calculations with respect to their interactions with other branches of government. For example, in *Butterworth v. Smith* (1990), the Court unanimously struck down, on Free Speech grounds, a Florida law that prohibited grand jury witnesses from disclosing their own testimony after the grand jury's term had ended. Chief Justice Rehnquist wrote the opinion for the unanimous Court. A potential argument is that by issuing a unanimous opinion—and by having the chief justice speak for the entire Court—the Court acted strategically to buttress the legitimacy of its decision to overturn a state law for violating the Constitution.

In terms of institutional context, we investigate whether four discrete changes in Court procedure influence the likelihood of consensus: addition of the syllabus, formalization of dissent assignment, changes in docket size, and changes in the number of law clerks assigned to each justice. We theorize that the addition of the syllabus in 1971, and the concurrent disappearance of the practice of acquiescence and notation, increased the likelihood of dissent. However, our initial examination of the data does not support this hypothesis. Before 1971, 36.5 percent of decisions were unanimous and 51.2 percent were either unanimous or highly consensual; after 1971, 41.1 percent were unanimous and 50.5 percent were either unanimous or highly consensual.

We also posit that the formalization of dissent assignment in 1975 would similarly lead to an increase in dissensus. Once again, we find no support for this hypothesis: before 1975, 36.5 percent of decisions were unanimous and 50.6 percent were either unanimous or highly consensual. After 1975, 41.8 percent of decisions were unanimous and 50.8 percent were either unanimous or highly consensual.

With respect to docket size—which shrank between 1953 and 2004—we assessed whether fluctuations over time influenced the degree of consensus. We find that as the docket grew smaller, the likelihood of consensus, perhaps surprisingly, grew, though the increase was rather slight. When the size of the docket was more than one standard deviation above the mean of 120 cases, unanimity occurred in 37 percent of cases and 47.7 percent were either unanimous or highly consensual. When the docket fell to more than one standard deviation below the mean, unanimity was achieved 44.1 percent of the time and 53.3 percent were either unanimous or highly consensual. Thus, our initial investigation suggests that having more time to consider each case aids the justices in achieving agreement though, again, the differences are relatively small.

The last institutional variable we consider is the effect of the number of law clerks, who increasingly aided in opinion writing during the study period. Here, the findings suggest that more law clerks result, somewhat paradoxically, in more consensus rather than less. When the number of clerks was more than one deviation below the mean, unanimity occurred 36.7 percent of the time. When the number jumped to more than one standard deviation above the mean, the justices were able to reach complete agreement 44.8 percent of the time. We thus see a small but consistent increase in the rate of unanimity as the number of law clerks grew, and these results are similar when examining unanimous or highly consensual cases. Taken together, these preliminary findings suggest, contrary to our expectations, that changes that increase the amount of time justices can devote to each case actually serve to increase the likelihood of agreement.

In terms of ideological considerations, we predict that the likelihood of unanimity will be more likely as the ideological compatibility of the justices increased. Our initial exploratory results support this hypothesis. When the justices were most compatible (i.e., when their ideological polarization scores were more than one standard deviation below the mean), unanimity occurred 43.2 percent of the time and either unanimous or highly consensual decisions occurred 54 percent of the time. The likelihood of unanimity was lower (34.5 percent) when the justices were more ideologically polarized (i.e., when their ideological polarization scores were more than one standard deviation above the mean), as was the likelihood of a unanimous or highly consensual decision (49.5 percent). Unanimity is thus aided by the justices being more ideologically aligned.

The attitudinal model more specifically suggests that unanimity should be a function of reversing an "extreme" lower court decision whereby every justice is either to the left or right of that decision and/or panel. We do not find, at least preliminarily, much support for this hypothesis. Only 38.8 percent of the cases where the Court reversed an "extreme" lower court decision were decided unanimously compared to 41 percent in which the Court reversed a "nonextreme" decision. These initial results seem to indicate that unanimity is not a function of the Supreme Court reacting to lower court decisions that are clearly outside the mainstream.

Finally, we seek to understand the influence of legal certainty on consensus. The preliminary assessment of our Legal Certainty Index points toward the utility of examining the level of legal certainty in order to understand agreement on the Court. Of the 1,667 cases found to contain a high level of legal certainty, 680, or 40.8 percent, were decided unanimously and 53.1 percent were either unanimous or highly consensual. If we examine the 2,115 cases that had a low level of legal certainty, 38.5 percent were unanimous and 48.5 percent were either unanimous or highly consensual. These results suggest that agreement is slightly more likely when the level of legal certainty facing the justices is high.

Kokoszka v. Belford (1974) presents an ideal example of a unanimous case based on the initial findings just presented. This case is one in which the chief justice ultimately authored the opinion, a high level of legal certainty existed, the question to be decided was statutory, the case concerned an economic issue, and the case was not found later to be salient to outside actors (and thus did not appear on the front page of the *New York Times*). In *Belford*, the Supreme Court unanimously determined that income tax refunds are to be considered "property," without any exceptions or exemptions under the Consumer Credit Protection Act.

Another prototypical example is *Nobelman v. American Savings Bank* (1993). Here a high level of legal certainty existed, the Court addressed a question of statutory law concerning an economic issue, the case did not appear on the front page of the *New York Times*, and the justices were fairly ideologically compatible. In a unanimous opinion, the Court determined that federal law does not allow a debtor who has filed for bankruptcy under Chapter 13 of the Bankruptcy Code to reduce an undersecured homestead mortgage to the fair market value of the mortgaged residence.

While these initial exploratory results suggest that a range of ideological, strategic, institutional, and legal factors all work to influence the likelihood of unanimity, the analysis just described is bivariate and descriptive. The question still to be answered is what explains the occurrence of unanimity on the Supreme Court when all of these factors are considered concurrently.

A Model of Consensus

We turn now to a more rigorous assessment of our theory of consensus. Our preliminary investigation, presented in the last section, looked at individual variables in isolation without considering how they might operate in tandem. The following analyses address these concerns, allowing us to determine the degree to which each variable in our model influences the likelihood of unanimity or a high degree of consensus when alternative explanations are simultaneously taken into account. The data are all orally argued federal cases that were granted certiorari by the Supreme Court.[3] We use logit to estimate the models because our two dependent variables are dichotomous. Our first dependent variable is whether the vote in the case was *Unanimous* (unanimous decisions were coded 1, and all others were coded 0); our second dependent variable is whether the vote in the case was *Unanimous or Highly Consensual* (abbreviated UHC), with highly consensual defined as one dissenting vote. Thus, cases with no dissenting votes or a sole dissenter are coded 1, and all cases with two or more dissenting votes are coded 0. In all of the models presented next, we utilize robust standard errors clustered on case citation.

Our purpose in this chapter is to investigate when consensus on the Supreme Court is most likely to occur in terms of votes on the merits. We conduct two levels of analysis. First we explore what predicts a unanimous and a highly consensual outcome. In these models, we test for the direct effect of each force on unanimous and highly consensual decisions. Next we examine the indirect effect of legal forces on the Court's ability to achieve consensus in order to assess whether the level of legal certainty constrains the operation of attitudes in some cases and, consequently, increases the likelihood of consensus.

Unanimous Decisions and Unanimous or Highly Consensual Decisions

Table 3.2 displays the parameter estimates for our models, indicating which factors increase or decrease the likelihood of a unanimous or a highly consensual decision. Model 1 uses the dependent variable for *Unanimous Decisions*. Model 2 uses the dependent variable for *Unanimous or Highly Consensual Decisions* (UHC). Since we also want to assess the substantive effects of the potential influences on unanimity and consensus, Table 3.3 presents a series of predicted probabilities associated with each of the statistically significant variables in the two models.[4] The baseline predicted probability of a unanimous decision is 0.272 and the baseline predicted probability of a unanimous or highly consensual decision is 0.383.

While the results presented in Models 1 and 2 are overall very similar, suggesting that the same factors that influence the likelihood of a unanimous decision also influence the likelihood of the Court achieving a high degree of consensus, there are also some notable differences. First, when investigating the role of legal certainty in consensual decision making, we find that as the level of legal certainty in a case increases, the likelihood of the Court achieving both unanimity and a highly consensual decision also increases.

TABLE 3.2

Logit models of unanimous and highly consensual decisions

Variable	MODEL 1: UNANIMOUS DECISIONS Coefficient (R.S.E.)	p-value	MODEL 2: UNANIMOUS OR HIGHLY CONSENSUAL DECISIONS Coefficient (R.S.E.)	p-value
Legal considerations				
Level of Legal Certainty	0.122 (0.038)	0.001	0.128 (0.038)	0.001
Attitudinal				
Ideological Polarization	−0.097 (0.051)	0.029	−0.053 (0.050)	0.145
Extreme Lower Court Decision	−0.005 (0.197)	0.980	0.003 (0.192)	0.987
Reversed Lower Court Decision	0.110 (0.079)	0.164	0.180 (0.078)	0.021
Extreme Lower Court Decision × Reversed	−0.162 (0.248)	0.743	−0.044 (0.242)	0.571
Strategic considerations				
Chief Justice Writes Opinion	0.275 (0.118)	0.010	0.294 (0.117)	0.006
Median Justice Writes Opinion	−0.165 (0.144)	0.252	−0.316 (0.138)	0.022
Altered Precedent	−0.130 (0.270)	0.630	−0.237 (0.258)	0.357
Declared Statute Unconstitutional	−0.246 (0.260)	0.344	−0.246 (0.246)	0.318
SG Party	0.067 (0.074)	0.184	0.069 (0.073)	0.171
Institutional context				
Addition of Syllabus	0.003 (0.211)	0.506	−0.071 (0.206)	0.366
Formalization of Dissent Assignment	−0.095 (0.170)	0.289	−0.177 (0.166)	0.143
Docket Size	0.000 (0.002)	0.433	−0.002 (0.002)	0.854
Number of Law Clerks	0.010 (0.025)	0.648	0.037 (0.025)	0.930
Rehnquist Court	0.393 (0.425)	0.356	−0.230 (0.416)	0.580
Burger Court	0.131 (0.341)	0.701	−0.209 (0.332)	0.530
Case factors				
Governmental Powers Issue	0.596 (0.094)	0.000	0.680 (0.093)	0.000
Economic Issue	0.492 (0.086)	0.000	0.508 (0.085)	0.000
Political Salience	−0.615 (0.120)	0.000	−0.589 (0.110)	0.000
Liberal Decision	0.555 (0.074)	0.000	0.468 (0.073)	0.000
Constant	−1.423 (0.609)	0.019	−1.253 (0.591)	0.034
N	3,425		3,425	

NOTE: R.S.E. = robust standard error clustered on case citation. *p*-values reflect one-tailed tests if directionality hypothesized.

The likelihood of a unanimous decision increases by 0.115 (0.201 to 0.316) when legal certainty increases from its lowest to its highest level. Similarly, the likelihood of a UHC decision increases by 0.146 (0.290 to 0.436). It is essential to note that the individual variables that make up this index may be capturing a combination of legal certainty and other forces given how difficult it is to disentangle law and policy. However, we believe that, by taking

TABLE 3.3
Predicted probabilities of unanimous and highly consensual decisions

Change in variable value	Predicted probability of a unanimous decision	Predicted probability of a unanimous or highly consensual decision
Legal Certainty (min → max)	0.201 → 0.316 [0.146, 0.255] → [0.255, 0.376]	0.290 → 0.436 [0.222, 0.358] → [0.370, 0.502]
Ideological Polarization (min → max)	0.346 → 0.218 [0.256, 0.435] → [0.147, 0.289]	n/a
Associate Justice Writes → Chief Justice Writes	0.272 → 0.330 [0.224, 0.320] → [0.262, 0.398]	0.383 → 0.454 [0.328, 0.437] → [0.380, 0.528]
Nonmedian Justice Writes → Median Justice Writes	n/a	0.383 → 0.311 [0.328, 0.437] → [0.238, 0.385]
Civil Liberties Issue → Governmental Powers Issue	0.272 → 0.404 [0.224, 0.320] → [0.340, 0.468]	0.383 → 0.550 [0.328, 0.437] → [0.486, 0.615]
Civil Liberties Issue → Economic Issue	0.272 → 0.379 [0.224, 0.320] → [0.319, 0.439]	0.383 → 0.507 [0.328, 0.437] → [0.445, 0.569]
Nonsalient Case → Salient Case	0.272 → 0.168 [0.224, 0.320] → [0.124, 0.212]	0.383 → 0.256 [0.328, 0.437] → [0.199, 0.313]
Conservative Decision → Liberal Decision	0.272 → 0.394 [0.224, 0.320] → [0.335, 0.453]	0.383 → 0.497 [0.328, 0.437] → [0.437, 0.558]

NOTE: Baseline probability of a unanimous decision = 0.272 [0.224, 0.320]. Baseline probability of a unanimous or highly consensual decision = 0.383 [0.328, 0.437]. Baselines computed by holding all continuous variables (such as the level of certainty) at their mean values, while holding all discrete variables (such as whether the solicitor general was a party) at their modal values.

the five variables together and by controlling for alternative explanations, the index aids us in understanding legal certainty's influence.

As for the role that attitudes play in the ability of the Court to reach consensus, we argue that a more ideologically compatible Court is more likely to decide cases either unanimously or highly consensually. Here is where an important difference emerges between unanimous and UHC decisions. Table 3.2 provides support for this hypothesis in terms of unanimous decisions: as ideological polarization increases, decision unanimity becomes less likely. Turning to the predicted probabilities, this likelihood decreases by 0.128 (0.346 to 0.218) when the Court is ideologically polarized as opposed to ideologically compatible. Thus, these findings suggest that the Court can indeed reach unanimity more easily if the justices are ideologically aligned. However, ideological polarization is not statistically significant in Model 2, suggesting that it does not influence whether the Court is able to achieve a highly consensual decision.

Additionally, we do not find any support for the idea of the Court reaching consensus when it reverses "extreme" lower court cases (those in which the lower court panel is more conservative or more liberal than even the most ideological justice). Thus, we have mixed findings with regard to ideological considerations. Although the degree of ideological polarization influences unanimous decisions, we do not find the Court reversing extreme lower court opinions. Thus, it appears that consensus is not the result of extreme lower court decisions being to the right or left of every justice, as the attitudinal model suggests, but it does seem to be correlated with an ideologically congruent Court.

We next examine the extent to which strategic factors influence unanimous and highly consensual decisions, finding that the Court is more likely to hand down both unanimous and highly consensual decisions when the chief justice authors the majority opinion. This finding suggests that chiefs can use their institutional power of self-assignment to ensure that the opinions they write command (and perhaps maintain) unanimity. Specifically, when the chief authors the majority opinion, the predicted probability of a unanimous decision increases by 0.058 (0.272 to 0.330) and the predicted probability of a UHC decision increases by 0.071 (0.383 to 0.454).

Whether the median justice writes the majority opinion appears to influence UHC decisions but not unanimous decisions. With respect to UHC decisions, the Court is less likely to reach them when the median justice writes the opinion. Specifically, the likelihood of a high degree of consensus drops by 0.072 (0.383 to 0.311). These findings, coupled with those about chief justice authorship, suggest that, while the chief justice is able to use his powers to encourage consensus, the median justice performs a different function: most likely, he or she plays in important role in keeping minimum-winning coalitions from fracturing during the opinion writing process.

While research has shown that the solicitor general is very successful when appearing before the Court, this success does not translate into more unanimity or a high degree of consensus when we control for alternative explanations. Moreover, whether the Court is altering precedent or declaring a statute unconstitutional does not appear to influence whether it is able to reach consensus, defined as either unanimity or a UHC decision.

Turning to the institutional variables, again we do not find that any of these influence the likelihood of either unanimity or a high degree of consensus. It may be that dissensus was so institutionally entrenched by 1953 that any additional changes in the institutional context had little effect on the overall rate of unanimity.

Salient cases, on the other hand, are less likely to result in unanimous and highly consensual decisions. The likelihood of achieving unanimity drops by 0.104 (0.272 to 0.168) for a case that is salient compared to one that is not. Similarly, salient cases are less likely than nonsalient cases to be decided in a highly consensual fashion. Specifically, the predicted probability of a unanimous or highly consensual decision decreases by 0.127 (0.383 to 0.256) for a salient case compared to a nonsalient one. In addition, civil liberties and rights cases—those we predicted would be most divisive because of the issues they involve—are indeed less likely to be decided unanimously or in a highly consensual fashion than are governmental powers (0.132 and 0.167 decrease, respectively) and economic cases (0.107 and 0.124 decrease, respectively). These findings highlight the reality that the issues and controversies that divide the other political branches and the electorate are likely to divide the Supreme Court as well and make achieving unanimity and consensus all the more difficult.

Finally, in concert with previous findings, we find that unanimity and a high degree of consensus are both more likely when the Court reaches a liberal decision. In fact, the predicted probability of a unanimous decision increases by 0.122 when the Court reaches a liberal result rather than a conservative result. Similarly, the probability of a UHC decision increases by 0.114 when the Court reaches a liberal result. It may be that during the period under study the Court was more predisposed to liberal outcomes in landmark cases or in those involving certain areas of the law, such as the Nixon Watergate tapes case or those involving school desegregation. Or perhaps conservative justices were more willing than liberals to join decisions that would seemingly contradict their ideology.

Overall, unanimity and highly consensual decisions are a function of multiple, concurrently operating forces. They are most likely when the level of legal certainty as to the strongest legal answer is high, when the chief justice authors the majority opinion, when the case before the Court concerns a governmental powers or economic issue, when the case is not considered salient, and when the result is in the liberal direction. Additionally, a high degree of consensus more easily occurs in cases where the median justice is not the opinion author.

United States v. Boyle (1985) is an excellent example of a unanimous case that reflects all of the findings reported. In this case, Boyle was named the executor of his mother's will. He hired an attorney to help him with a federal estate tax return, which was required to be filed within nine months of the decedent's death. However, the return was submitted three months late, apparently because of a clerical mistake that omitted the filing date from the attorney's calendar. Boyle was then assessed a penalty for a late return; such a penalty is assessed "unless it is shown that such failure is due to reasonable cause and not due to willful neglect." Boyle sued, arguing that the late filing was due to the reasonable cause of relying on his attorney. In a unanimous decision authored by Chief Justice Burger, the Court held that the failure to file a tax return in time is not excused by a taxpayer's reliance on an agent. Rather, the burden is on the taxpayer to ensure that any statutory obligations or deadlines are met. This case concerned a governmental powers issue, was decided in a liberal direction, was not viewed as salient, and had a high degree of legal certainty.

A prototypical example of a UHC decision is *United States v. Texas* (1993). This case concerned the federal Food Stamp Program, under which the U.S. Department of Agriculture gives coupons to the states to distribute to qualified individuals and households. If a state chooses to distribute the coupons through the mail, it must reimburse the federal government for part of the cost of replacing those that are lost or stolen. A substantial number of coupons sent by Texas through the mail were lost, and the state was told that prejudgment interest would begin to accrue on its debt unless payment was made within thirty days. Texas sued, arguing that the Debt Collection Act of 1982 prohibits the federal government from collecting prejudgment interest on debts owed to it by a state. The Supreme Court, in a 8–1 decision authored by Chief Justice Rehnquist, determined that the Act did not abrogate the states' obligation to pay prejudgment interest on such debts. Once again, the details of the case help to illuminate why the justices reached a highly consensual decision. It concerned a nonsalient governmental powers issue and was decided in a liberal direction. Furthermore, it reflected, *a priori*, a high level of legal certainty. Specifically, the case had a relatively low level of legal complexity, no outside amici, lacked any dissensus (nonideological or otherwise) in the lower court, and addressed a question of statutory law.

Both *Texas* and *Boyle* highlight the different forces that simultaneously influence the Supreme Court's ability to reach agreement on the important legal issues facing the nation. Notably, each force is a distinct and necessary piece of the explanation for consensus, and it is only by considering all of them in concert that we can unravel the mystery of unanimous decisions and understand how an ideologically polarized group of justices—entrenched in an era of dissensual norms and practices—is able to reach these decisions so often.

Understanding the Relationship between Attitudes and Legal Certainty

The theory presented in Chapter 2 suggests that attitudinal and legal forces operate concurrently in all cases and directly affect the Court's ability to achieve consensus; the findings outlined previously strongly support this theory. We also posit that the law exerts an *indirect* effect on judicial decision making: we propose that attitudes are the principal force but that they can be constrained by legal forces in certain cases. This causes the jaws of the vise to close and the operation of attitudes to be circumscribed (see Figures 2.1 and 2.2 in Chapter 2). Our theory therefore suggests not only that both attitudes and legal forces directly affect the likelihood of unanimous and highly consensual decisions but also that, as the strength of legal factors increases, the impact of attitudes lessens and vice versa. In other words, as the level of legal certainty increases, the influence of attitudes decreases; alternatively, when the level of legal certainty decreases, the influence of attitudes increases.

To test for this interactive relationship, we reran the models presented in Table 3.2 but with an important variation: we estimated them with the same independent variables except for level of legal certainty. We then altered the sample on which the model was estimated based on the level of legal certainty in the case. Thus, we estimated four distinct models: (1) a model of unanimity on all cases in which the level of legal certainty was high (greater than 3); (2) a model of unanimity on all cases in which the level of legal certainty was low (less than 4); (3) a model of UHC decisions in all cases in which the level of legal certainty was high; and (4) a model of UHC decisions in all cases in which the level of legal certainty was low.

In each of these models, our interest is in whether the variable for ideological polarization is significant. We expect that in the two models reflecting the sample of cases where the level of legal certainty is low, ideological polarization should be significant and substantively strong. Such a finding would suggest that when the justices are faced with a case in which there are many plausible options as to the strongest legal answer, their attitudes will play a strong role in influencing the Court's ability to achieve consensus. Alternatively, we expect that in the two models reflecting the sample of cases where the level of legal certainty is high, ideological polarization should

TABLE 3.4

Logit models of ideological and legal interaction: Unanimous decisions

	LOW LEGAL CERTAINTY		HIGH LEGAL CERTAINTY	
Variable	Coefficient (R.S.E.)	*p*-value	Coefficient (R.S.E.)	*p*-value
Attitudinal				
Ideological Polarization	**−0.186 (0.071)**	**0.005**	**−0.015 (0.072)**	**0.416**
Extreme Lower Court Decision	0.135 (0.270)	0.619	−0.204 (0.295)	0.488
Reversed Lower Court Decision	0.179 (0.106)	0.092	0.045 (0.121)	0.708
Extreme Lower Court Decision × Reversed	−0.237 (0.360)	0.744	0.047 (0.355)	0.448
Strategic considerations				
Chief Justice Writes Opinion	0.259 (0.153)	0.045	0.371 (0.196)	0.030
Median Justice Writes Opinion	−0.281 (0.196)	0.152	−0.040 (0.211)	0.851
Altered Precedent	0.026 (0.341)	0.938	−0.365 (0.470)	0.436
Declared Statute Unconstitutional	−0.395 (0.290)	0.172	0.294 (0.648)	0.650
SG Party	0.065 (0.100)	0.257	0.060 (0.111)	0.305
Institutional context				
Addition of Syllabus	0.234 (0.324)	0.765	−0.194 (0.282)	0.246
Formalization of Dissent Assignment	−0.237 (0.227)	0.149	0.034 (0.256)	0.553
Docket Size	0.001 (0.003)	0.350	−0.001 (0.004)	0.570
Number of Law Clerks	−0.009 (0.035)	0.398	0.022 (0.037)	0.726
Rehnquist Court	0.485 (0.613)	0.429	0.289 (0.599)	0.629
Burger Court	0.238 (0.499)	0.633	0.007 (0.470)	0.987
Case factors				
Governmental Powers Issue	0.562 (0.126)	0.000	0.647 (0.141)	0.000
Economic Issue	0.533 (0.118)	0.000	0.481 (0.128)	0.000
Political Salience	−0.861 (0.146)	0.000	−0.188 (0.213)	0.188
Liberal Decision	0.763 (0.100)	0.000	0.305 (0.113)	0.004
Constant	−0.422 (0.835)	0.613	−1.326 (0.849)	0.118
N	1,969		1,456	

NOTE: R.S.E. = robust standard error clustered on case citation. *p*-values reflect one-tailed tests if directionality hypothesized.

not be significant. In other words, a non-significant finding would suggest that when the level of legal certainty is high, and all information available to the justices points to a single legal answer, the influence of attitudes is necessarily constrained.

Tables 3.4 and 3.5 display the results of our test of the indirect influence of legal certainty. Looking at our key variable of interest, the results across all four models are in line with our predictions. First, when the level of legal certainty is low, attitudes significantly influence whether the decision will be unanimous or highly consensual. Alternatively, when the level of legal certainty is high, we find no effect for ideological polarization on the likelihood

TABLE 3.5
Logit models of ideological and legal interaction: Unanimous or highly consensual decisions

Variable	LOW LEGAL CERTAINTY Coefficient (R.S.E.)	LOW LEGAL CERTAINTY *p*-value	HIGH LEGAL CERTAINTY Coefficient (R.S.E.)	HIGH LEGAL CERTAINTY *p*-value
Attitudinal				
Ideological Polarization	**−0.137 (0.069)**	**0.023**	**0.021 (0.072)**	**0.386**
Extreme Lower Court Decision	0.115 (0.257)	0.654	−0.157 (0.294)	0.593
Reversed Lower Court Decision	0.191 (0.103)	0.065	0.181 (0.121)	0.134
Extreme Lower Court Decision × Reversed	−0.157 (0.341)	0.678	0.167 (0.355)	0.320
Strategic considerations				
Chief Justice Writes Opinion	0.178 (0.150)	0.118	0.562 (0.203)	0.003
Median Justice Writes Opinion	−0.363 (0.186)	0.051	−0.273 (0.205)	0.183
Altered Precedent	−0.260 (0.334)	0.437	−0.187 (0.412)	0.649
Declared Statute Unconstitutional	−0.452 (0.273)	0.098	0.640 (0.644)	0.320
SG Party	0.041 (0.097)	0.337	0.087 (0.111)	0.218
Institutional context				
Addition of Syllabus	0.086 (0.306)	0.610	−0.226 (0.283)	0.212
Formalization of Dissent Assignment	−0.290 (0.219)	0.093	−0.078 (0.252)	0.378
Docket Size	−0.002 (0.003)	0.736	−0.003 (0.004)	0.826
Number of Law Clerks	0.018 (0.034)	0.700	0.047 (0.036)	0.901
Rehnquist Court	−0.198 (0.588)	0.737	−0.190 (0.597)	0.750
Burger Court	−0.131 (0.478)	0.784	−0.266 (0.466)	0.568
Case factors				
Governmental Powers Issue	0.640 (0.124)	0.000	0.748 (0.142)	0.000
Economic Issue	0.480 (0.115)	0.000	0.580 (0.127)	0.000
Political Salience	−0.787 (0.134)	0.000	−0.236 (0.204)	0.124
Liberal Decision	0.659 (0.098)	0.000	0.208 (0.113)	0.033
Constant	−0.072 (0.799)	0.928	−1.183 (0.834)	0.156
N	1,969		1,456	

NOTE: R.S.E. = robust standard error clustered on case citation. *p*-values reflect one-tailed tests if directionality hypothesized.

of either a unanimous or a highly consensual decision. In other words, when the level of certainty as to the strongest legal answer is high, the jaws begin to close, hindering the operation of the justices' attitudes, and making unanimity and highly consensual decisions much more likely. In such situations, we argue that the high level of legal certainty leads the justices toward a single legal answer regardless of the degree of ideological polarization.

Put simply, the findings in these two tables suggest that even the most ideologically polarized Court finds agreement in cases in which the available information strongly points to a single legal answer. This test of the interactive effects of attitudes and legal certainty highlights how legal forces can constrain the justices' ability to vote their policy preferences and instead lead the Court to achieve unanimity. As a result, we suggest that models of judicial decision making need to account for both the direct and indirect force legal considerations exert on the justices' decisions and, in particular, their ability to render decisions that are unanimous or highly consensual.

Conclusion

In this chapter, we seek to explain unanimous decision making on the modern Supreme Court. Simply put, why do ideologically polarized justices ever agree, given the entrenched institutional norms promoting dissensus? Our findings indicate that consensus is shaped by multiple, concurrently operating forces. Most notably, unanimity and highly consensual decisions, all else being equal, are indeed a by-product of cases in which a stronger legal answer exists and thus law itself acts as a constraint. Our results suggest that when the justices are more certain about the strongest legal answer, the jaws of the vise are sufficiently tight and consensus is more likely, but when there is ambiguity and uncertainty, the jaws are wide open and dissensus is more likely because the justices are free to vote according to their personal policy preferences. Note that we do not claim that each variable used in the index alone captures legal considerations. However, by taking all five variables together, and by controlling for alternative explanations, our index successfully taps into the concept of legal certainty.

Furthermore, we show that the issues and controversies that divide the other political branches and the electorate are more likely to divide the Supreme Court as well and make achieving consensus more difficult. We also find that chief justices who wish to push for consensus can indeed achieve this goal even in the face of ideological polarization.

Taken together, our results suggest that both unanimous and highly consensual decisions reflect myriad forces. First, strategic considerations matter in terms of the justices' interactions; however, unanimity and consensus do not seem to be influenced by strategic responses to external actors. Second, personal policy preferences matter, even in unanimous decisions. However, the influence of attitudes is most apparent when we examine cases in which attitudes are least likely to be constrained by other forces. Furthermore, consistent with a previous study, we do not find that the justices are reversing "extreme" lower court cases; simply put, unanimity is not a function of the Court hearing and correcting cases that are far outside the legal mainstream.

Finally, legal considerations, as captured through the level of legal certainty, influence consensus. When the level of legal certainty is high—even controlling for attitudinal influences—unanimity and consensus are more likely. Legal certainty appears to constrain the operation of attitudes on justices' votes.

Thus, our results demonstrate that in order to fully understand unanimity and consensus, a model of judicial decision making must be used that takes into account various forces emanating from what are usually seen as competing models. Only by acknowledging the many influences on the justices' decisions can we gain a complete understanding of how the Court arrives at its final judgments and begin to disentangle the puzzle of unanimity.

In this chapter, we investigate the influence of a number of factors on the likelihood of the Supreme Court reaching a unanimous or highly consensual decision in terms of justices' votes on the merits. While a unanimous vote in a case may reflect agreement among all the justices, it may also obscure true disagreements. When a justice votes with the Court on the outcome of a case, but disagrees with the legal reasoning used by the other justices, he or she may author a concurrence that expresses this disagreement. Separate opinions, including concurrences, reveal important legal disputes. In Chapter 4, we take into account separate opinions and define consensus in terms of *opinion consensus* in order to further investigate why the justices agree to agree.

CHAPTER 4

Monolithic Solidarity

Consensus in Opinion Writing

On May 22, 1990, James Everett Smith, a Sacramento County sheriff's deputy, along with Murray Strapp, another officer, responded to a call to break up a fight. When Strapp returned to his patrol car, a motorcycle operated by Brian Willard and carrying Philip Lewis as a passenger approached at high speed. Strapp turned on the lights of his patrol car and yelled for the boys to stop; he moved his car close to Deputy Smith's so that the motorcycle would be forced to stop. However, Willard maneuvered the motorcycle between the two patrol cars and then sped off. Deputy Smith turned on his lights and siren and began pursuing the motorcycle, which reached speeds of up to 100 miles per hour through a residential neighborhood. The chase ended when Willard attempted to make a sharp left turn and the motorcycle tipped over. Deputy Smith slammed on his brakes, but skidded into Lewis at 40 miles per hour, and Lewis was killed. His parents brought an action under 42 U.S.C. §1983, alleging that Lewis was deprived of his substantive due process right to life under the Fourteenth Amendment. The district court granted summary judgment for Deputy Smith, but the Ninth Circuit reversed, holding that the appropriate degree of fault for substantive due process liability is deliberate indifference to, or reckless disregard for, a person's right to life.

In *County of Sacramento v. Lewis* (1998), the question before the Supreme Court was whether a police officer violates the Fourteenth Amendment's guarantee of substantive due process by causing death through deliberate or reckless indifference to life, or whether the police officer's conduct must shock the conscience. The Court unanimously reversed the Ninth Circuit's decision, holding that the Fourteenth Amendment was not violated by the conduct of Deputy Smith. Specifically, the Court held that, in order to find a due process violation in this case, "only a purpose to cause harm, unrelated to the legitimate object of arrest, will satisfy the element of arbitrary conduct shocking the conscience" (*Lewis*, 836).

Although the vote on the merits in *Lewis* was unanimous, the Court did not produce a single opinion reflecting the views of all of the justices. Rather, there were five separate concurrences in addition to the majority opinion, with seven of the justices either writing or joining them. These justices wrote separately to express certain individual thoughts or opinions regarding the case. For example, Justice John Paul Stevens's opinion concurring in the judgment agreed with the majority that the Ninth Circuit's decision should be reversed, but on the ground that Deputy Smith was entitled to qualified immunity because the relevant law was not clearly defined at the time of the incident. Justice Antonin Scalia also wrote a concurrence, joined by Justice Clarence Thomas, in which he expressed his vehement opposition to the shocks-the-conscience test: "[R]ather than ask whether the police conduct here at issue shocks my un-elected conscience, I would ask whether our Nation has traditionally protected the right respondents assert" (ibid., 862). Scalia and Thomas agreed with the result of the majority opinion, but argued for reversing the Ninth Circuit "on the ground that respondents offer no textual or historical support for their alleged due process right" (ibid., 865). Simply put, the unanimous vote on the merits in *Lewis* suggests widespread consensus among the justices. However, an examination of the concurrences reveals another reality: unanimous agreement that Deputy Smith was not liable but also strong disagreement as to the *reason* that he was not liable.

The justices' propensity to express themselves individually has exploded in the modern era. Figure 4.1 illustrates the dramatic shift in the Court's separate opinion writing behavior that, as we detail in Chapter 1, took root during the Roosevelt Court. The justices have been more than willing to justify this increase in individual expression. For example, in *Ferguson v. Moore McCormack Lines* (1957) Justice Felix Frankfurter stated, "Dissent is essential to an effective judiciary in a democratic society, and especially for a tribunal exercising the powers of this Court" (*Ferguson*, 528). But if separate opinions are easily justifiable and have come to be the rule rather than the exception, why are a significant proportion of cases without any separate opinions issued each term?

In Chapter 3, we investigated the influence of a number of factors on the likelihood of the Supreme Court reaching a unanimous or highly consensual decision in terms of the justices' votes on the merits. Discussions of the Court generally assume that a unanimous vote signals that the justices agreed on all facets of a case. However, while a unanimous vote may reflect agreement among all the justices, it may also conceal true disagreements, particularly with regard to legal reasoning. When a justice votes with the

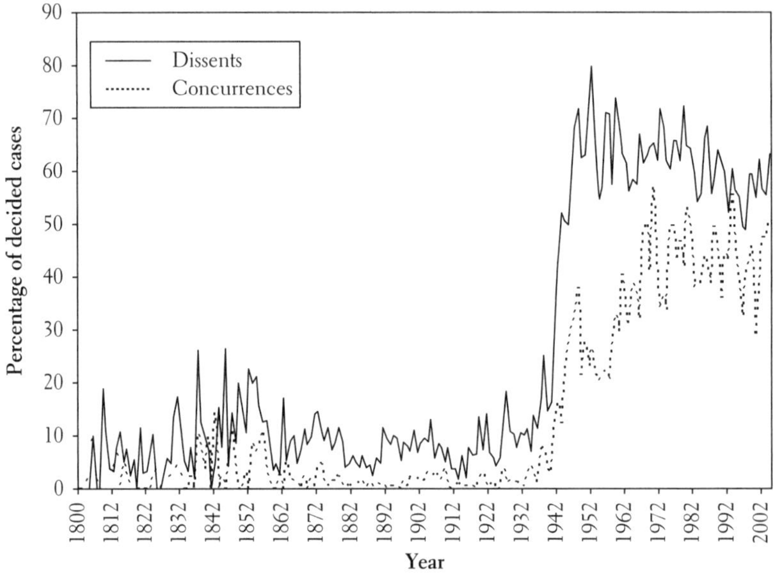

Figure 4.1. Separate opinion writing behavior: Supreme Court, 1800–2004
SOURCE: Data from Lee Epstein, Jeffrey A. Segal, Harold Spaeth, and Thomas G. Walker, *The Supreme Court Compendium: Data, Decisions and Developments*, 4th ed. (Washington, DC: CQ Press, 2007).

Court on the outcome of a case but disagrees with the legal reasoning of the other justices, he or she may author a concurrence in order to express this disagreement. Separate opinions, including concurrences, thus reveal important legal disputes.

To fully understand consensus on the Supreme Court, we need to consider separate opinions and thus examine *opinion consensus*. We take into account separate opinions because of their potential legal and political impact; they "may shake public confidence in the judiciary by bringing into question the certainty of the law" (Walker, Epstein, and Dixon 1988, 387). Also, any disagreement over the majority opinion "cancels the impact of monolithic solidarity on which the authority of a bench of judges so largely depends" (Hand 1958, 72). And while dissents are clearly detrimental to the authority of majority opinions, concurrences can be equally damaging. In fact, if a decision of the Court is accompanied by a concurrence that does not support the majority opinion, lower courts are less likely to comply with it (Corley 2010). Similarly, lower courts are less likely to follow plurality opinions, in which a majority of the justices concur in the result but not in the reasoning (Corley 2009).

Consider the Sixth Amendment Right to Counsel case *Argersinger v. Hamlin* (1973). After initially deciding to affirm the conviction of an indigent defendant who was denied counsel and sentenced to ninety days in jail, the justices changed their minds and voted unanimously to reverse. Yet they divided sharply over the extent to which the "loss of liberty" rationale should be extended to indigent defendants. William O. Douglas attempted to draft an opinion for the Court. Potter Stewart wrote him: "This case seems to me peculiarly one in which a Court opinion is essential—in order to give intelligible guidance to the countless courts in the country where the problem involved will arise every day. With that objective in mind, I take the liberty of expressing my difficulties with your opinion in its present form."[1] The justices labored to reach complete agreement but eventually fell short. Stewart, for example, ultimately joined Douglas's final opinion, but he also joined William Brennan's separate concurrence. Indeed, despite having authored the lead opinion, Douglas also joined Brennan's concurrence. Lewis Powell informed his colleagues: "Although the revision of the Court's opinion . . . meets some of my concerns, I still intend to concur in the result by a separate opinion."[2] Then Associate Justice William Rehnquist joined Powell's separate concurrence and Chief Justice Burger filed his own, concurring in the result only. Hence, the 8–0 vote for the result did not accurately reflect the level of disagreement among the justices, as revealed by Douglas's plurality opinion and the separate opinions issued by his colleagues.

To exemplify the important potential implications of separate opinions, consider how the Court treated the issue of criminal sodomy statutes. In *Bowers v. Hardwick* (1986), it narrowly upheld a Georgia state law proscribing the practice. While Justice Byron White wrote for the five-justice majority, two members of the coalition—Chief Justice Burger and Justice Powell—issued concurrences. Burger explained: "I write separately to underscore my view that, in constitutional terms, there is no such thing as a fundamental right to commit homosexual sodomy" (*Bowers*, 196). However, Powell's concurrence suggested that, while he agreed that there is no such fundamental right, there might be a legitimate Eighth Amendment challenge against excessive penalties for such acts, particularly since many states do not enforce them, "suggesting the moribund character" of such laws (ibid., 198). Justices Harry Blackmun and John Paul Stevens issued separate dissents. Blackmun argued that the right to privacy covers sexual intimacy, including consensual sodomy. Stevens suggested that sexual intimacy is a form of "liberty" protected by the Due Process Clause of the Fourteenth Amendment. These differing positions and arguments would prove important when the justices revisited the issue seventeen years later.

In 2003, the Court reviewed a Texas statute that criminalized homosexual sodomy in *Lawrence v. Texas*. The Court overturned its previous decision in *Bowers*, with Justice Anthony Kennedy issuing the 6–3 majority opinion. Notably, Kennedy's opinion made multiple, specific references to the divisions displayed in *Bowers*, including those among the justices in the *Bowers* majority. At the start of the opinion he noted: "The Court, in an opinion by Justice White, sustained the Georgia law. Chief Justice Burger and Justice Powell joined the opinion of the Court and filed separate, concurring opinions. Four Justices dissented . . . Blackmun . . . Brennan, Marshall, and Stevens" (*Lawrence*, 566). Kennedy criticized not only White's majority opinion but also Burger's concurrence: "The historical grounds relied upon in *Bowers* are more complex than the majority opinion and the concurring opinion by Chief Justice Burger indicate" (ibid., 571). Kennedy also used Powell's concurrence to undercut White's reasoning: "In *Bowers* the Court referred to the fact that before 1961 all 50 States had outlawed sodomy, and that at the time of the Court's decision 24 States and the District of Columbia had sodomy laws. . . . Justice Powell pointed out that these prohibitions often were being ignored, however" (ibid., 572). Finally, Kennedy bypassed Blackmun's *Bowers* dissent and instead chose to rely on Stevens's reasoning in that case: "Justice Stevens's analysis, in our view, should have been controlling in *Bowers* and should control here" (ibid., 578). Both *Bowers* and *Lawrence* demonstrate how separate opinions—both concurring and dissenting—can have a crucial impact on future legal developments.

Prior research investigating separate opinion writing on the Supreme Court has focused on three main areas of inquiry. A number of studies have examined whether dissensus decreases the legitimacy and authority of decisions (e.g., Gerber and Park 1997; Moorhead 1952; O'Brien 1999; Walker, Epstein, and Dixon 1988). Some have offered explanations for individual justices' decisions to author or join a separate opinion based on ideology (e.g., Segal and Spaeth 2002), institutional constraints (e.g., Ulmer 1986), strategic calculations (e.g., Epstein and Knight 1998; Murphy 1964), or a combination of these perspectives (e.g., Wahlbeck, Spriggs, and Maltzman 1999). Other studies have investigated aggregate patterns of opinion writing in an attempt to explain the rise in dissensus on the Court (e.g., Caldeira and Zorn 1998; Walker, Epstein, and Dixon 1988).

Building on these studies, Corley (2010) explored the justices' use of concurrences. While dissenting votes are generally explained by differences in ideology, explaining concurrences is not so easy. Corley investigated why particular types of concurrences are authored and attempted to determine their impact. She found that the decision to write or join a particular type of concurrence is a complex decision involving justice-specific, case-specific, and institutional factors, and that the factors influencing a justice's decision to write or join a concurrence depend on the type being written. Furthermore, she found that concurrences matter: lower court compliance decreases when a justice's concurrence strongly departs from the majority opinion. Moreover, the Supreme Court itself is less likely to positively interpret a precedent in future cases if it contains a concurrence expressing strong disagreement with the legal rationale for the Court's decision. Taken together, Corley's findings suggest that ignoring the influence of concurrences not only obscures potentially important disagreements over legal doctrine that may be missed by only examining votes on the merits, but also overlooks how disputes over legal reasoning can have important implications for lower court compliance and precedent vitality.

We draw on these findings to examine the issue of separate opinion writing from the vantage points of consensus and the collective output of the Court. In contrast to these previous studies, we investigate when the justices collectively are more likely to issue separate opinions—including in cases with seemingly consensual outcomes—to better understand the many facets of consensus on the Supreme Court.

Examining Opinion Consensus

To determine the degree of opinion consensus in each case, we utilize three dependent variables, all focused on the number of opinions issued in a particular case. The first dependent variable, *Fully Unanimous Opinions*, is defined as cases in which the vote was unanimous and there were no concurrences accompanying the majority opinion. Fully unanimous opinions are coded 1, and all other opinions are coded 0. The second and third dependent variables reflect highly consensual cases, which we define here in two ways. The second dependent variable, *UOC*, includes fully unanimous opinions and unanimous cases with only one concurrence, capturing cases with very high degrees of both voting and opinion consensus. To create this variable, we coded fully unanimous opinions and unanimous cases with a single concurrence as 1 and all other opinions as 0. The third dependent variable, *UOCD*, includes fully unanimous opinions, unanimous cases with only one concurrence, and cases with one dissent where there is only one justice dissenting. This variable captures cases in which there is a high degree of opinion consensus even though the vote in the case was not unanimous. Specifically, all fully unanimous opinions, unanimous cases with one concurrence, or cases with one dissent where only one justice actually dissented are coded 1; all others are coded 0.

Figure 4.2 displays the percentage of fully unanimous opinions by the Court for the period of our study. During Chief Justice Warren's tenure, 28 percent of cases were decided without a single concurrence. Similarly, 27 percent of Rehnquist Court opinions were fully unanimous. However, during Chief Justice Burger's tenure the justices achieved the lowest level of fully unanimous opinions, at 23 percent. Figure 4.2 also includes the percentage of unanimous cases that contained a single concurrence. The increase in concurring opinions issued in unanimous cases from Warren to Burger (from 8 to 10 percent) continued slightly under Rehnquist (11 percent). Finally, the figure includes the percentage of opinions in which there was one dissent with only one justice dissenting. Interestingly, the data show that the Warren Court was the most likely to achieve these highly consensual opinions (9 percent), which decreased from Burger (7 percent) to Rehnquist (4 percent).

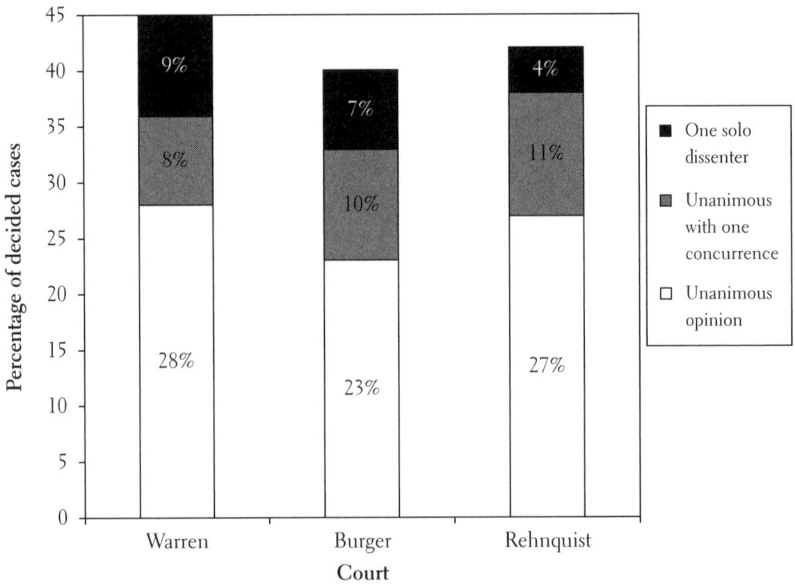

Figure 4.2. Comparing the Warren, Burger, and Rehnquist Courts: Percentage of unanimous and highly consensual opinions

Because our three dependent variables of opinion consensus are dichotomous, we use logistic regression with robust standard errors clustered on case citation. We again employ the variables described in Chapter 2 and the same data used in Chapter 3—that is, all federal cases granted certiorari and decided by the Supreme Court during the 1953–2004 terms. We use the data available through the Spaeth dataset.

Exploring Unanimous Opinions

We begin by exploring what cases with fully unanimous opinions look like as opposed to cases with multiple opinions: given the independent variables explicated in Chapter 2, what differences do we find? In this section, we assess the data in an exploratory fashion, and in the subsequent section we turn to a more rigorous, multivariate test of our theory.

What do fully unanimous or highly consensual opinions look like? We first hypothesize that certain case-specific factors influence whether the Court achieves them. In terms of issue areas, 33.2 percent of governmental powers cases and 31.9 percent of economic cases resulted in fully unanimous opinions, as opposed to only 17.4 percent of civil liberties cases (see Table 4.1). If we examine unanimous or highly consensual opinions, we again find a clear divide between economic and governmental powers cases on the one hand and civil liberties cases on the other. Of governmental powers cases, 52.5 percent resulted in a fully unanimous opinion, a unanimous opinion with a single concurrence, or one dissenting opinion with a single dissenting vote, while 48.7 percent of economic cases had such an outcome. Comparatively, only 31 percent of civil liberties cases resulted in high levels of opinion consensus.

Relatively unlikely to garner unanimous opinions were cases considered salient to outside actors (appearing on the front page of the *New York Times* the day after the decision was rendered). Of the 500 cases that appeared there, only 21 percent resulted in a fully unanimous opinion, a unanimous opinion with a single concurrence, or only one dissenting opinion with a single dissenting vote, as compared to 44.2 percent of nonsalient cases; a mere 12.2 percent of salient cases garnered a fully unanimous opinion.

In this chapter, we examine an additional case-specific variable that may influence the justices' ability to reach opinion consensus: time until end of term. Specifically, we posit that more time should lead to a decrease in opinion consensus because the justices have more time to craft separate opinions even if they agree on the merits. And we see preliminary support for

TABLE 4.1

Bivariate predictors of fully unanimous or highly consensual opinions

Independent variable	Percentage of fully unanimous opinions	Percentage of highly consensual opinions (UOC)[a]	Percentage of highly consensual opinions (UOCD)[b]
Civil Liberties and Rights Issue	17.4	26.8	31.0
Economic Issue	31.9	41.5	48.7
Governmental Powers Issue	33.2	44.6	52.5
Chief Justice Majority Opinion Author	24.5	35.6	40.4
Associate Justice Majority Opinion Author	25.4	35.2	41.3
Median Justice Majority Opinion Author	21.0	30.0	33.8
Solicitor General Party to Case	24.7	35.1	40.8
Solicitor General Not a Party to Case	25.7	35.4	41.5
Salient Case	12.2	18.8	21.0
Nonsalient Case	27.3	37.7	44.2
Altered Precedent	17.7	26.5	27.9
No Alteration of Precedent	25.5	35.4	41.4
Declared Statute Unconstitutional	4.4	17.8	23.3
No Declaration of Unconstitutionality	25.8	35.7	41.6
Before Addition of Syllabus	26.6	34.2	42.1
After Addition of Syllabus	24.7	35.7	40.8
Before Formalization of Dissent Assignment	25.7	33.8	41.4
After Formalization of Dissent Assignment	25.1	36.3	41.1
Larger Docket Size	22.0	33.3	40.1
Smaller Docket Size	28.6	38.0	42.6
Smaller Number of Law Clerks	27.1	34.5	42.2
Larger Number of Law Clerks	26.4	36.1	41.0
Ideologically Compatible Justices	26.7	36.0	42.7
Ideologically Polarized Justices	22.4	30.0	38.1
Reversed an "Extreme" Lower Court Decision	29.4	36.0	43.5
Reversed a "Nonextreme" Lower Court Decision	24.5	35.6	41.5
High Level of Legal Certainty	28.6	37.7	44.6
Low Level of Legal Certainty	22.4	33.1	38.4
Shorter Time until End of Term	26.1	36.3	41.9
Longer Time until End of Term	21.8	32.0	38.2

[a]UOC = unanimous opinions or highly consensual opinions (unanimous decisions with one concurrence).
[b]UOCD = unanimous opinions or highly consensual opinions (unanimous decisions with one concurrence or decisions with one dissent where there is only one justice dissenting).

this hypothesis: when the number of days until the end of term are relatively few (more than one standard deviation below the mean), fully unanimous opinions occurred in 26.1 percent of cases; comparatively, when the number of days are relatively many (more than one standard deviation above the mean), opinion unanimity was achieved in only 21.8 percent of cases.

We also predict that a number of strategic considerations might influence the likelihood of the Court issuing a fully unanimous or highly consensual opinion. The analysis in Chapter 3 reveals that cases in which the majority opinion was authored by the chief justice were more likely to result in unanimous decisions. However, when we look descriptively at these cases in terms of opinion consensus, we find a much different story: there is almost no difference in the percentage of cases resulting in fully unanimous or highly consensual opinions when the chief rather than an associate justice is the opinion author. This finding thus suggests that a significant number of the unanimous opinions authored by the chief did not result in true opinion consensus even if there was agreement reached on the merits. We do see, however, that opinion consensus is less likely when the median justice authors the majority opinion, as compared to either the chief or another associate justice.

Participation by the solicitor general (SG), at least descriptively, does not appear to influence the likelihood of opinion consensus, regardless of how we measure it. For example, while 40.8 percent of cases in which the SG was a party resulted in a highly consensual opinion (UOCD), 41.8 percent in which the SG did not participate achieved the same result.

We also predict that whether the Court struck down a statute or overturned a past precedent might influence the achievement of opinion consensus. We find, in this preliminary exploration, that opinion consensus is rare when the Supreme Court exercises judicial review. In only 4.4 percent of these cases was a fully unanimous opinion reached, as compared to 25.8 percent when there was no declaration of unconstitutionality; alternatively, as reported in the descriptive analysis in Chapter 3, 30 percent of cases striking down a law resulted in a unanimous vote on the merits. This finding suggests that when the Court exercises the power of judicial review, many of its members feel a need to express themselves separately or explain their reasoning further, perhaps underlining their recognition of the import of exercising that power. Regarding the overturning of precedent, we once again find that the Court more easily achieves opinion consensus when no alteration of precedent occurs. While a fully unanimous opinion was achieved in 25.5 percent of cases where precedent stood, the same was true in only 17.7 percent of cases where it was overturned.

However, we also see that opinion consensus is more likely when the justices strike down precedent as opposed to overturning statutes. This finding may be a function of the relative legal or political salience of the precedents that the Court overturns, or it may signal that the justices find it more important to show a completely united front when reversing precedent as compared to exercising judicial review.

In sum, our strategic variables reveal that a fully unanimous opinion is difficult to reach even when the justices agree on the merits of the case. We especially find a disconnect between voting unanimity and opinion unanimity in cases in which the Court struck down a statute as unconstitutional. These cases highlight how focusing simply on votes on the merits can obscure true disagreements—particularly disagreements over legal reasoning.

We theorize that a number of institutional developments influence the likelihood of opinion consensus on the Court. Specifically, we expect that two such developments—the addition of the syllabus and the formalization of dissent assignments—decrease the probability of the Court achieving opinion consensus. However, we find very little evidence to support these expectations. Concerning the addition of the syllabus, the likelihood of the Court issuing a fully unanimous opinion prior to 1971 was 26.6 percent; this dropped slightly to 24.7 percent after 1971 (see Table 4.1). If we examine cases that were fully unanimous or that contained one concurrence or one dissent with only one justice dissenting, the percentage before 1971 was 42.1 percent; after 1971 it was 40.8 percent. Similarly, we see little change as to the percentage of opinion consensus when we examine cases before and after 1975, when dissent assignments became formalized.

The other two institutional changes we explore concern the number of law clerks and the size of the Court's docket. In the time period under study, the number of law clerks assigned to the justices grew and the size of the Court's docket shrank. We therefore hypothesize that these changes likely increase the ability of the justices to write separately and thereby decrease the likelihood of fully unanimous opinions. The one potential finding that goes against our original hypothesis is that the justices were actually more likely to issue fully unanimous and highly consensual opinions with a smaller docket. This suggests that more time to decide cases may not inherently lead to more disunity and separate authorship. More specifically, when the size of the docket was one standard deviation above the mean, fully unanimous opinions resulted 22 percent of the time and highly consensual (UOC) opinions resulted 33.3 percent of the time. Oppositely, when the size of the docket was one standard deviation below the mean, the results were 28.6 percent and 38 percent, respectively. On the other hand, we find no discernible pattern—and relatively little change—when we vary the number of law clerks serving on the Court. It thus appears that the number of law clerks, in contrast to the size of the docket, has little bearing on the justices' ability to achieve opinion consensus.

Our hypothesis is that ideological compatibility among the justices should increase the likelihood of a fully unanimous opinion. Our initial investigation of the data supports this: the relationship between opinion consensus and ideological polarization was negative for fully unanimous and highly consensual opinions (see Table 4.1). When the justices were the most ideologically compatible (i.e., when the degree of polarization between them was more than one standard deviation below the mean), a fully unanimous opinion occurred 26.7 percent of the time. However, when the justices were the most ideologically polarized (i.e., when the degree of polarization was more than one standard deviation above the mean), a fully unanimous opinion occurred only 22.4 percent of the time. Similarly, highly consensual opinions (UOCs) occurred 36 percent of the time when the justices were most ideologically compatible as opposed to 30 percent when they were most ideologically polarized. These findings suggest that when they are more ideologically compatible the justices are better able to reach consensus on the legal reasoning in the case.

Following the assumptions of the attitudinal model, another hypothesis is that fully unanimous opinions should be more likely in cases where the justices are reversing a decision by an "extreme" lower court. We do find some evidence of such a phenomenon. When we examine cases that reversed decisions by lower courts considered "extreme," we find that 29.4 percent resulted in a fully unanimous opinion compared with only 24.5 percent in which the Court reversed a "nonextreme" decision. However, we see almost no difference in terms of whether the Court issued a fully unanimous opinion or a unanimous decision with one concurrence (36 percent versus 35.6 percent).

Finally, we theorize that fully unanimous opinions should occur more frequently in cases where the level of legal certainty as to the strongest legal answer is high. Our preliminary exploration reveals strong support for this hypothesis (see Table 4.1). Of those cases with high legal certainty (a score greater than 3), 28.6 percent resulted in fully unanimous opinions. Alternatively, a fully unanimous opinion was rendered in only 22.4 percent of cases with low legal certainty (a score less than 4). As these results indicate, opinion consensus is closely linked to the level of legal certainty: when the level is low, opinion consensus is difficult to achieve; when it is high, opinion consensus—and, indeed, a fully unanimous opinion—can be reached.

Given the preliminary findings just presented, a fully unanimous opinion appears to occur in the following types of cases: those that do not involve civil liberties issues, those that are not salient to outside actors, those that do not strike down statutes or alter precedent, those in which the majority decision is not authored by the median justice, those with less time before end of term, those that are decided with a high degree of ideological compatibility, and those that involve a high degree of legal certainty.

A prototypical example is *United States v. Orleans* (1976), which was decided by a fully unanimous opinion authored by Chief Justice Burger. This case involved a question of statutory interpretation with regard to a governmental powers issue, it was not reported on the front page of the *New York Times*, it was heard by a relatively ideologically compatible Court, and it concerned the highest possible level of legal certainty. Specifically, *Orleans* addressed whether the federal government can be sued under the Federal Torts Claims Act (FTCA) if an accident occurs under the auspices of a nonprofit organization that receives a percentage of its funds from the government. Orleans's minor child was injured in a car accident during an outing sponsored by an Ohio community organization. Orleans attempted to sue the federal government under the FTCA, alleging negligence. The Supreme Court held that, under the provisions of the FTCA, the organization was not a federal agency or instrumentality and its employees were not federal employees, thereby prohibiting the suit. Moreover, the justices were able to fully agree on both the outcome and the legal reasoning for their decision.

A Model of Opinion Consensus

The preceding analysis presents an initial picture of fully unanimous and highly consensual opinions. However, this picture does not help us understand how the different potential forces operate in conjunction or allow us to determine their relative influence. We therefore turn to multivariate analysis in order to test our theory of consensus by controlling simultaneously for multiple, competing influences on the likelihood of the Supreme Court issuing a fully unanimous opinion and thus achieving opinion consensus, not simply consensus on the merits.

Table 4.2 reports our estimation results. As a reminder, we utilize three distinct dependent variables to fully assess the Court's ability to reach agreement on the merits as well as on the legal reasoning. Model 1 indicates which factors increase or decrease the likelihood of the Court reaching a fully unanimous opinion (UO). Models 2 and 3 indicate which factors increase or decrease the likelihood of the Court reaching a highly consensual opinion—defined in Model 2 as a fully unanimous opinion or a unanimous decision

TABLE 4.2

Logit models of unanimous and highly consensual opinions

Variable	MODEL 1		MODEL 2		MODEL 3	
	Coefficient (R.S.E.)	*p*-value	Coefficient (R.S.E.)	*p*-value	Coefficient (R.S.E.)	*p*-value
Legal considerations						
Level of Legal Certainty	0.206 (0.044)	0.000	0.176 (0.040)	0.000	0.166 (0.039)	0.000
Attitudinal						
Ideological Polarization	−0.107 (0.057)	0.031	−0.085 (0.053)	0.054	−0.082 (0.051)	0.055
Extreme Lower Court Decision	0.080 (0.216)	0.711	−0.093 (0.205)	0.649	0.002 (0.199)	0.992
Reversed Lower Court Decision	−0.016 (0.089)	0.859	0.045 (0.081)	0.583	0.066 (0.080)	0.410
Extreme Lower Court Decision × Reversed	0.065 (0.273)	0.406	−0.016 (0.258)	0.524	−0.064 (0.250)	0.601
Strategic considerations						
Chief Justice Writes Opinion	0.101 (0.137)	0.232	0.147 (0.123)	0.116	0.118 (0.119)	0.161
Median Justice Writes Opinion	−0.303 (0.171)	0.076	−0.245 (0.149)	0.101	−0.335 (0.146)	0.022
Altered Precedent	−0.159 (0.333)	0.634	−0.247 (0.292)	0.397	−0.427 (0.284)	0.133
Declared Statute Unconstitutional	−1.599 (0.528)	0.002	−0.662 (0.300)	0.027	−0.441 (0.276)	0.111
SG Party	−0.065 (0.085)	0.776	0.001 (0.077)	0.495	−0.030 (0.075)	0.654
Institutional context						
Addition of Syllabus	0.036 (0.244)	0.558	0.128 (0.221)	0.719	−0.012 (0.215)	0.467
Formalization of Dissent Assignment	−0.087 (0.193)	0.326	−0.138 (0.176)	0.217	−0.217 (0.171)	0.102
Docket Size	−0.001 (0.002)	0.624	0.002 (0.002)	0.152	0.002 (0.002)	0.243
Number of Law Clerks	−0.025 (0.028)	0.188	0.007 (0.026)	0.601	0.023 (0.025)	0.825
Rehnquist Court	0.676 (0.463)	0.144	0.248 (0.428)	0.562	−0.043 (0.418)	0.918
Burger Court	0.337 (0.364)	0.353	−0.111 (0.340)	0.743	−0.225 (0.332)	0.498

(*continued*)

TABLE 4.2 *(continued)*

Variable	MODEL 1		MODEL 2		MODEL 3	
	Coefficient (R.S.E.)	*p*-value	Coefficient (R.S.E.)	*p*-value	Coefficient (R.S.E.)	*p*-value
Case factors						
Governmental Powers Issue	0.720 (0.105)	0.000	0.648 (0.096)	0.000	0.764 (0.094)	0.000
Economic Issue	0.714 (0.099)	0.000	0.596 (0.089)	0.000	0.656 (0.087)	0.000
Political Salience	−0.761 (0.158)	0.000	−0.781 (0.132)	0.000	−0.875 (0.126)	0.000
Liberal Decision	0.376 (0.084)	0.000	0.517 (0.077)	0.000	0.407 (0.075)	0.000
Time Left until End of Term	−0.001 (0.001)	0.029	−0.001 (0.001)	0.074	−0.001 (0.001)	0.066
Constant	−1.051 (0.681)	0.123	−1.686 (0.634)	0.008	−1.492 (0.615)	0.015
N	3,391		3,391		3,391	

NOTE: Model 1: Unanimous opinions.
Model 2: Unanimous opinions or highly consensual opinions (unanimous decisions with one concurrence).
Model 3: Unanimous opinions or highly consensual opinions (unanimous decisions with one concurrence or decisions with one dissent where there is only one justice dissenting).
R.S.E. = robust standard error clustered on case citation. *p*-values reflect one-tailed tests if directionality is hypothesized.

that contains one concurrence (UOC) and defined in Model 3 as a fully unanimous opinion, a unanimous decision that contains one concurrence, or a decision in which there is one dissent with only one justice dissenting (UOCD). Table 4.3 presents a series of predicted probabilities associated with each statistically significant variable in each model.

We first investigate the role that the level of legal certainty plays in the Supreme Court's ability to reach a fully unanimous or a highly consensual opinion. As shown in Table 4.2, we find that as the level of legal certainty increases, the likelihood of a fully unanimous or a highly consensual opinion increases as well.[3] Turning to the predicted probabilities in Table 4.3, the likelihood of opinion unanimity increases by 0.124 (UO) and the likelihood of a highly consensual opinion increases by 0.143 (UOC) and 0.157 (UOCD) when legal certainty is high compared to when legal certainty is low. Thus, even when defining consensus in terms of separate opinion writing as opposed to votes on the merits, legal certainty plays a substantial role in whether the Court reaches consensus. Although our index is admittedly an imperfect proxy for the law's influence, it is important for scholars to attempt to measure concepts such as legal certainty in order to advance our understanding of the influence of law on the Court. We propose that our Legal Certainty Index works to isolate the influence of legal forces on judicial decision making and that our results illuminate the importance of law to the Supreme Court.

We next explore the role of attitudes in the ability of the Court to reach a fully unanimous or highly consensual opinion. Specifically, we expect that as the degree of ideological polarization increases, the likelihood of a fully unanimous or highly consensual opinion decreases. Our results again support this proposition: a fully unanimous or a highly consensual opinion, defined both ways, is significantly less likely when the justices are ideologically distant. Looking again at Table 4.3, if the Court is ideologically polarized, the predicted probability of reaching a fully unanimous opinion is 0.119 whereas if the Court is ideologically compatible, the predicted probability is 0.219. Likewise, if the Court is ideologically polarized, the likelihood of reaching a highly consensual opinion decreases by 0.103 (UOC) and by 0.115 (UOCD). Thus, it appears that the Supreme Court can reach opinion consensus more easily if the justices are ideologically aligned. However, contrary to our expectations, we do not find any support for the idea of the Court reaching opinion consensus more easily when reversing an "extreme" lower court case. These results mirror the findings from Chapter 3.

We also examine the extent to which strategic factors influence the likelihood of opinion consensus. In Chapter 3, we find that the chief justice can

TABLE 4.3

Predicted probabilities of unanimous and highly consensual opinions

Change in variable value	MODEL 1: UNANIMOUS OPINION	MODEL 2: UNANIMOUS OR HIGHLY CONSENSUAL OPINION (UOC)[a]	MODEL 3: UNANIMOUS OR HIGHLY CONSENSUAL OPINION (UOCD)[b]
	Predicted probability	Predicted probability	Predicted probability
Level of Legal Certainty (min → max)	0.087 → 0.211 [0.056, 0.118] → [0.158, 0.264]	0.140 → 0.283 [0.098, 0.183] → [0.225, 0.341]	0.185 → 0.342 [0.134, 0.236] → [0.280, 0.404]
Ideological Polarization (min → max)	0.219 → 0.119 [0.140, 0.299] → [0.069, 0.169]	0.286 → 0.183 [0.199, 0.374] → [0.119, 0.248]	0.348 → 0.233 [0.253, 0.442] → [0.159, 0.308]
Nonmedian Justice Writes → Median Justice Writes	0.157 → 0.121 [0.121, 0.194] → [0.077, 0.166]	0.225 → 0.185 [0.181, 0.268] → [0.130, 0.240]	0.280 →0.218 [0.232, 0.329] → [0.157, 0.279]
No Declaration of Unconstitutionality → Declaration of Unconstitutionality	0.157 → 0.036 [0.121, 0.194] → [−0.001, 0.074]	0.225→ 0.130 [0.181, 0.268] → [0.059, 0.202]	—
No Formalization of Dissent Assignment → Formalization of Dissent Assignment	—	—	0.326 → 0.280 [0.261, 0.392] → [0.232, 0.329]
End of Term Close → End of Term Far Away	0.228 → 0.200 [0.177, 0.279] → [0.153, 0.248]	0.339 →0.315 [0.280, 0.399] → [0.257, 0.373]	0.382 → 0.356 [0.322, 0.443] → [0.296, 0.416]
Civil Liberties Issue → Governmental Powers Issue	0.157 → 0.277 [0.121, 0.194] → [0.218, 0.337]	0.225→ 0.357 [0.181, 0.268] → [0.294, 0.419]	0.280 → 0.455 [0.232, 0.329] → [0.390, 0.521]
Civil Liberties Issue → Economic Issue	0.157 → 0.276 [0.121, 0.194] → [0.220, 0.333]	0.225 → 0.345 [0.181, 0.268] → [0.286, 0.404]	0.280 → 0.429 [0.232, 0.329] → [0.367, 0.491]
Nonsalient Case → Salient Case	0.157 → 0.080 [0.121, 0.194] → [0.051, 0.109]	0.225 → 0.117 [0.181, 0.268] → [0.082, 0.152]	0.280 → 0.140 [0.232, 0.329] → [0.101, 0.178]
Conservative Decision → Liberal Decision	0.157 → 0.214 [0.121, 0.194] → [0.167, 0.261]	0.225 → 0.327 [0.181, 0.268] → [0.271, 0.383]	0.280 → 0.369 [0.232, 0.329] → [0.312, 0.427]

NOTE: Baseline probability of a unanimous opinion = 0.157 [0.121, 0.194]. Baseline probability of a unanimous or highly consensual opinion (UOC) = 0.225 [0.181, 0.268]. Baseline probability of a unanimous or highly consensual opinion (UOCD) = 0.280 [0.232, 0.329]. Baselines computed by holding all continuous variables (such as the level of certainty) at their mean values, while holding all discrete variables (such as whether the solicitor general was a party) at their modal values.

[a]UOC = unanimous opinions or highly consensual opinions (unanimous decisions with one concurrence).

[b]UOCD = unanimous opinions or highly consensual opinions (unanimous decisions with one concurrence or decisions with one dissent where there is only one justice dissenting).

influence the Court's ability to reach a unanimous *decision* through his powers of self-assignment, but he does not appear to influence whether the Court achieves a unanimous *opinion* or a decision with a high level of *opinion* consensus. However, if the median justice is the majority opinion author, such opinions are less likely.[4] If the median justice authors the majority opinion, the predicted probability of a unanimous opinion decreases by 0.036; that of a UOC highly consensual opinion decreases by 0.040; and that of a UOCD highly consensual opinion decreases by 0.062.

While previous research showed that the solicitor general (SG) is very successful when appearing before the Court, that success does not translate into more opinion consensus. Moreover, the Court is not more likely to reach a fully unanimous or a highly consensual opinion when the Court is altering precedent. These results mirror those in Chapter 3. However, although declaring a statute unconstitutional does not influence whether a unanimous decision is reached, the Court is less likely to reach a fully unanimous opinion or a highly consensual opinion (UOC) when declaring a statute unconstitutional. While one argument is that the Court is more likely to reach a fully unanimous or highly consensual opinion when declaring a statute unconstitutional due to legitimacy concerns, our results suggest that, when the Court is striking down legislation passed by an elected legislature, the justices feel compelled to separately explain their reasons for doing so in a concurrence, which can be interpreted as strategic behavior vis-à-vis external political actors.

Turning to the institutional variables in the models, we do not find that these variables, with the exception of formalization of dissent assignment, influence the likelihood of a fully unanimous or highly consensual opinion. With respect to UOCD highly consensual opinions, the Court was less likely to reach consensus in the period after the dissent process was formalized.

We do, however, find support for each of the case-specific factors. Salient cases are less likely to result in fully unanimous or highly consensual opinions. The likelihood of achieving opinion unanimity drops by 0.077 when the case is salient compared to when it is not. There is a decrease of 0.108 for the predicted probability of achieving a highly consensual opinion (UOC) and a 0.140 decrease for the predicted probability of achieving a highly consensual opinion (UOCD).

In addition, governmental powers cases and economic cases are more likely to result in a fully unanimous or highly consensual opinion than is a case involving civil liberties and rights. We also find that these opinions are more likely when the Court reaches a liberal decision. In fact, the predicted probability of a fully unanimous opinion increases by 0.057 when the Court reaches a liberal rather than a conservative result.

Finally, as the end of the term draws closer, the Court is more likely to reach a fully unanimous or highly consensual opinion. Our results suggest that when the justices lack sufficient time, they are less likely to write separately. Specifically, when the end of term is close, the predicted probability of a fully unanimous opinion is 0.228; when it is far away, the predicted probability is 0.200.

Overall, fully unanimous opinions and highly consensual opinions (UOC) in the 1953–2004 terms were a function of the following: a high degree of legal certainty; a less ideologically polarized Court; a relatively short time before the end of the term; and cases that did not address civil liberties issues, did not declare a statute unconstitutional, were decided in a liberal direction, did not appear on the front page of the *New York Times*, and were not written by the median justice. A highly consensual opinion (UOCD) was influenced by the same factors, with the exception of declaring a statute unconstitutional, which is not statistically significant in Model 3. Additionally, a UOCD was less likely after the dissent process was formalized.

An example of a fully unanimous opinion reflecting each of these factors is the *Republic of Argentina v. Weltover, Inc.* (1992), which concerned whether the federal courts had jurisdiction under the Foreign Sovereign Immunities Act of 1976 to address a claim concerning bonds issued by Argentina but which utilized banks in New York as the place of transfer and payment. Justice Scalia authored the sole opinion for the unanimous Court (which was relatively more ideologically compatible at this time). *Argentina* concerned a governmental powers issue, was decided in a liberal direction, was not salient, and did not declare a statute unconstitutional. It was also decided relatively close to the end of the term. Finally, the case had the highest level of legal certainty. In particular, it concerned a question of statutory interpretation, had the lowest level of legal complexity, had no amicus briefs filed, was decided unanimously by the lower court, lacked any nonideological dissensus between the lower court judges, and did not involve an unimportant conflict between lower courts (suggesting that the conflict was not due to disagreement about the law).

Unanimity on the Merits versus Opinion Consensus

The next question we address in this section is how the findings discussed here compare with those reported in Chapter 3. The premise underlying this chapter is that solely examining votes on the merits can obscure important information about disagreement among the justices. This is particularly true

TABLE 4.4

Summary of main model results from Chapters 3 and 4

Variable	Unanimous decision model	Unanimous or highly consensual decision model	Unanimous opinion model	Unanimous or highly consensual opinion (UOC)[a] model	Unanimous or highly consensual opinion (UOCD)[b] model
Legal considerations					
Level of Legal Certainty	More likely	More likely	More likely	More likely	More likely
Attitudinal					
Ideological Polarization	Less likely	No effect	Less likely	Less likely	Less likely
Extreme Lower Court Decision	No effect	No effect	No effect	No effect	No effect
Reversed Lower Court Decision	No effect	More likely	No effect	No effect	No effect
Extreme Lower Court Decision × Reversed	No effect	No effect	No effect	No effect	No effect
Strategic considerations					
Chief Justice Writes Opinion	More likely	More likely	No effect	No effect	No effect
Median Justice Writes Opinion	No effect	Less likely	Less likely	Less likely	Less likely
Altered Precedent	No effect	No effect	No effect	No effect	No effect
Declared Statute Unconstitutional	No effect	No effect	Less likely	Less likely	No effect
SG Party	No effect	No effect	No effect	No effect	No effect
Institutional context					
Addition of Syllabus	No effect	No effect	No effect	No effect	No effect
Formalization of Dissent Assignment	No effect	No effect	No effect	No effect	Less likely
Docket Size	No effect	No effect	No effect	No effect	No effect
Number of Law Clerks	No effect	No effect	No effect	No effect	No effect
Rehnquist Court	No effect	No effect	No effect	No effect	No effect
Burger Court	No effect	No effect	No effect	No effect	No effect
Case factors					
Governmental Powers Issue	More likely	More likely	More likely	More likely	More likely
Economic Issue	More likely	More likely	More likely	More likely	More likely
Political Salience	Less likely	Less likely	Less likely	Less likely	Less likely
Liberal Decision	More likely	More likely	More likely	More likely	More likely
Time Left until End of Term	—	—	Less likely	Less likely	Less likely

[a]UOC = unanimous opinions or highly consensual opinions (unanimous decisions with one concurrence).

[b]UOCD = unanimous opinions or highly consensual opinions (unanimous decisions with one concurrence or decisions with one dissent where there is only one justice dissenting).

when the disagreement is legal in nature and thus presented in concurrences rather than dissents. Table 4.4 provides a summary of the findings for each of the five main models estimated in this chapter and in Chapter 3 in order to shed light on how consensus on the merits differs in substance from opinion consensus.

The results reported in Table 4.4 show that the determinants of consensus on the merits and opinion consensus are relatively similar. With both, cases concerning governmental powers or economic issues as opposed to civil liberties issues are more likely to be decided with a high degree of consensus, as are cases decided in a liberal direction and those that are not subsequently discussed on the front page of the *New York Times*.

Perhaps most notable is the consistent influence of legal certainty on the achievement of both voting consensus and opinion consensus. In every model estimated, regardless of how we operationalize the dependent variable, legal certainty exerts a strong, positive effect on the Court's ability to reach consensus. These findings thus indicate that unanimity and consensus, in terms of both votes and opinions, are in part a function of the attributes of the case having a high degree of certainty as to the strongest legal answer; they also indicate that scholars of judicial decision making must consider the influence of law when assessing the justices' decisions, including the decision to author a separate opinion.

We also find some interesting differences among the models. First, increased ideological polarization decreases the likelihood of unanimous decisions, fully unanimous opinions, and highly consensual opinions, but not highly consensual decisions. This suggests that the direct effect of ideological compatibility matters for unanimous decisions and opinion consensus but not for highly consensual decisions on the merits. Whether the Court declares a statute constitutional negatively affects the likelihood of its issuing a UOC opinion but not a UOCD opinion; it also does not influence the achievement of consensus on the merits regardless of how voting consensus is measured. We suggest that when the Court exercises its power of judicial review, the likelihood of disagreement over the legal reasoning for such a decision is relatively high, leading to concurring opinions. This finding in particular showcases the necessity of studying opinion consensus along with consensus on the merits.

The final set of differences concerns opinion authorship. Both unanimous and highly consensual decisions are significantly more likely when the chief justice authors the opinion, suggesting that the chief can indeed use his self-assignment powers to help the Court reach agreement. However, chief justice authorship does not influence the likelihood of opinion consensus in any of our three models. As a result, while the chief may be able to bridge divides on the merits, he does not seem to hold the same sway when attempting to forestall separate opinions, especially concurring opinions expressing disagreements over legal reasoning. On the other hand, while authorship by the median justice does not influence unanimous decisions, it does negatively influence the probability of a highly consensual decision, a fully unanimous opinion, and a highly consensual opinion (UOC and UOCD). It may well be that the median author's most influential role is not to garner broader consensus but to preserve the unity of minimum-winning coalitions.

All told, unanimous and highly consensual decisions and opinions appear to be a function of law, attitudes, strategic considerations, and case factors. While we do see some differences between consensus on the merits and opinion consensus, the underlying story is the same: consensus is a function of a number of simultaneous influences, and any discussion of judicial decision making needs to recognize the role played by each one.

Understanding the Relationship between Attitudes and Legal Certainty

Our final set of empirical analyses addresses the relationship between attitudes and law with respect to opinion consensus. The theory presented in Chapter 2 suggests that attitudinal and legal forces operate simultaneously in all cases and directly affect consensus on the Court; we find strong support for this suggestion. We also posit that law exerts an *indirect* effect on judicial decision making: attitudes are the principal force but they can be constrained by legal considerations in certain cases, thus causing the jaws of the vise to close and the operation of attitudes to be circumscribed. Specifically, we should find that when the level of legal certainty increases, the influence of attitudes decreases; alternatively, when the level of legal certainty is low, the influence of attitudes is high.

As we did in the preceding chapter, we reran the models presented in Table 4.3 but with an important variation: we estimated the models with the same independent variables except for the level of legal certainty variable. We then altered the sample on which the model was estimated based on the level of legal certainty in the case. Thus, for each of the three dependent variables we reran the original regressions, first on the sample of cases where legal certainty was low (a score less than 4) and then on the sample of cases where it was high (a score greater than 3). We expect that in the three models reflecting the sample of cases where the level of legal certainty is low, ideological polarization will be significant and substantively strong. Alternatively, we expect that in the three models reflecting the sample of cases where the level of legal certainty is high, ideological polarization will not be significant. In other words, a non-significant finding indicates that when the level of legal certainty is high, and all of the information available to the justices points in the direction of a single legal answer, the influence of attitudes necessarily becomes constrained.

Table 4.5 reports the estimation results for the fully unanimous opinions (UO) model, while Table 4.6 reports those for the two unanimous opinion and highly consensual opinion (UOC and UOCD) models. Consistent with the results from the previous chapter, we find that the degree of ideological polarization significantly influences whether the Court is able to achieve a UOC or UOCD opinion when the level of legal certainty is low; however, the level of ideological polarization does not influence the likelihood of opinion consensus when the level of legal certainty is high. However, in the fully unanimous opinion model, ideological polarization is not statistically significant even at a low level of legal certainty (p-value = 0.060). Given that a fully unanimous opinion does not contain concurrences, it is not surprising that the degree of polarization does not influence the ability of the justices to reach consensus. Overall, these findings suggest that the influence of attitudes is constrained when the level of legal certainty is high and legal considerations act as a vise, limiting the justices' discretion to follow their attitudes and express disagreements through separate opinions.

Conclusion

The goal of this chapter is to further explain, by examining opinion consensus on the Court, why and how the justices are able to agree. We find that opinion consensus is explained by a set of factors that similarly explain unanimity and consensus on the merits. Consistent with the findings reported in Chapter 3, opinion consensus is a function of multiple, simultaneously acting forces—each exerting an important influence on the Court's operation. We therefore find strong support for our comprehensive theory of consensus.

Our findings have important implications for the study of judicial decision making. First and foremost, they consistently support the proposition that law—measured as the degree of legal certainty present in each case—influences opinion consensus both directly and indirectly. When the level of legal certainty is high, opinion consensus—as well as consensus on the

TABLE 4.5

Logit models of ideological and legal interaction: Unanimous opinions

	MODEL 1: UNANIMOUS OPINIONS			
	LOW LEVEL OF LEGAL CERTAINTY		HIGH LEVEL OF LEGAL CERTAINTY	
Variable	Coefficient (R.S.E.)	*p*-value	Coefficient (R.S.E.)	*p*-value
Attitudinal				
Ideological Polarization	**−0.131 (0.084)**	**0.060**	**−0.112 (0.079)**	**0.077**
Extreme Lower Court Decision	0.132 (0.311)	0.670	−0.029 (0.312)	0.929
Reversed Lower Court Decision	0.035 (0.123)	0.777	−0.083 (0.132)	0.531
Extreme Lower Court Decision × Reversed	0.101 (0.408)	0.402	0.167 (0.381)	0.331
Strategic considerations				
Chief Justice Writes Opinion	−0.075 (0.193)	0.652	0.345 (0.203)	0.044
Median Justice Writes Opinion	−0.197 (0.232)	0.396	−0.420 (0.248)	0.091
Altered Precedent	−0.414 (0.468)	0.377	0.118 (0.488)	0.809
Declared Statute Unconstitutional	−1.458 (0.535)	0.006	—	
SG Party	−0.017 (0.117)	0.557	−0.110 (0.122)	0.810
Institutional context				
Addition of Syllabus	0.213 (0.376)	0.710	−0.156 (0.323)	0.315
Formalization of Dissent Assignment	−0.193 (0.263)	0.232	0.004 (0.282)	0.506
Docket Size	−0.003 (0.003)	0.788	0.002 (0.004)	0.298
Number of Law Clerks	−0.043 (0.041)	0.148	−0.021 (0.039)	0.291
Rehnquist Court	0.639 (0.704)	0.364	0.824 (0.621)	0.185
Burger Court	0.409 (0.563)	0.467	0.312 (0.479)	0.515
Case factors				
Governmental Powers Issue	0.762 (0.143)	0.000	0.674 (0.154)	0.000
Economic Issue	0.855 (0.136)	0.000	0.612 (0.142)	0.000
Political Salience	−0.991 (0.209)	0.000	−0.397 (0.246)	0.054
Liberal Decision	0.485 (0.116)	0.000	0.255 (0.122)	0.019
Time Left until End of Term	−0.000 (0.001)	0.350	−0.002 (0.001)	0.011
Constant	0.058 (0.966)	0.952	−0.263 (0.924)	0.776
N	1,957		1,424	

NOTE: R.S.E. = robust standard error clustered on case citation. *p*-values reflect one-tailed tests if directionality is hypothesized. When *Declared Statute Unconstitutional* equaled 1, failure perfectly predicted and 10 observations not used.

TABLE 4.6

Logit models of ideological and legal interaction: Unanimous or highly consensual opinions

	MODEL 2				MODEL 3			
	LOW LEGAL CERTAINTY		HIGH LEGAL CERTAINTY		LOW LEGAL CERTAINTY		HIGH LEGAL CERTAINTY	
Variable	Coefficient (R.S.E.)	*p*-value	Coefficient (R.S.E.)	*p*-value	Coefficient (R.S.E.)	*p*-value	Coefficient (R.S.E.)	*p*-value
Attitudinal								
Ideological Polarization	**−0.136 (0.075)**	**0.036**	**−0.068 (0.074)**	**0.179**	**−0.117 (0.072)**	**0.052**	**−0.082 (0.074)**	**0.134**
Extreme Lower Court Decision	0.103 (0.282)	0.715	−0.377 (0.307)	0.219	0.196 (0.266)	0.460	−0.254 (0.302)	0.401
Reversed Lower Court Decision	0.076 (0.110)	0.490	0.017 (0.124)	0.892	0.034 (0.107)	0.751	0.109 (0.122)	0.374
Extreme Lower Court Decision × Reversed	−0.135 (0.375)	0.640	0.279 (0.368)	0.224	−0.228 (0.356)	0.739	0.207 (0.362)	0.283
Strategic considerations								
Chief Justice Writes Opinion	0.002 (0.164)	0.495	0.411 (0.197)	0.019	−0.145 (0.161)	0.815	0.552 (0.197)	0.003
Median Justice Writes Opinion	−0.268 (0.206)	0.194	−0.229 (0.214)	0.283	−0.295 (0.198)	0.136	−0.392 (0.211)	0.062
Altered Precedent	−0.267 (0.383)	0.486	−0.211 (0.468)	0.638	−0.511 (0.384)	0.183	−0.324 (0.450)	0.471
Declared Statute Unconstitutional	−0.964 (0.345)	0.005	0.436 (0.662)	0.510	−0.741 (0.317)	0.019	0.715 (0.632)	0.258
SG Party	−0.032 (0.105)	0.622	0.034 (0.114)	0.381	−0.064 (0.101)	0.735	0.000 (0.112)	0.500
Institutional context								
Addition of Syllabus	0.478 (0.348)	0.915	−0.176 (0.290)	0.272	0.316 (0.330)	0.831	−0.338 (0.290)	0.122
Formalization of Dissent Assignment	−0.174 (0.239)	0.234	−0.160 (0.260)	0.269	−0.218 (0.229)	0.170	−0.259 (0.256)	0.156
Docket Size	0.002 (0.003)	0.285	0.003 (0.004)	0.172	−0.000 (0.003)	0.563	0.004 (0.004)	0.109
Number of Law Clerks	−0.024 (0.037)	0.255	0.028 (0.037)	0.776	−0.008 (0.036)	0.406	0.042 (0.036)	0.879
Rehnquist Court	0.324 (0.640)	0.612	0.208 (0.596)	0.727	−0.111 (0.613)	0.857	0.126 (0.596)	0.832
Burger Court	0.005 (0.519)	0.992	−0.228 (0.463)	0.622	−0.183 (0.498)	0.714	−0.267 (0.461)	0.562

Case factors								
Governmental Powers Issue	0.642 (0.131)	0.000	0.676 (0.144)	0.000	0.788 (0.126)	0.000	0.755 (0.143)	0.000
Economic Issue	0.702 (0.121)	0.000	0.527 (0.131)	0.000	0.712 (0.118)	0.000	0.640 (0.129)	0.000
Political Salience	−1.075 (0.169)	0.000	−0.318 (0.218)	0.073	−1.045 (0.158)	0.000	−0.584 (0.216)	0.004
Liberal Decision	0.706 (0.104)	0.000	0.267 (0.114)	0.010	0.555 (0.101)	0.000	0.188 (0.113)	0.049
Time Left until End of Term	−0.000 (0.001)	0.460	−0.002 (0.001)	0.019	−0.000 (0.001)	0.372	−0.002 (0.001)	0.021
Constant	−0.420 (0.890)	0.637	−1.308 (0.869)	0.132	0.033 (0.849)	0.969	−1.374 (0.854)	0.108
N	1,957		1,434		1,957		1,434	

NOTE: Model 2: Unanimous opinion or highly consensual opinion (unanimous decisions with one concurrence).
Model 3: Unanimous opinion or highly consensual opinion (unanimous decisions with one concurrence or decisions with one dissent where there is only one justice dissenting).
R.S.E. = robust standard error clustered on case citation. *p*-values reflect one-tailed tests if directionality was hypothesized.

merits—is much more likely and, furthermore, the influence of attitudes on opinion consensus is mitigated. While our measure of legal certainty is an admittedly imperfect proxy for the influence of law, the consistent results we find across the different model specifications suggest that understanding judicial decision making requires a theory that takes into account not just how law influences decision making but also how attitudes and law interact.

Second, we find that case factors influence whether the Court achieves opinion consensus. Specifically, cases involving governmental powers and economic issues are more likely to result in opinion consensus than are cases involving civil liberties and rights. Moreover, the Court is less likely to achieve opinion consensus if the case is salient.

Third, we find limited support for the theory that strategic considerations influence whether the Court is able to achieve opinion consensus. When the Court declares a statute unconstitutional, opinion consensus is less likely, perhaps because justices feel compelled to write separately to explain their vote. Furthermore, opinion consensus is less likely when the median justice writes the opinion. Finally, the institutional context in which the justices work does not appear to influence whether they are able to achieve opinion consensus. The one exception to this finding is formalization of the dissent process for the UOCD model.

The findings presented here and in Chapter 3 illuminate the multiple, competing forces that influence Supreme Court decision making and, in particular, the way in which the level of legal certainty as to the strongest legal answer influences whether the justices are able to achieve consensus, if not complete unanimity. These findings also spark an important question concerning the Supreme Court's discretionary jurisdiction: If the Court is more likely to achieve consensus when the level of legal certainty is high, and thus many indicators suggest that one legal answer is stronger and more plausible than any other, why do the justices decide to take these cases in the first place? In the next chapter, we explore the answer to this question.

CHAPTER 5

An Opportunity to Clarify

Unanimity and Agenda Setting

The analysis in the previous chapters reveals that unanimous and highly consensual decisions occur frequently on the Supreme Court and that myriad factors explain why the Court is able to reach consensus. However, our findings also raise an important question: If the Supreme Court's role is to solve difficult and vexing legal questions—questions that likely divide the lower courts, the public, and elected officials—why does it grant certiorari in cases that are ultimately decided unanimously? This chapter provides an initial exploration of this crucial query.

For example, *Sisson v. Ruby* (1990) involved an economic activity issue and did not appear on the front page of the *New York Times*—two factors that increase the likelihood of unanimity. In this case, the Court unanimously held that the federal district courts have maritime jurisdiction over activities that bear a substantial relationship to traditional maritime activities. The justices explained that these activities include fires on noncommercial vessels docked at marinas on navigable waterways because they can potentially endanger maritime commerce. Of the 4,919 petitions the Court received during that term, why did they agree to decide this case? The cert pool law clerk who initially reviewed the petition drafted a memo to the justices that argued in favor of granting cert: "This case . . . presents the Court with an opportunity to clarify just how far admiralty jurisdiction extends when noncommercial vessels are involved."[1] In short, it appears that the justices were persuaded that existing law needed to be clarified.

Until now, our investigation of the puzzle of unanimity has centered on the Court's role in *deciding* cases. But the Court also possesses the power to *choose* the cases it decides. Originally, the Court's appellate jurisdiction, as determined by Congress, was predominantly mandatory, whereby the justices were forced to decide cases appealed from lower courts. As discussed in previous chapters, the Judges' Bill of 1925 allowed the Supreme Court increased control over its docket. Over time, Congress continued to reduce the Court's mandatory jurisdiction. By 1988, mandatory appeals cases were basically eliminated, and since then the vast majority of the Court's docket has been discretionary.

Numerous studies have investigated the Court's certiorari process to determine why some petitions are granted and others denied. The questions we explore in this chapter are somewhat distinct: Why does the Court choose to hear cases that are ultimately decided unanimously, and is there something different about these cases that can be pinpointed at the agenda-setting stage? We undertake this analysis not to definitively explain the Court's certiorari decisions but rather to understand why the Court spends so much time every term on cases that, according to conventional wisdom, it simply should not hear.

Usually discussions of the Supreme Court emphasize its role in answering hard, divisive legal questions that require an ultimate, national decision. These questions are ones in which the justices—much like lower court judges and the public—are likely to be divided. According to Posner (2005, 40), "it is rarely possible to say with a straight face of a Supreme Court constitutional decision that it was decided correctly or incorrectly." How then do we explain the fact that the Court chooses to hear a significant number of cases, including a not insubstantial number of constitutional cases, that ultimately result in decisions where all of the justices, liberal and conservative, reach the same legal answer?

This chapter considers this question. We begin with an overview of the Court's agenda-setting process. We then briefly discuss studies of the agenda-setting stage and lay out the hypotheses we derive from them regarding the link between certiorari and consensus. Finally, the heart of this chapter provides an exploratory analysis of whether there is something unique at the cert stage about cases that are granted and subsequently decided unanimously compared to those that are granted but ultimately result in divided decisions. We do so by examining the cert pool memos written for all cases decided during the 1989 term. We investigate these memos to determine what the memo author concluded with regard to a number of subjective measures of certworthiness, and then we compare the results for ultimately unanimously decided cases versus cases that led to nonunanimous decisions.

Based on our examination of these pool memos, we reach the following preliminary conclusions. First, unanimously decided cases are just as likely as nonunanimous cases to concern circuit splits and important issues; the distinction we uncover is that the memo authors are more likely in unanimously decided cases to emphasize the need for the Court to issue a final, national ruling that resolves the legal question at hand. Second, unanimous cases are more likely than nonunanimous cases to be viewed as "bad" vehicles, usually because the memo author feels that the case needs more time to percolate in the lower courts. Finally, the memo author is more likely to conclude that the lower court's decision was correctly decided in unanimous cases than nonunanimous cases. This finding suggests that unanimous cases are not, as some may assume, about error correction but rather about the Court recognizing the need to clarify or emphasize an important point of law. Overall, our results point once again toward the influence of law on Supreme Court justices: they not only are influenced by legal forces when deciding cases but are also concerned with clarifying law when deciding which cases to hear in the first place. We turn now to our exploration of the certiorari process and its link with consensus on the Court.

So Untenable: The Certiorari Process

Cases seeking a writ of certiorari are appealed to the Supreme Court from lower federal and state courts. In general, those traveling through the federal system reach the Court only after both the applicable district court (the federal trial court) and the circuit court (the federal intermediate appeals court) have rendered decisions. In a few instances, the case may be appealed to the Supreme Court straight from the district court. For cases stemming from a state court system, which must involve a federal question, appeals are usually allowed only after all state avenues have been exhausted and the state's high court has issued a final ruling.

When a writ of certiorari is filed, each party to the case submits a brief to the Court outlining why cert should or should not be granted. Sometimes both parties argue for the Court to hear the case; however, usually, the winning party argues against granting cert. Also, amicus curiae—"friend of the Court"—briefs arguing for or against cert may be filed. After the justices and clerks review the cert petitions and briefs, the justices meet to discuss them and vote on whether or not to grant plenary review. If four justices vote to hear the case, the writ is granted. Importantly, this means that only a minority is necessary to hear a case while a majority is needed to actually decide it. Additionally, as noted by Schubert (1962), justices who vote against granting certiorari still participate in oral arguments and the final decision unless they recuse themselves. Although a denial of certiorari is intended to convey no information about the relative merits of the case, its legal implication is that the last lower court ruling stands.[2]

The Supreme Court currently receives, on average, 8,000 to 10,000 appeals every term, granting approximately 80 of them. Thus, one of the Court's most important functions as an institution is to decide which cases receive a full hearing on the merits. To efficiently review and rule on these requests, the Court has adopted a number of procedures to aid the winnowing process.

The first stage of agenda setting is the creation of the "discuss list." The discuss list is initiated by the chief justice and then passed to the associate justices, who may add any cases they wish to it. Once a case is listed, it is formally reviewed and voted on at Conference; approximately forty to fifty cases are discussed at each Conference. Cases not placed on the discuss list are seen as nonmeritorious and denied without further consideration.

In response to the ever-growing number of certiorari petitions, the process of creating the discuss list has subtly but importantly changed over time. While originally the members of the Court discussed every petition in Conference, after the Judges' Bill gave them a largely discretionary docket, they soon realized that formal consideration of every petition was not necessary. In 1935, Chief Justice Hughes created a "special list," which soon became known as the "dead list" as cases placed on it were not discussed and therefore automatically denied (Ward and Weiden 2006). In 1950, Chief Justice Vinson stopped circulating the growing dead list in favor of the discuss list (Provine 1980, 28–29). Notably, the justices generally agree that the vast majority of petitions concern frivolous cases—perhaps because the Court lacks jurisdiction or a case concerns an issue of settled law—and so the dead and discuss lists allow them to more expeditiously review nonfrivolous petitions while also providing a mechanism for each justice to ensure that cases he or she thinks worthy of further consideration are reviewed by the Court as a whole (Perry 1991). In one of the few studies of the discuss list, Caldeira and Wright (1990, 827) found that a wide variety of factors influence which cases are listed, suggesting both that there is little risk to adding cases and that the list reflects "a series of individual calculations largely free of collective interaction."

Second, most of the justices have ceded to their clerks the task of reading each petition for certiorari and its accompanying briefs. Furthermore, most justices belong to the so-called "cert pool," which was created at the start of the Burger Court at the request of Justice Lewis Powell (Wilkinson 1974). Clerks of justices belonging to the cert pool divide petitions among themselves, thereby reducing the number they must fully review individually. Pool clerks review the cert petitions and briefs for each case they are assigned and draft a memorandum outlining their arguments for why the case should or should not be granted cert. This memo is then sent to each justice who is a member of the pool. Usually the justice's clerks also review the memorandum and make an additional recommendation (Perry 1991; Rehnquist 1987).

In Justice Ruth Bader Ginsburg's view, this process allows the justices to concentrate on the most important petitions: "We read pool memos with care and the judgment that comes with experience. . . . The law clerks are highly intelligent, very able, uncommonly diligent. They save us hours upon hours of labor. But most of them are also young and in need of the seasoning the experiences in life and in law practice afford. Whenever I think a case may be cert. worthy, I will do the homework required and will not rely solely on a pool memorandum" (Liptak 2008).

During his tenure on the Court, Justice John Paul Stevens never joined the cert pool. In an interview with Brian Lamb for C-SPAN (Stevens 2009), Stevens stated that while his clerks reviewed all of the cert petitions, they only prepared memos for those "they think I would be interested in—that really have a likelihood of granting." He also commented that he did not originally join the cert pool because he felt that he and his clerks could process the cert petitions more efficiently: "The memos [the clerks in the cert pool] prepare are very thorough and very carefully written but they're a lot longer than I thought was necessary in order to make a decision on whether to vote to grant or to deny" (ibid.). In addition, justices have raised concerns that having too many justices in the pool may allow for more errors in processing. For example, in 1991, after Thurgood Marshall announced his retirement, concerns were raised that Justice Stevens was the only justice not belonging to the pool. As Justice Harry Blackmun explained, "So long as there [were] four or three [justices] not in the Pool, there was a brake against errors that might be committed by Pool writers."[3] He also noted that as a safeguard he had his clerks independently review all pool memos and offer an independent analysis of the certworthiness of each petition. As Justice Stevens neared retirement, Justice Samuel Alito announced that he would operate outside the pool, thereby ensuring that the "brake" Blackmun and others were concerned about would continue (Liptak 2008).

The importance of these filtering processes grows when we consider that, at least from the justices' perspective, a large percentage of certiorari petitions are flagrantly unworthy. As Justice John Marshall Harlan II (1958, 14) explained, "Of the total petitions acted on I think it must be said that more than one-half were so untenable that they never should have been filed." Similarly, in his interviews with justices' clerks, Perry (1991, 52) heard many comments like the following: "When writing the pool memo, you can often just look at cases and see they're frivolous. But even though the case is frivolous and you know that there is no way in hell the Court is going to grant this thing, it still might take a day to write the cert. memo." Thus, one of the major tasks that justices and their clerks undertake is to discern which of the more than 8,000 appealed cases are worthy of plenary review by the Court.

The Cert Pool Memos

The clerk-written cert pool memos offer a window into this winnowing process. They present factual information about appealed cases as well as more subjective determinations of a case's "certworthiness." Pool memos first provide basic information about whether the case is on certiorari or appeal; if the petition was filed in a timely manner; the court below; the name of the judges on the lower court panel; who wrote the opinion; and who dissented or concurred. Each memo then summarizes the facts of the case and the decisions rendered by the lower courts, followed by the arguments offered by the petitioner as to why the case should be granted as well as the respondent's reply. The memo ends with a discussion section laying out the writer's conclusions concerning certworthiness and his or her recommendations.

From the information offered by pool memos, we can begin to explore whether systematic patterns distinguish unanimously decided cases from other cases. We read each pool memo from the Court's 1989 term and collected data on the subjective conclusions reached by the pool clerk as to the certworthiness of the case.[4]

For this investigation, we read the memos for all cases granted cert and then orally argued and decided with a written opinion by the Court.[5] Our focus on a single term obviously precludes an examination of possible changes over time; however, the 1989 term is representative of the modern Court. Also, we examine only the memos for cases that were subsequently granted cert. While denials would provide additional information, they would not help answer our core question, as our interest is not in determining what distinguishes grants from denials. Rather, our ultimate goal is to understand how the Court achieves consensual decisions and opinions on the merits. Toward that end, our aim in this chapter is to illuminate potential differences at the agenda-setting stage between granted cases that result in consensus and granted cases that lead to divided decisions.

We obtained the cert pool memos through the Blackmun Archives, compiled and made available to the public by Lee Epstein, Jeffrey A. Segal, and

Harold Spaeth (2001). For each case appealed to the Court, Justice Harry Blackmun preserved the docket sheet with his handwritten notations as to each justice's vote in conference and the merits vote if the case was granted. He also preserved his copies of cert pool memos, which contain his handwritten notations and the private recommendations (sometimes handwritten, sometimes typed) provided by his clerks.

Ending the Confusion: Certworthiness and Consensus on the Merits

Research has shown that certain factors play a significant role in the decision to grant certiorari. Some are subjective in that clerks and justices can disagree about whether or not they are present in a given case. Two of these subjective indicators come from Supreme Court Rule 10, which focuses on whether the lower court decision creates a conflict—a so-called "circuit split"—and whether the case presents an important federal question. Caldeira and Wright (1988) found that whenever an actual conflict is present, the likelihood of granting certiorari increases dramatically. Other research has shown that some more objective case aspects—facts that are not disputable—are also influential in determining which cases are ultimately granted. For example, if the solicitor general (SG) petitions for cert, the Court is more likely to grant cert (e.g., Salokar 1992). In addition, amicus briefs filed in support or even in opposition to the petition increase the likelihood that the Court will grant review (Caldeira and Wright 1988).

In addition to these indicators, other factors influence particular justices' certiorari decisions, such as a their personal interest in certain areas of law, their ideological preferences on the legal issue, and their strategic calculations as to whether their answer to the question presented can ultimately prevail on the merits (see, e.g., Boucher and Segal 1995; Brenner 1979). In fact, Ulmer (1972) argued that the decision to grant cert and the decision on the merits are linked rather than wholly distinct processes affected by different considerations. We posit that there may also be a connection between the cert process—why the Court chooses to hear the case in the first place—and whether it is able to reach a unanimous decision. Is it possible that cases that ultimately result in unanimity are more likely than those that result in divided opinions to involve important issues or to have been decided incorrectly by the court below? The former would suggest an emphasis on the Court's role in providing national guidance on important legal issues, while the latter would point to the Court recognizing the need for error correction.

TABLE 5.1
Summary of measures of certworthiness

Measure	Description
Circuit split	Did the memo writer address whether the case involved conflicting lower court decisions on the same legal question? And, what conclusion did he or she reach?
Important issue	Did the memo writer note that the case raised an important issue, whether due to its legal, political, social, economic impacts or other, similar implications?
Lower court confusion	Did the memo writer note that the core legal question posed in the case was a difficult one to resolve or was causing confusion among the inferior courts?
Bad vehicle	Did the memo writer address whether the case was one that would allow the justices to easily address the legal questions or one that would be difficult? And, what conclusion did he or she reach?
Lower court incorrect	Did the memo writer address whether he or she believed the lower court reached the "correct" legal decision? And, what conclusion did he or she reach?

Thus, investigating the cert stage will hopefully aid us in better understanding why the Court reaches consensus on so many cases each term.

We derive a number of possible indicators of certworthiness from the existing literature as well as from our analyses in the previous chapters. Since our question is whether unanimously decided cases differ from nonunanimously decided cases at the certiorari stage, we focus on identifying factors that might show why these cases are different or, alternatively, why the Court would take cases that ultimately result in unanimous decisions at all. Specifically, we note five potential indicators of subjective certworthiness: whether the case raised an important issue, presented a good vehicle, suggested a lower court conflict, demonstrated confusion in the lower court, or was wrongly decided by the lower court. Table 5.1 presents a summary of how we measure each indicator.

Subjective Case Characteristics: Theory

The first indicator we examine is whether the pool clerk noted a *Conflict between Lower Courts*. Supreme Court Rule 10 provides that a conflict between circuits is a compelling reason to grant certiorari. Furthermore, Tanenhaus et al. (1963) asserted that cases are more likely to be granted when a lower court conflict exists. Ulmer (1984) explored the role of conflict in influencing decisions to grant and found that the Supreme Court is more likely to grant cert when a case involves a conflict between two circuit court decisions. He maintained that the Court must closely assess a party's claim of conflict to determine whether it is genuine, and he noted that this likely leads to "a large role for law clerks in distinguishing genuine conflict cases from those in which the claim is too tenuous to warrant the Court's attention" (911). Caldeira and Wright (1990), in a study of both the discuss list and the decision to grant, found that cases are more likely to be placed on the discuss list if a conflict is alleged, but once a case receives more scrutiny, only instances of actual conflict increase the likelihood of cert being granted. Similarly, Black and Owens (2009, 1070) found that justices "are increasingly compelled by the presence of conflict and norms of legal clarity to grant review." Thus, it appears that "the single most important generalizable factor in assessing certworthiness is the existence of a conflict or 'split' in the circuits" (Perry 1991, 246).

Given the importance of resolving lower court splits over law, this factor is undoubtedly a key one for justices when considering cert petitions and is the one most likely to be alleged by petitioners and disputed by respondents. As a result, memo writers often devote significant attention to whether a split actually exists. For example, according to the memo writer in *Baltimore City Department of Social Services v. Bouknight* (1990), "Notwithstanding DSS's [Department of Social Services's] assertions to the contrary, none of the state court cases cited by it are really in direct conflict with the decision rendered below." For this reason, we analyze the cert pool data in terms of whether or not the memo writer noted, and subsequently concluded, that a split among lower courts existed.

We also note whether the memo writer stated that the case raised an *Important Issue*. According to Perry (1991), important cases are more likely to be granted. He identified three types: (1) one-of-a-kind important cases, such as the presidential election case *Bush v. Gore* (2000); (2) cases that have a huge impact on society, such as the racial segregation case *Brown v. Board of Education* (1954); and (3) cases that are important to law, such as the maritime jurisdiction case we mentioned at the start of this chapter, *Sisson v. Ruby* (1990). Additionally,

> Importance is often determined by the breadth of effect rather than the depth. In other words, if a ruling below has a potential impact on large numbers of people, that helps establish importance. If it has a large impact on one corporation or individual, that alone does not make it important. A second though related criterion is the effect something has on the federal government. When the solicitor general claims that a ruling or policy has a large effect on the government, and he urges review, such a case is almost always believed to be important. (Perry 1991, 254)

In the memo for *Bouknight*, for example, the pool clerk stressed breadth of effect. Specifically, the memo quoted from Chief Justice Rehnquist's initial opinion to stay the lower court's decision holding that imprisoning a mother for refusing to produce her previously abused child violates her Fifth Amendment right against compulsory self-incrimination: "'Protecting infants from child abuse seems to . . . rank in order of social importance with the regulation and prevention of traffic accidents.'" The memo for *John Doe Agency v. John Doe Corp.* (1989) is an example of the SG arguing that a case would have a large impact on the federal government. *John Doe* concerned a Freedom of Information Act request for documents from a government agency, and the pool clerk noted that "the SG represents that a great number of federal agencies have alerted the Justice Department that law enforcement efforts may be handicapped by CA2's [2nd Circuit Court of Appeals] ruling [denying the agency's request to withhold documents from release]."

Additionally, we investigate whether the memo writer noted that there was *Confusion in the Lower Courts* over the correct legal answer. Here we focus on whether the question was one that might be hard to resolve or one that gave the lower courts difficulty. In particular, we look for whether the memo writer discussed problems that the lower courts were having in answering a particular legal question, or whether he or she simply suggested that the legal question was a "confusing" one. For example, the memo writer for *Jimmy Swaggart Ministries v. Board of Equalization of California* (1990) stated, "The answer to this question [whether applying a sales tax to religious publications sold by religious organizations violates the Free Exercise Clause] is not obvious." Similarly, in *Tafflin v. Levitt* (1990), the pool memo writer noted: "Even though the majority of cts (including CA4) has reached what seems to be the correct resolution—that RICO does not meet the rigorous test for finding exclusive federal jurisdiction—it seems prudent for this Ct to end the confusion now surrounding this issue, especially since this confusion causes hardship for litigants." Thus, in order to end uncertainty, justices may be more likely to grant cert in a situation in which there is lower court confusion.

Another indicator we look at is if the memo writer commented on whether the case presented a *Bad Vehicle* or, conversely, a *Good Vehicle*. According to one clerk interviewed by Perry (1991, 235), "The justices like cases with simple facts—very simple and very clean—that is the type of case they want. And also if the decision below was clear; that's of interest to them." More specifically:

> [B]eing a good vehicle is determined by such things as: is the issue clear and "squarely" presented? Is the record below clear? Is the fact situation nonambiguous? Can the

primary issue be reached, or will some confounding issue have to be decided first, which would preclude a decision on the major issue? (ibid., 279)

The memo writer might therefore discuss whether the facts of the case are straightforward or whether the legal question can be easily reached. For example, in the antitrust case *Texaco v. Hasbrouck* (1990), the pool clerk wrote: "I doubt that one could reasonably hope for a significantly better vehicle than the present case." Oppositely, the memo writer concluded in *Minnesota v. Olson* (1990), a case concerning the legality of a warrantless arrest, that "the case does not present any clean legal issues."

Also part of what makes a case a good vehicle is whether the issue is "ripe," or has percolated through various courts and other institutions: "It is good jurisprudence and makes good sense to put off rendering an interpretation as long as possible—or more precisely, as long as the benefits of avoidance outweigh the problems—so that the Court can benefit from analysis by others" (Perry 1991, 231). Thus, if cases that are ultimately decided unanimously are more likely than nonunanimous cases to be good vehicles, this may provide us with some understanding about why the Court chooses to hear these cases in the first place.

Finally, we note whether the memo writer suggested that the *Lower Court Decision was Incorrect*. Although the Court claims that it does not grant cert in order to correct errors, Chief Justice Rehnquist (1987, 127) admitted that "the most common reason members of our Court vote to grant certiorari is that they doubt the correctness of the decision of the lower court." And Perry (1991, 265) noted that "an egregious result below sometimes prompted review." For example, in *Selvage v. Collins* (1990), a case concerning a defendant convicted of capital murder, the memo writer stated: "On the merits, the *voir dire* claim appears to have been correctly resolved below." Comparatively, in *Preseault et ux. v. Interstate Commerce Commission* (1990), a case involving the Takings Clause and the question of reversionary ownership, the memo writer suggested that "CA2's analysis of the takings question is somewhat questionable."

Returning to *Sisson v. Ruby* (1990), the cert pool memo offers some hints as to why a case about maritime jurisdiction that ultimately resulted in a unanimous decision was heard. First, it noted the potentially broad implications of the decision in the case: "The principles involved may seem archaic, but the answer to the jurisdiction question can have serious consequences. In this case, if admiralty law applies, [Petitioner] apparently will be liable for only $800; if it doesn't, he may have to cough up $275,000 or more under ordinary state law tort remedies." The writer also highlighted the confusion generated by the Court's previous decision in *Foremost Insurance Co. v. Richardson* (1982): "Judge Ripple, in his CA7 concurrence, observed that the lower courts have been left in a 'quagmire' and have struggled to resolve the ambiguities gendered by *Foremost*." Similarly, Justice Blackmun's clerk noted the necessity of clarifying the law for future cases: "It looks like the lower cts need some guidance on the factors to use when deciding if a case comes under admiralty juris when pleasure crafts are involved. This case, with its narrow fact pattern, would be a good vehicle to explain the somewhat vague nexus test of *Executive Jet* and *Foremost* and to give content to 'maritime activity' in the pleasure boat context."

Thus, the clerks reviewing the petition for certiorari in *Sisson* routinely returned to the argument that the case needed to be heard in order to clarify the law. These remarks suggest—and the justices seem to have agreed given that all of them except Stevens voted ultimately to grant the petition—that the Court is often asked to elucidate what the law is and how the lower courts should apply it in future cases. The *Sisson* petition—and, as we will see, many others—suggests that even if the Court ultimately agrees on the legal answer to the issue raised by a case, it also often believes that it is important to hear the case and issue a final, national ruling that clarifies the law.

Subjective Case Characteristics: Results

As noted earlier, we examine the cert pool memos for all 130 cases that were granted certiorari and decided during the 1989 term. Of these, 43 (33 percent) were ultimately decided unanimously. In the following analyses of our subjective measures of certworthiness (see Table 5.1), we compare our findings for these 43 unanimous cases against our findings for the 87 cases that resulted in more dissensual decisions.

Turning to our first subjective case characteristic, Figure 5.1 illustrates that slightly more memos (65 percent vs. 54 percent) concluded that a split existed for unanimous cases as opposed to nonunanimous cases. This finding indicates that unanimous cases are more likely to concern circuit splits. It may be that unanimity lends a Supreme Court decision more legitimacy in the eyes of disagreeing lower courts. The justices may also see cases involving circuit splits as more in need of a unanimous, legally certain decision in order to ensure compliance.

With regard to whether the case concerned an important issue, 77 percent of pool memos for unanimous cases and 68 percent of those for nonunanimous cases concluded that an important issue existed. Once again, there is

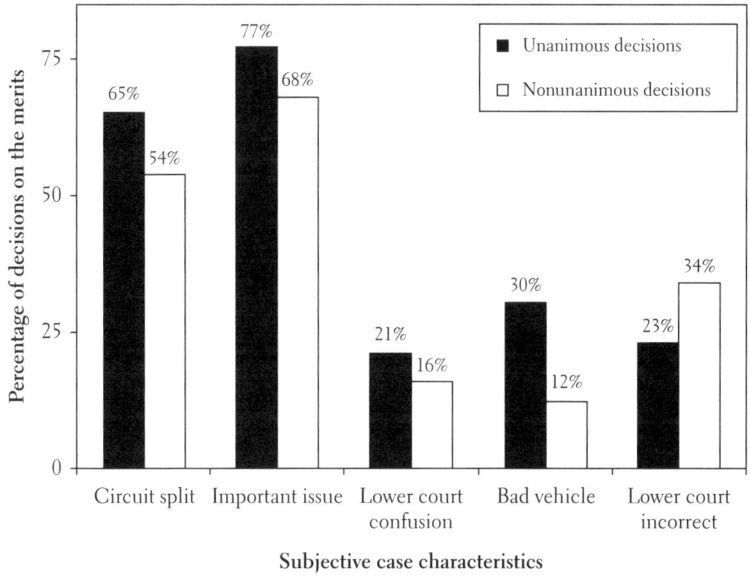

Figure 5.1. Subjective case characteristics: Unanimous versus nonunanimous cases

not a strong difference between unanimously and nonunanimously decided cases at the certiorari stage in terms of this case characteristic. For example, in *Hasbrouck*, which was subsequently decided unanimously, the memo writer noted that the lower court's decision "is potentially of enormous consequences" and referred later to the "significant and economically costly uncertainty" that would exist if the case were to be left unheard. Similarly, in *Tafflin*—another case decided unanimously on the merits—the memo writer argued that "because of the widespread use of civil RICO actions and the importance of uniformity and certainty in the enforcement of such actions, this Ct should grant cert on this question." In fact, what may be most striking is that we find unanimous cases to be more likely than cases ultimately decided by a divided Court to be characterized as concerning an important issue.

However, although these quantitative results suggest that the vast majority of granted cases concern important issues—a finding in line with the literature on Supreme Court agenda setting—a more qualitative assessment of the statements that describe *why* the issue was deemed important reveals noticeable variation between subsequently unanimous and nonunanimous cases. In particular, in the 1989 term, memos for unanimously decided cases were more likely to highlight a need for the Court to resolve the pending legal issue. The memo for the contingency fee case *Venegas v. Mitchell* (1990), for example, concluded: "Thus, given the diversity of these approaches, a S.Ct. opinion would be useful to provide greater uniformity." Similarly, the memo for *United States Department of Labor v. Triplett* (1990), concerning the constitutionality of the Black Lung Act's attorney fee allocation system, noted: "There is something unacceptable about a federal law that remains effective but that states will not enforce." In *Taylor v. United States* (1990), concerning the definition of "burglary," the desire for the Supreme Court to issue an opinion seemed great: "The CA's are truly in disarray on this issue, having adopted three definitions of burglary. . . . At least four cert petitions currently before this Court . . . request this Court to define 'burglary.'" Finally, the memo for *General Motors Corp. v. United States* presented a fairly straightforward argument for granting cert: "On balance, however, the need for a uniform federal rule probably outweighs any prudential reasons for deferring review."

We propose that the pool memo writers believed these cases to reflect not only important issues but specifically the importance of determining the proper legal rule. Thus, a tentative conclusion is that cases that are ultimately decided unanimously are selected in part because they are those in which the justices find it necessary to clarify the law even if the ultimate legal answer is one they all agree on.

Regarding confusion in the lower courts, pool clerks concluded that it was present in 21 percent of the granted cases that were ultimately decided unanimously on the merits and in 16 percent of the granted cases that were ultimately decided nonunanimously. The memo in *Tafflin v. Levitt* is a prototypical example of lower court confusion: "Even though the majority of cts (including CA4) has reached what seems to be the correct resolution—that RICO does not meet the rigorous test for finding exclusive federal jurisdiction—it seems prudent for this Ct to end the confusion now surrounding this issue, especially since this confusion causes hardship for litigants."

When it comes to whether the case provided a good vehicle for cert, the pool memos reached relatively similar conclusions for unanimously and nonunanimously decided cases (30 and 29 percent, respectively). However, unanimously decided cases were substantially more likely to be denoted "bad" test cases: the memo writers concluded that 30 percent of them were bad vehicles as opposed to only 12 percent of nonunanimous cases. A review of the pool memos for unanimously decided cases reveals that many of the concerns raised about whether the case offered a good vehicle were perhaps those the Court was less likely to be swayed by.

A number of memos for cases that were eventually decided unanimously suggest that the memo writers were concerned about percolation, or whether the issue needed more time to develop in the lower courts. For example, in *Butterworth v. Smith* (1990)—a case involving the constitutionality of a Florida statute concerning grand jury secrecy under the First Amendment—the memo writer stated that since "there is literally no lower court development on this important issue, I recommend that the Court deny certiorari to allow further percolation." It was therefore not an unimportant legal question—the clerk noted that "the petition . . . raises a First Amendment issue which is far from frivolous"—but rather one on which the Court might wish to see further doctrinal development. Similarly, in *General Motors Corp. v. United States* (1990)—asking whether the EPA can enforce an existing State Implementation Plan (SIP) when it had failed to act on a revised SIP in a timely manner—the memo writer stated, "[T]he Court could well wait for other Circuits to express their views on the subject (CA6, for example, has a case pending that presents this issue). The effect of proposed legislation on this case is unclear—although the Court could always dismiss the case if newly enacted legislation mooted the question presented, Congress may well stay its hand if the Court grants certiorari."

Finally, in *United States v. Munoz-Flores* (1990), concerning the constitutionality of the passage of the Special Assessment on Convicted Persons statute under the Origination Clause, the memo writer noted that the Court would most likely "eventually grant cert on this question," but also believed that "the eventual disposition of the complex issues in this case would be well served by further development." Strikingly, however, the justices voted unanimously on the question of whether to grant certiorari in *Munoz-Flores*, which suggests that they felt the time was right to address these complex issues. It may also be that such cases were granted simply because the Court felt it could not wait: for example, in *Yellow Freight System v. Donnelly* (1990), concerning whether state and federal courts have concurrent jurisdiction over Title VII claims, the pool clerk argued against a grant, "unless the Conference feels that it is important to weigh in on this issue immediately." Clearly, they *did* believe that weighing in immediately was necessary, as six of the justices voted to grant cert.

Finally, the pool memo writers concluded that the decision below was incorrect in only 23 percent of the granted cases that were decided unanimously, compared to 34 percent of the granted cases that were decided nonunanimously. Thus, at least based on the 1989 pool memos, it appears that the Court does not engage in error correction. More notably, these results suggest that unanimous cases are not simply instances in which the Court finds it necessary to correct egregiously wrong decisions by the lower courts; rather, for subsequently unanimous cases the memo writers were more likely to view the lower court decision as correct.

Overall, this investigation of the subjective conclusions reached by the pool memo writers reveals interesting similarities and differences between unanimous and nonunanimous cases. First, granted cases generally involve splits between lower courts and unanimously decided cases are slightly more likely to involve them. Second, unanimous cases are slightly more likely to involve important issues; a more in-depth examination reveals that the memo writers saw the legal issues presented in these cases as those particularly requiring guidance from the Court. Third, slightly more unanimous cases involved confusion. And, fourth, unanimous cases were less likely to involve judgments of lower court error.

Thus, the reason the Court chooses to hear unanimous cases does not seem to be egregious lower court errors. Rather, these cases seem to be those that require an ultimate, decisive decision—those in which the Court likely feels a duty to resolve a pressing legal issue. This notion is summarized nicely in the pool memo for *Commissioner of INS v. Jean* (1990), concerning the awarding of attorney fees under the Equal Access to Justice Act: "In short there is a clear split involving several CAs on a question of considerable importance in litigation involving the government."

Fearing Horrible Things: The Recommendations of Blackmun's Clerks

We collected data on any additional recommendations that were provided by Blackmun's clerks when reviewing the pool memos; these recommendations were usually written in pencil on the memo itself and provided Blackmun with extra guidance on whether to vote in favor of granting cert. We find that, since these recommendations were private and directed at Blackmun only, unlike the more general recommendations written for all of the justices belonging to the pool, they were more candid and often more overtly strategic and tactical.

Blackmun became increasingly suspicious of pool clerks injecting partisanship into their memos, and in 1986 he began requiring that his clerks add additional information when marking them up. Specifically, next to the last name of the pool-memo writer—which appeared at the end of each memo—Blackmun clerks were required to add the pool clerk's first name, law school attended, last name and (sometimes court) of any lower court judge he or she had clerked for, and the name of the justice for whom the clerk was currently working. For example, "McAllister" became "Steve McAllister (BRW/Kansas/Posner)." Given Blackmun's instructions, it is not surprising that his clerks provided candid, strategic analyses in addition to their objective recommendations.

Examining the recommendations of Blackmun's clerks also highlights the reality that cert decisions, too, are inherently strategic. As numerous studies (e.g., Brenner and Krol 1989; Krol and Brenner 1990; Linzer 1979) as well as the justices' own accountings attest, cert decisions are not made in a vacuum. Rather, they take into account numerous factors beyond certworthiness, including the justices' personal views on how the case should be decided and their calculations of whether they can gain the necessary fifth vote to see their favored outcome become law. We review these private recommendations to determine how strategic calculations influenced Blackmun's decision to grant or deny each case, as well as to see whether differences emerged between cases that were granted and decided unanimously compared to those that were granted but decided with dissenting votes on the merits.

With regard to the granted and unanimous cases, clerks often noted the size of the docket. For example, in *Keller v. State Bar of California* (1990), concerning the use of state bar compulsory membership dues for political activities, Blackmun's clerk stated, "I was torn about recommending a grant or deny on this one. The issue is definitely a certworthy one. The question seems whether to decide it now or later. I saw no pressing need to decide it now, but with the docket low I can see adding this case to the calendar. Perhaps you should vote J3 ["join three," or grant if three other justices vote to grant]?" Similarly, in *Franchise Tax Board v. Alcan Aluminum Ltd.* (1990), the clerk disagreed with the pool memo recommendation to "deny" and argued that "[t]he Court's docket has empty spaces and I think the California government deserves to be heard on the standing issue—since it shouldn't have to litigate the case on the merits if CA7 messed up on the standing issue." Finally, in *General Motors Corp. v. United States*, the recommendation focused on both the importance of the issue and the relatively few cases currently on the docket: "Although the issue doesn't especially excite me, I think the question is an important one. . . . Especially with the docket low, I think the case is worth hearing."

At times, the comments by Blackmun clerks were much more strategic, particularly with regard to the potential outcome of the case on the merits. Many of these cases, perhaps unsurprisingly, were eventually decided with dissenting votes. Thus, in the death penalty case *Blystone v. Pennsylvania* (1990), Blackmun's clerk noted, "Justice Stevens has been interested in this issue for a long time and will almost certainly vote to grant. I think the question presented is interesting and important, but am somewhat worried about how the Court would resolve it." In the National Labor Relations Act case *Golden State Transit Corp. v. City of Los Angeles* (1989), Blackmun's clerk was similarly concerned about the possible outcome: "I am also uncertain where the Ct would go with this issue, but I doubt it would be favorable to [Section] 1983 claimants." Blackmun clerks also referenced the actions of the other justices: in *McCoy v. North Carolina* (1990), another death penalty case, the clerk wrote: "Justice [Byron] White is the critical vote on the issue. He provided the 5th vote in *Mills*. If he is inclined to send this to habeas, you might want to follow suit. I know JPS's [John Paul Stevens's] clerk recommended a Grant."

Blackmun's clerks turned out at times to be quite prescient. For example, in *Jimmy Swaggert Ministries*, one stated, "I never thought that the 'another day' referenced in *Texas Monthly* would arrive so soon—and with Jimmy Swaggert as the religious taxpayer! The one advantage of having Swaggert as appellant is that it puts the consequences of *Murdock* and *Follett* . . . in its starkest terms. The disadvantage is that the Free Exercise position will not be well briefed (at least if the [jurisdictional statement] is any indication). . . . Perhaps this Court will affirm 9–0, but it should at least hear the arguments." In the end the Court did indeed unanimously affirm.

Overall, the memos written by Blackmun's clerks acted as a check on the pool memos, providing private recommendations to the justice. They anticipated potential ideological biases in the pool memos, were far more forthcoming about their own concerns, and provided information from other chambers gleaned through the clerk network. They also helped Blackmun think strategically in anticipating the final votes on the merits. For these reasons, our findings lend support to previous research suggesting that the cert pool has fundamentally changed the certiorari process, with pool clerks emphasizing circuit splits at the expense of candid political and strategic analysis.

With regard to unanimity, the additional information provided by Blackmun's clerks shows that at times they pushed for certain cases to be granted when the docket had space; many of these cases were subsequently decided unanimously. This finding suggests that clerks play a role in ensuring that the Court addresses crucial but nondivisive legal issues. Blackmun's clerks were also concerned about how the Court might rule on certain questions, and their strategic calculations generally correctly foreshadowed more divided decisions. An interesting question for future research is the extent to which justices follow or ignore the strategic considerations their clerks pose.

Conclusion

This chapter investigates why the justices vote to grant cert in cases that they ultimately decide unanimously. We theorize that at the agenda-setting stage unanimous cases are different from nonunanimous cases. We find some preliminary yet important differences between cases granted certiorari that ultimately resulted in unanimous decisions and those that resulted in nonunanimous decisions. As a result, these findings help us understand why an ideologically divided Court, entrenched in an era of dissensus, is able to achieve such a high degree of consensus year in and year out, as well as why the Court elects to hear cases that are ultimately decided unanimously.

Our examination of the pool memos from cases decided during the 1989 term focuses on subjective case characteristics discussed routinely by the authors that provide information about the case's certworthiness. In analyzing these memos to understand why the Supreme Court accepts cases for which it ultimately issues a unanimous opinion, some interesting findings emerge. First, while almost all granted cases are deemed to involve important issues, we find variation between those that were decided unanimously and those that were decided nonunanimously as to how the importance of the issue was explained. In particular, the emphasis in ultimately unanimous cases was on the need for the Court to issue a final, national ruling.

Second, unanimously decided cases are less likely to be determined by the pool memo writer as incorrectly decided by the lower courts. This finding suggests that unanimous cases are not about correcting egregious errors but rather about the Court finding it necessary at the certiorari stage to hear the case even if a unanimous decision is likely.

From this investigation of the 1989 term cert pool memos we conclude overall that unanimous cases are those in which the justices believe it is important to clarify the law and issue a final, national ruling on a legal question of great importance, and in which a single, unified answer can be reached. In the next chapter, we discuss the implications of our findings, for both the cert and merits stages, not only for debates about the nature of Supreme Court decision making but also for how the Court's decisions affect the larger political environment.

CHAPTER 6

Conclusion

Our goal in this book has been to explain the puzzle of unanimity on the United States Supreme Court. Given that attitudes explain a majority of justices' votes, how does the Court ever arrive at a unanimous decision? In other words, if the justices vote on the basis of their personal policy preferences, why would we ever expect to see a staunch conservative such as Justice Antonin Scalia agree with a liberal such as Justice Thurgood Marshall? Thus, we undertook the task—suggested by Epstein, Segal, and Spaeth (2001) and Hensley and Johnson (1998)—of determining what drives Supreme Court decision making in unanimous and highly consensual cases in the modern era.

We argue that consensus on the Supreme Court is a function of multiple, simultaneously operating forces. We test our theory on all cases decided by the Court between 1953 and 2004. We find that unanimity most commonly occurs in cases with a high degree of legal certainty as to the strongest legal answer, that involve nonsalient economic or governmental power issues, and in which the Court ultimately reaches a liberal decision. For example, in *Willy v. Coastal Corp.* (1992), the issue was whether a federal district court can impose sanctions pursuant to Rule 11 of the Federal Rules of Civil Procedure in a case in which the district court is later determined to be without subject matter jurisdiction. The Court unanimously held that it can do so. This case illustrates that unanimity is in part a function of the type of case the Court considers. Every decision handed down "is a judgment about the specific dispute brought to it, an interpretation of the legal issues in that dispute, and a position on the policy questions that are raised by the legal issues" (Baum 2007, 3). Thus, it is only by examining the multitude of forces that influence each decision that we can understand how the Court arrives at its final decision and achieves consensus in a substantial proportion of cases. In this chapter we review our findings and discuss their potential implications for researchers as well as for the larger legal and political environment in which the Supreme Court operates.

Findings

While the bulk of our investigation focuses on the modern era of dissensus, we note that consensus was the norm on the Supreme Court in the eighteenth and early nineteenth centuries. To more fully understand why consensus occurs today, we investigate why that norm broke down during the mid-twentieth century. Chapter 1 examines the breakdown of consensus on the Roosevelt Court. Based on our investigation of the personal papers of Chief Justice Harlan Stone and Justice William O. Douglas, we conclude that the era of dissensus began during Stone's tenure and was firmly entrenched by the time Earl Warren became chief. Most notably, while Stone's leadership style almost certainly exacerbated discord, it was a series of institutional changes, both internal and external to the Court, that ultimately helped usher in this new era. Outside the Court, the influence of legal realism and President Franklin Roosevelt's appointment of justices who were critical of traditional jurisprudential philosophy laid the foundation for individual expression. Within the Court, changes in traditional practices, including the erosion of acquiescence and delays in opinion circulation fostered dissensus as well. Importantly, the implication of our argument is that the levels of dissensus characterizing the Court at this time could not be erased simply by installing a chief with a style vastly different from Stone's; rather, the internal and external institutional changes instituted during the Roosevelt Court so fundamentally altered it that a return to the norm of consensus was virtually impossible.

As Chapter 1 showcases, the transition from the norm of consensus to the modern era of dissensus resulted from transformative institutional changes, the effects of which are apparent today. However, while Chapter 1 highlights this shift from consensus to dissensus, we recognize that the level of consensus on the Court is still surprisingly high: approximately one-third of the cases each term since 1953 have been decided unanimously. For this reason, Chapters 2 through 5 are devoted to investigating why, in spite of these entrenched institutional developments, consensus occurs so frequently.

In Chapter 2, we present our comprehensive theory of consensus and detail how we measure each of the forces that we contend play a role in influencing whether the justices can achieve unanimity or a high degree of consensus. We begin by exploring the literature on judicial decision making in order to highlight the multiple forces previous scholars illuminated in the quest to understand judicial decision making. We then discuss previous attempts to understand why the Court is able to achieve consensus even in the midst of contentious cases and ideological polarization. The chapter ends with a detailed discussion of our theory of consensus and our conceptualization of legal certainty.

Our theory of consensus is premised on the notion that multiple forces simultaneously operate in each case and that it is only by assessing these forces in tandem—rather than as mutually exclusive—that we can uncover how consensus occurs. We start with the presumption that attitudes are the driving force behind the decisions of the Supreme Court. However, they are not the only influence: we argue in particular that consensus on the modern Court is also a reflection of legal, strategic, and case-specific forces. And while these forces are often discussed as competing explanations, we suggest that they work simultaneously to influence the justices' decisions, many times in a complex, interactive fashion. What may differ is the degree to which certain forces influence the justices or how they operate in tandem in certain types of cases.

An important component of our theory is the recognition that law plays an essential role in judicial decision making. We argue that legal forces directly affect the Court's decisions, and we further contend that they indirectly influence judicial decision making either by enabling or by constraining the extent to which attitudes influence the justices. Specifically, we see legal considerations as a type of "vise" through which attitudes must pass. When the jaws of the vise are open, indicating that the legal factors operating in the case are not influential, attitudes pass through relatively unhindered. In such cases, the justices are free to vote their attitudes and the likelihood of dissensus is high. However, when legal forces are significantly at play, the jaws are tightly closed; in these instances, the justices' attitudes are more constrained and consequently the likelihood of consensus increases.

Additionally, Chapter 2 presents a novel way to conceive of law and its influence on judicial decision making. We first assess previous attempts to measure the law. Constructing such a measure is difficult because of two concerns: ensuring that law is not reduced to a static, mechanistic process and guarding against narrowly conceptualizing it such that its influence is minimized or even obscured. Thus, we propose a way to overcome these concerns: measuring the level of legal certainty facing the justices as to the strongest legal answer, arguing for C. Herman Pritchett's (1941) original postulation that unanimous cases occur when the law is relatively clear. Specifically, when legal certainty is high, there is likely to be less confusion and debate over the strongest legal answer to the question raised, resulting in a greater probability of consensus. However, when legal certainty is low, and thus multiple legal answers are possible (if not wholly defensible), dissensus is much more probable. We introduce a Legal Certainty Index for capturing the level of legal certainty in each case in order to determine whether legal considerations influence the ability of the Court to achieve consensus. Importantly, our index is based on information readily available to the justices while they are deciding the case, and therefore it enables us to better understand the occurrence of consensus *a priori*.

After laying out our theory of consensus in Chapter 2, as well as explicating how we measure the different theoretical concepts, we turn to an investigation of consensus on the modern Court. Chapter 3 begins the empirical test of our theory by exploring when the Supreme Court is most likely to achieve a unanimous or highly consensual decision on the merits. We find that consensual decisions indeed reflect the influence of myriad forces. Specifically, we find them to be a function of personal policy preferences, the level of legal certainty, and certain strategic and case-specific factors. Furthermore, although attitudes help explain unanimous decisions, the magnitude of their influence is depressed in these cases as opposed to cases that ultimately result in divided decisions. The level of legal certainty also matters: when legal certainty is high—even controlling for attitudinal influences—unanimity and consensus are much more likely.

We find that legal forces indirectly influence judicial decision making by constraining the operation of the justices' attitudes. It appears that when the level of legal certainty is high, ideological considerations do not influence the Court's ability to achieve consensus and so the jaws of the vise are shut tightly. On the other hand, when legal certainty is low, the jaws of the vise are open wide and ideological considerations predominate. Legal certainty thus constrains the operation of attitudes on the justices' votes and illuminates how legal forces can significantly influence judicial decision making. Additionally, when the chief justice authors the majority opinion, the likelihood of unanimity and consensus is high, which suggests that chiefs can use their formal powers to encourage agreement. Finally, a number of case-specific forces aid consensus: unanimity and consensus are more likely when the case concerns a non-civil-liberties issue, is not salient to outside actors, and is decided in a liberal direction. Unanimous and highly consensual decisions are thus a function of multiple, concurrently operating forces, and it is only by examining all of them that we can truly understand agreement on the Court.

In Chapter 4, we turn our attention to the notion of opinion consensus by taking into account the number of separate opinions that accompany the majority opinion. Since the Supreme Court, like all appellate courts, issues not only a vote on the outcome but also an opinion detailing the reasoning behind it, it is not uncommon for the justices to agree on the outcome but disagree as to why it is the correct one. As a result, examining opinion consensus reveals when disagreements may exist even when the vote on the merits is unanimous.

For example, in *eBay Inc. v. MercExchange, L.L.C.* (2006), the Court unanimously held that an injunction should not be automatically issued based on a finding of patent infringement. However, while the majority opinion stated that there should be no general rule for issuing an injunction, two separate concurrences, joined by three and four justices respectively, suggested guidelines for doing so. The two concurrences differed in their proposals for how to determine when injunctions should be granted, and as a consequence, differed as to the required level of showing necessary to result in an injunction. While neither carried the force of law, they clearly highlighted the level of disagreement on the Court as to the correct standard to judge when injunctions are the proper remedy.

In some instances, a justice may decide to write separately to emphasize or clarify a particular point. For example, in *Argersinger v. Hamlin* (1972), the Court unanimously ruled that the Sixth Amendment Right to Counsel for indigent defendants established in *Gideon v. Wainwright* (1963) extends to any person facing imprisonment regardless of the severity of the offense. This decision created the so-called "loss of liberty" rule. Justice Lewis Powell concurred in the decision to express his concern that it might overburden an already strained criminal justice system.[1]

Such concurrences occur in nonunanimous cases as well: in *Hamdan v. Rumsfeld* (2006), the Supreme Court ruled 5–3 that the military commissions created by the George W. Bush administration to try detainees being held at Guantanamo Bay were unconstitutional because the congressional Authorization for the Use of Military Force Act and the Uniform Code of Military Justice did not give the president the necessary statutory authorization to create such tribunals. Justice Stephen Breyer wrote separately to emphasize that such commissions are not categorically unconstitutional if the president is granted the necessary legislative authority by Congress.

As these examples show, looking simply at votes on the merits may obscure the true amount of disagreement on the Court in a particular case. Furthermore, since the reasoning explicated by the majority is part and parcel of understanding the law itself, disagreements—even within a unanimous decision—can lead to uncertainty and instability for lower courts and the public regarding how to proceed in the future. We therefore analyze what factors influence the likelihood of unanimity and consensus in a particular case, but define consensus to take into account separate opinions.

We find that opinion consensus is similarly explained by a combination of attitudinal, legal, strategic, and case-specific influences. Furthermore, an institutional force—time—is also a factor. We find that both attitudes and the level of legal certainty are influential in that high degrees of legal certainty constrain the operation of attitudes, leading to increased opinion consensus. We further find that when the median justice writes the opinion, opinion consensus is less likely. It is also less likely when the justices exercise judicial review and declare statutes unconstitutional. Once again, in non-civil-liberties cases, nonsalient cases, and cases decided in a liberal direction, the likelihood of opinion consensus increases. Finally, opinion consensus is a function of time: justices are more likely to author separate opinions the greater the amount of time left until the end of term.

The implication of the results presented in Chapters 3 and 4 is that unanimity and consensus, and hence agreement on the Court, are explained by our comprehensive theory of consensus. When we account for the totality of forces that may influence the achievement of consensus, we find that unanimity, voting consensus, and opinion consensus are a reflection of numerous factors working in tandem. The justices' personal preferences influence the likelihood of consensus, but so do strategic, legal, and case-specific factors. Additionally, consensus reflects a complex interaction between legal and attitudinal forces. Specifically, legal considerations can exert increased pressure on the Court and consequently mitigate the influence of personal policy preferences. In our conceptualization of law in terms of legal certainty, when the level of legal certainty is high, the justices' ability to vote their attitudes is constrained and so consensus is more likely; alternatively, they are free to vote their preferences when legal uncertainty and ambiguity abound.

These findings further suggest that unanimous cases are neither uninteresting nor boring. Rather, they reflect the myriad forces that influence the justices on every case before the Court, and they illuminate how understanding judicial decision making necessitates an examination of all of them. They also highlight instances in which law, as captured by the notion of legal certainty, plays an important role in influencing justices' decisions. Our findings suggest that we need to continue recent attempts to bring law back into discussions and examinations of judicial decision making to ensure that we possess a complete understanding of how the Supreme Court decides the important legal questions of our time.

Our results raise an important question vis-à-vis the role of the Supreme Court in the American political system: Why do the justices vote to grant certiorari in cases that are ultimately decided unanimously? In other words, why do they spend so much time on cases in which, if the findings presented in Chapters 3 and 4 are correct, the level of legal certainty as to the strongest legal answer is quite high? In Chapter 5, we explore this phenomenon through an investigation of the cert pool memos written for the justices for all cases granted during the 1989 term. We theorize that unanimous cases may differ in notable ways from nonunanimous cases at the agenda-setting stage, and we find that important differences do indeed exist—specifically, unanimous cases were more likely to be considered "bad vehicles," usually because the pool memo author concluded that the legal issue required more percolation in the lower courts. Perhaps most notable, however, we find no difference between unanimous cases and nonunanimous cases with respect to whether they involve a lower court conflict or an important issue. Differences did arise as to the type of important issue highlighted in the pool memos for unanimous as opposed to nonunanimous cases: memos for ultimately unanimous cases often expressed the need to resolve the pending legal issue to provide guidance to the lower courts and to ensure clarity in the law.

Implications

The ultimate goal of this book has been to investigate, and hopefully begin to unravel, the puzzle of unanimity. Our findings suggest that unanimity, and consensus more generally, is a function of multiple concurrently operating forces. One of the central forces driving unanimity is law. Furthermore, the fact that the Supreme Court achieves unanimity or a high degree of consensus as frequently as it does indicates that we need further study on the role the Court plays in national policy making. Is it the Court's responsibility to defend minority interests, to legitimize the national ruling coalition, or to provide clear guidance as to the state of the law, or is it some crucial combination of all of these? Do unanimous or highly consensual decisions affect the larger political environment differently than do divided cases?

Our results suggest that the Supreme Court pursues many goals when handing down a decision, such as reinforcing legal norms, validating legal principles, and providing a final, ultimate answer to important legal questions. It is the latter goal that is perhaps most intriguing. In a substantial proportion of cases, we believe that the Court recognizes that the nation will benefit from its decisions. Furthermore, even if the level of *legal* certainty as to the strongest legal answer is high, it does not necessarily reflect *popular* agreement about how to resolve the issue. Consider *Brown v. Board of Education* (1954), which stands as the foremost example of a case in which all of the justices agreed on the legal answer but with which many others expressed disagreement both in the elected branches and in the states (e.g., Katznelson 2005; Rosenberg 1991). Earl Warren (1977, 2–3) recalled: "At the weekly conference after arguments in the case, the members, [were] conscious of its gravity and far-reaching effects. . . . I have never seen a group of men more conscious of the seriousness of a situation, more intent upon resolving it with as little disruption as possible, or with a greater desire for unanimity."

While one might argue that *Brown* is the exception rather than the rule, many other unanimously decided cases also dealt with highly important, yet potentially divisive, issues. For example, in *Washington v. Glucksberg* (1997), the Court unanimously held that there is no fundamental right to, or liberty interest in, assisted suicide. The Court upheld Washington state's ban despite the growing assisted-suicide movement and the fact that 46 percent of Washington voters cast ballots to overturn the law (Annas 1994). Another example is *Clinton v. Jones* (1997), in which the justices ruled unanimously that the popular, newly reelected president was not immune from participating in legal proceedings during his term in office.

Thus, it can be seen that members of the Court take seriously their role as jurists through a concern for the broader institution of the Court as well as for the rule of law itself. As Gillman and Clayton (1999, 5) noted, "justices' behavior might be motivated not only by a calculation about prevailing opportunities and risks but also by a sense of duty or obligation about their responsibilities to the law and the Constitution and by a commitment to act as judges."

Additionally, we believe that our findings speak more broadly to the fact that even justices recognize the central importance of law: "While it is true that life tenure might make it easier to promote policy preferences, it may also be central to a judge's sense of duty to resist political pressure and decide a case in accordance with the law" (Gillman 1999, 83). By taking cases in which the legal answer is relatively clear, the Court plays a vital role in underscoring the value of law itself. And, by deciding these cases, the Court works to preserve the role of law in ensuring stability, predictability, and consistency across the United States.

Law is not merely a set of political beliefs, nor is it simply a neutral arbiter of actions. However, it does represent the authoritative, government-made rules that order society and our daily activities. If these rules are not stable, predictable, and clear, individuals, groups, companies, and the government itself will act blindly and so may be more likely to violate the rights of others. In the United States it has long been settled that the job of the courts is to interpret the law. The justices still approvingly cite Chief Justice John Marshall's statement from *Marbury v. Madison* (1803, 177): "It is emphatically the duty and province of the judicial department to say what the law is." Recently, the Iowa Supreme Court, in unanimously striking down a law banning gay marriage, reinforced the idea that the courts act to interpret laws and to make sure that the prevailing winds of public opinion do not serve to undercut the rights of a less powerful minority:

> A statute inconsistent with the Iowa Constitution must be declared void, even though it may be supported by strong and deep-seated traditional beliefs and popular opinion. . . . It is also well established that courts must, under all circumstances, protect the supremacy of the constitution as a means of protecting our republic form of government and our freedoms. . . . Our responsibility, however, is to protect constitutional rights of individuals from legislative enactments that have denied those rights, even when the rights have not yet been broadly accepted, were at one time unimagined, or challenge a deeply ingrained practice or law viewed to be impervious to the passage of time. (Justice Cady, majority opinion in *Varnum v. Brien* (2009), 13–15)

Similarly, in the Free Speech, flag salute case *West Virginia State Board of Education v. Barnette* (1943), Justice Robert Jackson stated that the Constitution limits the power of the elected branches of government precisely "to withdraw certain subjects from the vicissitudes of political controversy, to place them beyond the reach of majorities and officials and to establish them as legal principles to be applied by the courts" (*Barnette*, 638). The Supreme Court's unanimous decisions thus serve to remind us that sometimes the justices are relatively certain about the legal answer but that the principles expressed and reinforced are still important.

Federal courts are designed to be divorced from politics and the Supreme Court was particularly created to be free from the pressures of the political branches and the public. This freedom, however, enables the justices to vote according to their personal policy preferences. At the same time, the Court's duty is to interpret the law and, in doing so, reinforce key legal norms. Thus, we must recognize that, although the Court is a political institution, it is also a legal institution.

Appendix

In this appendix, we present the results of a series of models that reflect alternative operationalizations of key independent and dependent variables discussed in Chapters 3 and 4. In Chapter 3, we examine what explains unanimity and consensus on the merits. In Table A.1 we reestimate the models for the unanimous and highly consensual decisions originally presented in Table 3.2. However, instead of using the Legal Certainty Index itself, we use each of the five variables that comprise it.

To fully explore how the Supreme Court achieves consensus in an age of dissensus, we also model the degree of consensus the Court reaches in each case. Thus, in Table A.2 we once again reestimate the model presented in Table 3.2 but use as our dependent variable *the amount of consensus in the final vote.* Here we are interested in decisions in which a relatively high degree of consensus was achieved, even if the final decision was not unanimous, as compared to decisions with a split vote. We measure the level of consensus achieved in each case on a scale of 1 to 5, with 1 representing the least consensus and 5 representing the most.[1] Given the ordered nature of our dependent variable, a partial proportional odds model (PPO) is used. PPO is preferred here because of its ability to handle independent variables that violate the parallel lines assumption associated with the ordered logit model, while also fitting the most parsimonious model possible.

Using the Brant test, we determined that some of our independent variables violated the parallel lines assumption, which means that the use of ordered logit was not advisable. However, since not all of our variables violated this assumption, we used the PPO model—specifically, gologit2, a user-written Stata command created by Richard Williams (2006), which relaxes the parallel lines constraint only for variables where it is not justified, thus providing a more parsimonious model than would be produced with generalized ordered logit. As a result, the model estimates one set of coefficients for variables that do not violate the parallel lines assumption (as would be the case when using ordered logit), and generates a different coefficient for each cutpoint of the dependent variable for those variables that do violate the assumption. The coefficients of the variables that meet the parallel lines assumption are interpreted in the same manner as are the ordered logit results. For the other variables, an examination of the pattern of coefficients across the different categories of the dependent variable reveals information that would be obscured or distorted if a parallel lines model were estimated instead.

Table A.2 reports $M - 1$ sets of coefficients for each of the levels of consensus (where M denotes the number of the levels of consensus). The first column, labeled

TABLE A.1

Logit models of unanimous and highly consensual decisions, without Legal Certainty Index

Variable	MODEL 1: UNANIMOUS DECISIONS Coefficient (R.S.E.)	*p*-value	MODEL 2: UNANIMOUS OR HIGHLY CONSENSUAL DECISIONS Coefficient (R.S.E.)	*p*-value
Legal considerations				
Legally Noncomplex	0.250 (0.091)	0.003	0.180 (0.087)	0.020
Lack of Amicus Participation	0.001 (0.083)	0.496	0.053 (0.082)	0.260
Lack of Legal Dissensus in Lower Court	0.220 (0.080)	0.003	0.237 (0.077)	0.001
Statutory Interpretation	0.102 (0.078)	0.096	0.164 (0.076)	0.016
Lack of Legal Conflict	0.014 (0.085)	0.434	−0.082 (0.084)	0.834
Attitudinal				
Ideological Polarization	−0.096 (0.051)	0.030	−0.056 (0.050)	0.130
Extreme Lower Court Decision	−0.003 (0.197)	0.986	−0.002 (0.192)	0.991
Reversed Lower Court Decision	0.121 (0.080)	0.130	0.203 (0.078)	0.010
Extreme Lower Court Decision × Reversed	−0.161 (0.248)	0.742	−0.038 (0.243)	0.562
Strategic considerations				
Chief Justice Writes Opinion	0.278 (0.119)	0.010	0.303 (0.117)	0.005
Median Justice Writes Opinion	−0.172 (0.144)	0.235	−0.326 (0.139)	0.019
Altered Precedent	−0.131 (0.273)	0.632	−0.231 (0.262)	0.377
Declared Statute Unconstitutional	−0.218 (0.264)	0.409	−0.182 (0.249)	0.466
SG Party	0.066 (0.074)	0.189	0.063 (0.073)	0.194
Institutional context				
Addition of Syllabus	−0.027 (0.211)	0.450	−0.111 (0.206)	0.295
Formalization of Dissent Assignment	−0.101 (0.171)	0.278	−0.182 (0.167)	0.137
Docket Size	0.001 (0.002)	0.337	−0.002 (0.002)	0.792
Number of Law Clerks	0.008 (0.025)	0.620	0.035 (0.025)	0.917
Rehnquist Court	0.363 (0.428)	0.397	−0.255 (0.419)	0.543
Burger Court	0.119 (0.343)	0.730	−0.203 (0.336)	0.546
Case factors				
Governmental Powers Issue	0.581 (0.094)	0.000	0.658 (0.094)	0.000
Economic Issue	0.470 (0.089)	0.000	0.479 (0.087)	0.000
Political Salience	−0.615 (0.122)	0.000	−0.562 (0.112)	0.000
Liberal Decision	0.544 (0.075)	0.000	0.450 (0.074)	0.000
Constant	−1.404 (0.613)	0.022	−1.135 (0.595)	0.057
N	3,425		3,425	

NOTE: R.S.E. = robust standard error clustered on case citation. *p*-values reflect one-tailed tests if directionality hypothesized.

TABLE A.2

Partial proportional odds model of factors explaining level of voting consensus

Variable	c_1		c_2		c_3		c_4	
	Coefficient (R.S.E.)	*p*-value	Coefficient (R.S.E.)	*p*-value	Coefficient (R.S.E.)	*p*-value	Coefficient (R.S.E.)	*p*-value
Legal considerations								
Level of Legal Certainty	0.129 (0.033)	0.000	0.129 (0.033)	0.000	0.129 (0.033)	0.000	0.129 (0.033)	0.000
Attitudinal								
Ideological Polarization	−0.290 (0.059)	0.000	−0.241 (0.048)	0.000	−0.092 (0.047)	0.025	−0.088 (0.049)	0.036
Extreme Lower Court Decision	0.090 (0.163)	0.582	0.090 (0.163)	0.582	0.090 (0.163)	0.582	0.090 (0.163)	0.582
Reversed Lower Court Decision	0.380 (0.098)	0.000	0.227 (0.080)	0.004	0.204 (0.077)	0.008	0.112 (0.078)	0.149
Extreme Lower Court Decision × Reversed	−0.147 (0.205)	0.764	−0.147 (0.205)	0.764	−0.147 (0.205)	0.764	−0.147 (0.205)	0.764
Strategic considerations								
Chief Justice Writes Opinion	0.237 (0.102)	0.010	0.237 (0.102)	0.010	0.237 (0.102)	0.010	0.237 (0.102)	0.010
Median Justice Writes Opinion	−0.746 (0.156)	0.000	−0.392 (0.139)	0.005	−0.316 (0.135)	0.019	−0.199 (0.142)	0.161
Altered Precedent	−0.216 (0.221)	0.329	−0.216 (0.221)	0.329	−0.216 (0.221)	0.329	−0.216 (0.221)	0.329
Declared Statute Unconstitutional	−0.360 (0.232)	0.120	−0.360 (0.232)	0.120	−0.360 (0.232)	0.120	−0.360 (0.232)	0.120
SG Party	0.065 (0.065)	0.156	0.065 (0.065)	0.156	0.065 (0.065)	0.156	0.065 (0.065)	0.156
Institutional context								
Addition of Syllabus	−0.075 (0.182)	0.340	−0.075 (0.182)	0.340	−0.075 (0.182)	0.340	−0.075 (0.182)	0.340
Formalization of Dissent Assignment	−0.891 (0.174)	0.000	−0.543 (0.155)	0.000	−0.198 (0.153)	0.098	0.047 (0.156)	0.617
Docket Size	−0.001 (0.002)	0.733	−0.001 (0.002)	0.733	−0.001 (0.002)	0.733	−0.001 (0.002)	0.733
Number of Law Clerks	0.010 (0.021)	0.687	0.010 (0.021)	0.687	0.010 (0.021)	0.687	0.010 (0.021)	0.687
Rehnquist Court	0.255 (0.330)	0.439	0.255 (0.330)	0.439	0.255 (0.330)	0.439	0.255 (0.330)	0.439
Burger Court	0.176 (0.260)	0.499	0.176 (0.260)	0.499	0.176 (0.260)	0.499	0.176 (0.260)	0.499
Case factors								
Governmental Powers Issue	0.614 (0.084)	0.000	0.614 (0.084)	0.000	0.614 (0.084)	0.000	0.614 (0.084)	0.000
Economic Issue	0.451 (0.077)	0.000	0.451 (0.077)	0.000	0.451 (0.077)	0.000	0.451 (0.077)	0.000
Political Salience	−0.544 (0.092)	0.000	−0.544 (0.092)	0.000	−0.544 (0.092)	0.000	−0.544 (0.092)	0.000
Liberal Decision	0.245 (0.096)	0.001	0.356 (0.077)	0.000	0.467 (0.073)	0.000	0.551 (0.074)	0.000
Constant	2.398 (0.560)	0.000	0.937 (0.514)	0.068	−0.679 (0.507)	0.181	−1.31 (0.513)	0.010
N	3,425		3,425		3,425		3,425	

NOTE: R.S.E. = robust standard error clustered on case citation. *p*-values reflect one-tailed tests if directionality hypothesized (*p*-value/2). If the effect is in the opposite direction than as predicted, *p*-values are calculated by subtracting the *p*-value (divided by 2) from 1.

C_1 (for cutpoint 1), gives the coefficient estimates for a decision above the first cutpoint (i.e., score = 2, 3, 4, 5) versus below it (i.e., score = 1); the second column, labeled C_2, gives the coefficient estimates for a decision above the second cutpoint (i.e., score = 3, 4) versus below it (i.e., score = 1, 2); the third column, labeled C_3, gives the coefficient estimates for a decision above the third cutpoint (i.e., score = 4, 5) versus below it (i.e., score = 1, 2, 3); and the fourth column, labeled C_4, gives the coefficient estimates for a decision above the fourth cutpoint (i.e., score = 5) versus below it (i.e., score = 1, 2, 3, 4). Thus, positive coefficients indicate that higher values of the explanatory variable make it more likely that the decision is in a higher category than the current one, while negative coefficients indicate that higher values on the explanatory variable increase the likelihood of the decision being in the current or a lower category. In other words, positive coefficients indicate that the existence of the explanatory variable increases the likelihood of a higher level of consensus, while negative coefficients indicate that the existence of the explanatory variable decreases that likelihood. However, for those variables that did not violate the parallel lines assumption, the coefficients remain constant across the categories and can be interpreted in the same manner as are ordered logit coefficients.

In Chapter 4, we investigate opinion consensus, or consensus in terms of the number of separate opinions authored by the justices. Table A.3 reports a reestimation of the models presented originally in Table 4.2 showing the factors that predict fully unanimous as well as highly consensual opinions. While Table 4.2 uses the Legal Certainty Index, Table A.3 includes instead each of the five separate variables that comprise it.

In Table A.4, we once again reestimate the models originally presented in Table 4.2, but use as our dependent variable the *level of opinion consensus*. We are interested in cases in which a relatively high degree of opinion consensus was achieved, even if the final vote was not unanimous. Additionally, we wish to account for the fact that even unanimous decisions on the merits may not reflect total agreement and so we include both dissenting and concurring opinions in our measure. We measure the level of opinion consensus on a scale of 1 to 5, with 1 representing the lowest level and 5 representing the highest. This scale reflects the opinion consensus on the Court in each case as reflected by the number of separate opinions filed. In our data, the number of separate opinions ranges from 0 to 9. If this number was 4 or higher, the level of opinion consensus was coded 1; if it was 3, the level of opinion consensus was coded 2; if it was 2, the level of opinion consensus was coded 3; if it was 1, the level of opinion consensus was coded 4; and if there were no separate opinions (meaning that the case was fully unanimous), the level of opinion consensus was coded 5. Although the vote may have been unanimous, the decision may have been bracketed by many concurring opinions, which indicates less consensus than a unanimous decision with no separate opinions.

Given the ordered nature of our dependent variable, we again use a PPO model to estimate this model. Table A.4 reports the results of the PPO model and is interpreted in the same manner as Table A.2 (described previously).

TABLE A.3

Logit models of unanimous and highly consensual opinions, without the Legal Certainty Index

	MODEL 1		MODEL 2		MODEL 3	
Variable	Coefficient (R.S.E.)	*p*-value	Coefficient (R.S.E.)	*p*-value	Coefficient (R.S.E.)	*p*-value
Legal considerations						
Legally Noncomplex	0.510 (0.113)	0.000	0.389 (0.096)	0.000	0.279 (0.093)	0.002
Lack of Amicus Participation	0.174 (0.096)	0.035	0.073 (0.086)	0.198	0.111 (0.084)	0.093
Lack of Legal Dissensus in Lower Court	0.103 (0.092)	0.133	0.179 (0.083)	0.016	0.196 (0.081)	0.008
Statutory Interpretation	0.229 (0.090)	0.006	0.234 (0.081)	0.002	0.280 (0.079)	0.000
Lack of Legal Conflict	0.059 (0.095)	0.270	−0.018 (0.087)	0.581	−0.135 (0.086)	0.942
Attitudinal						
Ideological Polarization	−0.110 (0.058)	0.028	−0.089 (0.053)	0.048	−0.090 (0.052)	0.041
Extreme Lower Court Decision	0.067 (0.214)	0.753	−0.104 (0.204)	0.612	−0.014 (0.199)	0.945
Reversed Lower Court Decision	−0.007 (0.090)	0.936	0.062 (0.082)	0.448	0.097 (0.081)	0.229
Extreme Lower Court Decision × Reversed	0.096 (0.271)	0.362	0.006 (0.258)	0.491	−0.040 (0.250)	0.564
Strategic considerations						
Chief Justice Writes Opinion	0.094 (0.138)	0.249	0.150 (0.123)	0.112	0.128 (0.119)	0.141
Median Justice Writes Opinion	−0.317 (0.171)	0.064	−0.260 (0.150)	0.084	−0.353 (0.147)	0.017
Altered Precedent	−0.141 (0.334)	0.673	−0.230 (0.296)	0.436	−0.405 (0.291)	0.164
Declared Statute Unconstitutional	−1.495 (0.530)	0.005	−0.556 (0.303)	0.065	−0.298 (0.279)	0.286
SG Party	−0.061 (0.085)	0.765	−0.001 (0.077)	0.507	−0.037 (0.075)	0.691
Institutional context						
Addition of Syllabus	0.014 (0.245)	0.523	0.088 (0.222)	0.655	−0.069 (0.217)	0.375
Formalization of Dissent Assignment	−0.109 (0.195)	0.287	−0.163 (0.178)	0.178	−0.241 (0.172)	0.081
Docket Size	−0.000 (0.002)	0.546	0.003 (0.002)	0.094	0.002 (0.002)	0.166
Number of Law Clerks	−0.028 (0.028)	0.161	0.004 (0.026)	0.560	0.021 (0.025)	0.794
Rehnquist Court	0.699 (0.464)	0.132	0.233 (0.430)	0.589	−0.056 (0.424)	0.894
Burger Court	0.369 (0.364)	0.311	−0.100 (0.342)	0.770	−0.197 (0.337)	0.559

(continued)

TABLE A.3 *(continued)*

Variable	MODEL 1		MODEL 2		MODEL 3	
	Coefficient (R.S.E.)	*p*-value	Coefficient (R.S.E.)	*p*-value	Coefficient (R.S.E.)	*p*-value
Case factors						
Governmental Powers Issue	0.695 (0.106)	0.000	0.619 (0.097)	0.000	0.730 (0.095)	0.000
Economic Issue	0.694 (0.103)	0.000	0.558 (0.092)	0.000	0.613 (0.090)	0.000
Political Salience	−0.737 (0.161)	0.000	−0.762 (0.134)	0.000	−0.828 (0.128)	0.000
Liberal Decision	0.368 (0.084)	0.000	0.497 (0.077)	0.000	0.379 (0.076)	0.000
Time Left until End of Term	−0.001 (0.001)	0.034	−0.001 (0.001)	0.089	−0.001 (0.001)	0.078
Constant	−1.059 (0.682)	0.120	−1.626 (0.637)	0.011	−1.328 (0.620)	0.032
N	3,391		3,391		3,391	

NOTE: Model 1: Unanimous opinions.
Model 2: Unanimous opinions or highly consensual opinions (unanimous decisions with one oncurrence).
Model 3: Unanimous opinions or highly consensual opinions (unanimous decisions with one concurrence or decisions with one dissent where there is only one justice dissenting).
R.S.E. = robust standard error clustered on case citation. *p*-values reflect one-tailed tests where directionality hypothesized.

TABLE A.4

Partial proportional odds model of factors explaining level of opinion consensus

	c_1		c_2		c_3		c_4	
Variable	Coefficient (R.S.E.)	*p*-value	Coefficient (R.S.E.)	*p*-value	Coefficient (R.S.E.)	*p*-value	Coefficient (R.S.E.)	*p*-value
Legal considerations								
Level of Legal Certainty	0.257 (0.034)	0.000	0.257 (0.034)	0.000	0.257 (0.034)	0.000	0.257 (0.034)	0.000
Attitudinal								
Ideological Polarization	−0.108 (0.046)	0.009	−0.108 (0.046)	0.009	−0.108 (0.046)	0.009	−0.108 (0.046)	0.009
Extreme Lower Court Decision	−0.039 (0.182)	0.830	−0.039 (0.182)	0.830	−0.039 (0.182)		−0.039 (0.182)	0.830
Reversed Lower Court Decision	−0.059 (0.069)	0.390	−0.059 (0.069)	0.390	−0.059 (0.069)	0.390	−0.059 (0.069)	0.390
Extreme Lower Court Decision × Reversed	0.047 (0.231)	0.420	0.047 (0.231)	0.420	0.047 (0.231)	0.420	0.047 (0.231)	0.420
Strategic considerations								
Chief Justice Writes Opinion	−0.348 (0.234)	0.931	0.063 (0.163)	0.351	−0.133 (0.119)	0.869	0.094 (0.140)	0.251
Median Justice Writes Opinion	−0.280 (0.125)	0.026	−0.280 (0.125)	0.026	−0.280 (0.125)	0.026	−0.280 (0.125)	0.026
Altered Precedent	−0.681 (0.253)	0.004	−0.681 (0.253)	0.004	−0.681 (0.253)	0.004	−0.681 (0.253)	0.004
Declared Statute Unconstitutional	−0.328 (0.178)	0.065	−0.328 (0.178)	0.065	−0.328 (0.178)	0.065	−0.328 (0.178)	0.065
SG Party	−0.039 (0.066)	0.724	−0.039 (0.066)	0.724	−0.039 (0.066)	0.724	−0.039 (0.066)	0.724
Institutional context								
Addition of Syllabus	0.045 (0.194)	0.591	0.045 (0.194)	0.591	0.045 (0.194)	0.591	0.045 (0.194)	0.591
Formalization of Dissent Assignment	−0.073 (0.149)	0.312	−0.073 (0.149)	0.312	−0.073 (0.149)	0.312	−0.073 (0.149)	0.312
Docket Size	0.008 (0.003)	0.006	0.005 (0.002)	0.014	0.006 (0.002)	0.002	0.001 (0.002)	0.252
Number of Law Clerks	−0.051 (0.025)	0.022	−0.049 (0.022)	0.015	−0.045 (0.022)	0.019	−0.024 (0.022)	0.142
Rehnquist Court	0.666 (0.361)	0.065	0.666 (0.361)	0.065	0.666 (0.361)	0.065	0.666 (0.361)	0.065
Burger Court	0.152 (0.288)	0.598	0.152 (0.288)	0.598	0.152 (0.288)	0.598	0.152 (0.288)	0.598
Case factors								
Governmental Powers Issue	0.768 (0.084)	0.000	0.768 (0.084)	0.000	0.768 (0.084)	0.000	0.768 (0.084)	0.000
Economic Issue	0.826 (0.078)	0.000	0.826 (0.078)	0.000	0.826 (0.078)	0.000	0.826 (0.078)	0.000
Political Salience	−0.928 (0.104)	0.000	−0.928 (0.104)	0.000	−0.928 (0.104)	0.000	−0.928 (0.104)	0.000
Liberal Decision	0.267 (0.067)	0.000	0.267 (0.067)	0.000	0.267 (0.067)	0.000	0.267 (0.067)	0.000
Time Left until End of Term	−0.002 (0.000)	0.001	−0.002 (0.000)	0.001	−0.002 (0.000)	0.001	−0.002 (0.000)	0.001
Constant	3.396 (0.825)	0.000	2.314 (0.614)	0.000	0.676 (0.546)	0.215	−1.367 (0.553)	0.013

NOTE: R.S.E. = robust standard error clustered on case citation. N = 3,391. *p*-values reflect one-tailed tests where directionality is hypothesized.

Index of Cases

Argersinger v. Hamlin, 407 U.S. 25 (1973)

Baltimore City Department of Social Services v. Bouknight, 493 U.S. 549 (1990)
Betts v. Brady, 316 U.S. 455 (1942)
Blystone v. Pennsylvania, 494 U.S. 299 (1990)
Board of Comm'rs of Jackson County v. United States, 308 U.S. 343 (1939)
Booth v. Maryland, 482 U.S. 496 (1987)
Bowers v. Hardwick, 478 U.S. 186 (1986)
Bray v. Alexandria Clinic, 506 U.S. 263 (1993)
Brown v. Allen, 344 U.S. 443 (1953)
Brown v. Board of Education, 347 U.S. 483 (1954)
Bush v. Gore, 531 U.S. 98 (2000)
Butterworth v. Smith, 494 U.S. 624 (1990)

Chaplinsky v. New Hampshire, 315 U.S. 568 (1942)
Chesapeake & Ohio v. Leitch, 276 U.S. 429 (1928)
Clinton v. Jones, 520 U.S. 681 (1997)
Commissioner of INS v. Jean, 496 U.S. 154 (1990)
Commissioner of Internal Revenue v. National Alfalfa Dehydrating and Milling Co., 417 U.S. 134 (1974)
Coolidge v. Long, 282 U.S. 582 (1930)
County of Sacramento v. Lewis, 523 U.S. 833 (1998)

Davis v. United States, 328 U.S. 582 (1946)
Driscoll v. Edison Light & Power Co., 307 U.S. 104 (1939)

East Carroll Parish School Board v. Marshall, 424 U.S. 636 (1976)
Eaton v. City of Tulsa, 415 U.S. 697 (1974)
eBay Inc. v. MercExchange, L.L.C., 547 U.S. 388 (2006)
Ex parte Quirin, 317 U.S. 1 (1942)

Federal Power Commission v. Hope Natural Gas, 320 U.S. 591 (1944)
Federal Trade Commission v. Eastman Kodak Co., 274 U.S. 619 (1927)
Ferguson v. Moore McCormack Lines, 352 U.S. 521 (1957)
Foremost Insurance Co. v. Richardson, 457 U.S. 668 (1982)
Franchise Tax Board v. Alcan Aluminum Ltd., 493 U.S. 331 (1990)

Garcia v. Elf Atochem North America, 28 F.3d 466 (5th Cir. 1994)
General Motors Corp. v. United States, 496 U.S. 530 (1990)
Gideon v. Wainwright, 372 U.S. 335 (1963)
Golden State Transit Corp. v. City of Los Angeles, 493 U.S. 103 (1989)
Gregg Cartage & Storage Co. v. United States, 316 U.S. 74 (1942)

Hamdan v. Rumsfeld, 548 U.S. 557 (2006)
Hawk v. Olson, 326 U.S. 271 (1945)
Higgins v. Smith, 308 U.S. 473 (1939)
Hiibel v. Sixth Judicial District Court of Nevada, 542 U.S. 177 (2004)
Hirabayashi v. United States, 320 U.S. 81 (1943)

Jewell Ridge Coal Corp v. United Mine Workers of America, 325 U.S. 161 (1945)
Jimmy Swaggart Ministries v. Board of Equalization of California, 493 U.S. 378 (1990)
John Doe Agency v. John Doe Corp., 493 U.S. 146 (1989)

Keller v. State Bar of California, 496 U.S. 1 (1990)
Kokoszka v. Belford, 417 U.S. 642 (1974)
Korematsu v. United States, 323 U.S. 214 (1944)

Lawrence v. Texas, 539 U.S. 558 (2003)
Leach v. Peirson, 275 U.S. 120 (1927)
Little v. Streater, 452 U.S. 1 (1981)
Lynce v. Mathis, 519 U.S. 443 (1997)

Marbury v. Madison, 5 U.S. 137 (1803)
Maryland v. Pringle, 540 U.S. 366 (2003)
McCoy v. North Carolina, 494 U.S. 433 (1990)
Medo Photo Supply Corp. v. Labor Board, 321 U.S. 678 (1944)
Mercoid Corporation v. Mid-Continent Investment Co., 320 U.S. 661 (1944)
Minersville School District v. Gobitis, 310 U.S. 586 (1940)
Minnesota v. Olson, 495 U.S. 91 (1990)
Moore v. City of East Cleveland, 431 U.S. 494 (1977)
Morehead v. New York ex rel. Tipaldo, 298 U.S. 587 (1936)
Municipal Investors Assn. v. Birmingham, 316 U.S. 153 (1942)
Murdock v. Pennsylvania, 319 U.S. 105 (1943)

National Broadcasting Co. v. United States, 319 U.S. 190 (1943)
National Labor Relations Board v. Boeing Co. et al., 412 U.S. 67 (1973)
Nobelman v. American Savings Bank, 508 U.S. 324 (1993)

Oklahoma Press Publishing Co. v. Walling, 327 U.S. 186 (1946)
Olmstead v. United States, 277 U.S. 438 (1928)
Oncale v. Sundowner Offshore Services, 523 U.S. 75 (1998)

Payne v. Tennessee, 501 U.S. 808 (1991)
Polish National Alliance v. Labor Board, 322 U.S. 643 (1944)
Preseault et ux. v. Interstate Commerce Commission, 494 U.S. 1 (1990)

Railroad Retirement Board v. Alton Railroad Co., 295 U.S. 330 (1935)
Republic of Argentina v. Weltover, 504 U.S. 607 (1992)
Richards v. Wisconsin, 520 U.S. 385 (1997)
Roe v. Wade, 410 U.S. 113 (1973)

Schneiderman v. United States, 320 U.S. 118 (1943)
Scott v. Illinois, 440 U.S. 367 (1979)
Selvage v. Collins, 494 U.S. 108 (1990)
Sisson v. Ruby, 497 U.S. 358 (1990)
Skinner v. Oklahoma, 316 U.S. 535 (1942)
Smith v. Allwright, 321 U.S. 649 (1944)
Sorrells v. United States, 287 U.S. 435 (1932)
South Carolina v. Gathers, 490 U.S. 805 (1989)
State of Maryland v. Baltimore Radio Show, 338 U.S. 912 (1950)
Swann v. Charlotte-Mecklenburg, 402 U.S. 1 (1971)

Tafflin v. Levitt, 493 U.S. 455 (1990)
Taylor v. United States, 495 U.S. 575 (1990)
Texaco v. Hasbrouck, 496 U.S. 543 (1990)
Texas v. Florida, 306 U.S. 398 (1939)
Tinker v. Des Moines, 393 U.S. 503 (1969)

United States Department of Labor v. Triplett, 494 U.S. 715 (1990)
United States v. Boyle, 469 U.S. 241 (1985)
United States v. Classic, 313 U.S. 299 (1941)
United States v. Munoz-Flores, 495 U.S. 385 (1990)
United States v. Nixon, 418 U.S. 683 (1974)
United States v. Orleans, 425 U.S. 807 (1976)
United States v. Southeastern Underwriters Assn., 322 U.S. 533 (1944)
United States v. Texas, 507 U.S. 529 (1993)
Utah v. Aldrich, 316 U.S. 174 (1942)

Vacco v. Quill, 521 U.S. 793 (1997)
Varnum v. Brien, 763 N.W.2d 862 (Iowa 2009)
Venegas v. Mitchell, 495 U.S. 82 (1990)

Washington v. Glucksberg, 521 U.S. 702 (1997)
West Virginia State Board of Education v. Barnette, 319 U.S. 624 (1943)
Wickard v. Filburn, 317 U.S. 111 (1942)
Willy v. Coastal Corp., 503 U.S. 131 (1992)

Yellow Freight System v. Donnelly, 494 U.S. 820 (1990)

Notes

INTRODUCTION

1. As detailed by the Supreme Court in its opinion, the Fifth Circuit held that same-sex sexual harassment claims are never cognizable under Title VII; the Fourth Circuit held that these claims are actionable only if the plaintiff can prove the person harassing him or her is gay; and the Seventh Circuit held that any harassment claim in the workplace is actionable regardless of the sex of the victim or the harasser.

2. Full case citations are provided in the Index of Cases.

3. Justice Byron White to colleagues on the Supreme Court, June 28, 1993. http://law.onecle.com/ussc/justices/509usix-retirement-of-justice-white.html. Accessed September 15, 2012.

CHAPTER 1

1. Eventually, the Court reached a record of 30 percent one-vote margin cases by the close of the 2000 term.

2. 43. Stat. 936, February 13, 1925.

3. For example, mandatory appeals from state high courts were limited to instances in which the state high court declared a federal statute invalid or denied a claim that a state law was unconstitutional. Direct appeals from the federal district courts to the Supreme Court were eliminated in most instances. Instead, parties needed to file a writ of certiorari asking the Court to hear their case, and the decision to grant these writs was left to the Court itself.

4. Felix Frankfurter to Hugo Black, December 15, 1939, Douglas Papers, Box 39. Manuscript Division, Library of Congress, Washington, DC.

5. Harlan F. Stone to Edward Sanford, May 13, 1927, Stone Papers, Box 76. Manuscript Division, Library of Congress, Washington, DC.

6. Stone to Charles Evans Hughes, November 28, 1932, Stone Papers, Box 75.

7. Stone to Charles Evans Hughes, November 2, 1938, Stone Papers, Box 75.

8. James McReynolds to Harlan F. Stone, April 2, 1930, Stone Papers, Box 76.

9. Stone to James McReynolds, April 3, 1930, Stone Papers, Box 76.

10. William Howard Taft to Harlan F. Stone, January 26, 1927, Stone Papers, Box 76.

11. Stone to William Howard Taft, January 26, 1927, Stone Papers, Box 76.

12. Stone to Owen Roberts, December 16, 1930, Stone Papers, Box 76.

13. Felix Frankfurter to Harlan F. Stone, April 23, 1942, Stone Papers, Box 74.
14. William O. Douglas to Harlan F. Stone, January 6, 1944, Stone Papers, Box 74.
15. Taft to William Lyon Phelps, May 30, 1927. Quoted in Danelski (1960, 6).
16. Stone to Stanley Reed, December 27, 1939, Stone Papers, Box 76.
17. Frankfurter to Harlan F. Stone, May 3, 1939, Stone Papers, Box 74.
18. Frankfurter to Harlan F. Stone, December 12, 1939, Douglas Papers, Box 39.
19. Stone to Felix Frankfurter, October 12, 1941, Stone Papers, Box 74.
20. Frankfurter to Harlan F. Stone, October 21, 1942, Stone Papers, Box 74.
21. Frankfurter to the Brethren, October 22, 1942, Stone Papers, Box 74.
22. Stone to Felix Frankfurter, June 7, 1944, Stone Papers, Box 74.
23. Wiley Rutledge to Harlan F. Stone, June 21, 1943, Stone Papers, Box 76.
24. Stone to Wiley Rutledge, June 24, 1943, Stone Papers, Box 76.
25. For example, Stone wrote the other justices on February 23, 1944:

> Should we increase the length of the next recess in order to catch up with opinion writing? On Saturday February 26th we will have completed 21 weeks of the 34 week term. During that period we have handed down 55 full opinions. As of this date 10 opinions have been circulated, in most of which there will probably be concurrences or dissents, or both. There are 23 cases assigned for opinion in which no opinion has been circulated. Unless we catch up with our opinion writing soon we will be in serious difficulties as we approach the end of the term. We ought to avoid, if possible, the accumulation of unwritten opinions at the end of the term which embarrassed us so seriously last year. (Stone Papers, Box 77)

26. Stone to James F. Byrnes, November 1, 1941, Stone Papers, Box 74.
27. Stone to Felix Frankfurter, April 1, 1943, Stone Papers, Box 74.
28. Stone to Robert H. Jackson, March 31, 1943, Stone Papers, Box 75.
29. Stone to William O. Douglas, March 20, 1944, Stone Papers, Box 74.
30. Stone to Charles Evans Hughes, January 3, 1941, Stone Papers, Box 75.
31. Robert H. Jackson to Harlan F. Stone, April 10, 1942, Stone Papers, Box 75.
32. Frankfurter to Harlan F. Stone, February 24, 1939, Stone Papers, Box 74.
33. Frankfurter to Harlan F. Stone, November 10, 1945, Stone Papers, Box 75.
34. Rutledge to the Conference, January 3, 1946, Stone Papers, Box 76.
35. Rutledge to Harlan F. Stone, January 15, 1946, Stone Papers, Box 76.
36. Rutledge to Harlan F. Stone, January 15, 1946, Stone Papers, Box 76.
37. Stone to Wiley Rutledge, January 16, 1946, Stone Papers, Box 76.
38. Frankfurter to Harlan F. Stone, May 26, 1942, Stone Papers, Box 74.
39. Jackson to Harlan F. Stone, May 25, 1942, Stone Papers, Box 74.
40. Stone to the Conference, May 27, 1942, Stone Papers, Box 74.
41. Frankfurter to Harlan F. Stone, March 6, 1939, Stone Papers, Box 74.
42. Frankfurter to Hugo Black, December 15, 1939, Douglas Papers, Box 39.
43. Frankfurter to Harlan F. Stone, April 14, 1939, Stone Papers, Box 74.
44. Oliver Wendell Holmes, Jr., to Harlan F. Stone, November 16, 1927, Stone Papers, Box 75.
45. Stone to Oliver Wendell Holmes, Jr., March 22, 1928, Stone Papers, Box 75.
46. Stone to Felix Frankfurter, January 25, 1945, Stone Papers, Box 75.

47. Frankfurter to Harlan F. Stone, May 15, 1944, Stone Papers, Box 74.
48. Stone to Felix Frankfurter, May 16, 1944, Stone Papers, Box 74.
49. Stone to the Conference, March 6, 1946, Stone Papers, Box 75.
50. Jackson to Harlan F. Stone, January 17, 1944, Stone Papers, Box 75.
51. Frankfurter to Harlan F. Stone, March 17, 1944, Stone Papers, Box 74.
52. Stone to Robert H. Jackson, April 3, 1942, Stone Papers, Box 75.
53. Frankfurter to Harlan F. Stone, December 28, 1943, Stone Papers, Box 74.
54. Frankfurter to Harlan F. Stone, March 16, 1943, Stone Papers, Box 74.
55. Rutledge wrote: "Last week I promised that I would give further consideration to this case and indicate my conclusions to you during the present week. I have done so and after going through the record with some care . . . I feel I must dissent. . . . While I regret, again the necessity of dissenting from an opinion of yours, I feel that this case simply goes too far." Rutledge to Harlan F. Stone, March 30, 1944, Stone Papers, Box 76.
56. Stone to Wiley Rutledge, March 31, 1944, Stone Papers, Box 76.
57. Owen Roberts to the Conference, December 1, 1944, Stone Papers, Box 76.
58. *New York Herald Tribune*, "Danger in Dissent," January 6, 1944, collected in Stone Papers, Box 77.
59. *New York Herald Tribune*, "'Rift' in the Court," January 6, 1944, collected in Stone Papers, Box 77.
60. Stone to the Conference, January 13, 1944, Stone Papers, Box 77.
61. Frankfurter to Harlan F. Stone, March 8, 1944, Stone Papers, Box 74.
62. Stone to Felix Frankfurter, March 27, 1944, Stone Papers, Box 74.
63. Frankfurter to the Brethren, November 10, 1944, Stone Papers, Box 74.

CHAPTER 2

1. Connecticut General Statute § 46b-160 (1981) stated that "if such mother or expectant mother continues constant in her accusation, it shall be evidence that the respondent is the father of such child." Furthermore, in *Mosher v. Bennett* (108 Conn. 671 [1929]) the Connecticut Supreme Court held: "The mother still has the right to rely upon the *prima facie* case made out by constancy in her accusation. . . . The *prima facie* case so made out places upon the reputed father the burden of showing his innocence of the charge, and, under our practice, he must do this by other evidence than his own" (*Mosher*, 674).
2. From 1941 to 1954, Pritchett published a series of articles, the first of which was "Division of Opinion Among Justices of the U.S. Supreme Court, 1939–1941," published in the *American Political Science Review* in 1941. His first book was *The Roosevelt Court*, published in 1948, and his second book was *Civil Liberties and the Vinson Court*, published in 1954. These are considered Pritchett's most important contributions to explaining and understanding judicial behavior (Baum 2003).
3. Warren E. Burger to the Conference, January 21, 1974, Rehnquist Papers, Box 7. Hoover Institution, Stanford University, Stanford, CA.
4. Collins (2008) coded a case as salient if the case appeared on the front page of the *New York Times* the day following the decision.

5. We thank Paul Collins for providing the data from 1953 through 2001 and for providing the coding instructions that we used to code the 2002–2006 terms.

6. Specifically, we relied on the "cert" variable in the Spaeth dataset (2007). This variable denotes the reason for the Court granting certiorari, which includes conflict between the lower courts and whether the case was granted to resolve an important or significant question.

7. To be sure, justices and their clerks read lower court opinions. For example, in the reapportionment case *East Carroll Parish School Board v. Marshall* (1976), Rehnquist wrote White: "I have come to the conclusion, with understandable reluctance, that you are right and I was wrong in the Conference discussion of your proposed *per curiam* in this case. After rereading the opinion of the Court of Appeals for the Fifth Circuit, I now realize that petitioner here does not challenge the original invalidation of its own apportionment law, but simply argues as to whether the District Court's own plan should have been upheld by the Court of Appeals." William H. Rehnquist to Byron R. White, June 20, 1975, Rehnquist Papers, Box 7.

8. While Giles, Hettinger, and Peppers (2001) created a more variable measure of lower federal court judge ideology, the correlation between this measure and a simple dummy reflecting the party of the appointing president is almost perfect. We therefore utilize the simple partisan dummy given its ease of use with respect to ultimately creating a dummy variable reflecting whether nonideological disagreement exists on the lower court.

9. For the interested reader, an Appendix is included which reestimates the models presented in Chapters 3 and 4, but reports each variable comprising the Legal Certainty Index's independent influence on consensus.

10. The Martin-Quinn scores place justices on a common ideological continuum and are based on merits votes derived from the Spaeth dataset. Because these scores are dynamic, they allow the position of each justice to evolve over time. In addition, they have been shown to classify votes well across all legal issues, while other measures are typically limited to civil rights and liberties cases.

11. For the JCS scores, see http://epstein.usc.edu/research/JCS.html; for the scores for district court judges, see http://clboyd.net/ideology.html.

12. Specifically, we relied on the "win" variable, which measures which party prevailed, the petitioner or the respondent (McGuire et al. 2009).

13. Harold H. Burton to Earl Warren, May 17, 1954, Warren Papers, Box 82. Manuscript Division, Library of Congress, Washington, DC.

14. Sherman Minton to George Braden, February 15, 1954, Braden Papers, Box 2. Truman Library, Independence, MO.

15. Burger to Harry A. Blackmun, Lewis Powell, and William H. Rehnquist, April 2, 1973, Rehnquist Papers, Box 5.

16. Rehnquist to Warren Burger, March 8, 1974, Rehnquist Papers, Box 71.

17. Harry A. Blackmun to John Paul Stevens and Sandra Day O'Connor, October 21, 1991. Blackmun Papers, Box 607. Manuscript Division, Library of Congress, Washington, DC.

18. David Kendall to William H. Rehnquist, undated, Rehnquist Papers, Box 3.

19. Rehnquist to the Conference, June 2, 1994, Rehnquist Papers, Box 144.

20. Alternatively, we have no reason to believe that workload considerations influence the decision of how to vote. Votes on the merits are in and of themselves costless, and justices are not required to author a dissenting opinion. Opinion authorship, on the other hand, requires energy and time. Previous studies have found that, while justices may not be influenced by time constraints when voting, they are influenced by such constraints when deciding whether to write a separate opinion; this is especially true when the decision concerns whether to author a concurring opinion (e.g., Wahlbeck, Spriggs, and Maltzman 1999).

CHAPTER 3

1. After the arrest, Pringle waived his *Miranda* rights and confessed to possession of the cocaine. He stated that the driver and the other passenger of the car did not know about the drugs, and they were subsequently released.

2. Because of the specific hypotheses we test, as explained in detail in Chapter 2, appeals cases and cases appealed from state courts were necessarily excluded from the analysis.

3. Certain variables have missing data because of the appointment of judges by a president before Eisenhower (these judges lack Judicial Common Space scores) and because some lower court judges were not listed for the lower court case or the lower court case was not available.

4. For interested readers, the statistical results of a partial proportional odds model with level of consensus as the dependent variable appear in the Appendix. The Appendix also includes the statistical results of the models in Table 3.2 when reestimated with logit using the individual variables that make up the Legal Certainty Index rather than the index itself.

CHAPTER 4

1. Potter Stewart to William O. Douglas, April 12, 1972, Rehnquist Papers, Box 24.

2. Lewis Powell to the Conference, April 25, 1972, Rehnquist Papers, Box 24.

3. For the interested reader, the Appendix includes the results of our logit reestimation of the models in Table 4.2 using the individual variables that make up the Legal Certainty Index rather than the index itself. Additionally, the Appendix contains the statistical results of a partial proportional odds model with level of opinion consensus as the dependent variable.

4. The p-values for the unanimous opinion model and the UOC model are 0.076 and 0.101 respectively.

CHAPTER 5

1. *Sisson v. Ruby*, No. 88-204, Lee Epstein, Jeffrey A. Segal, and Harold J. Spaeth, "The Digital Archive of the Papers of Justice Harry A. Blackmun" (2007), available at: http://epstein.usc.edu/research/blackmunMemos/1989/GM-1989-pdf/88-2041.pdf.

2. Even the justices themselves debate what information a denial of certiorari provides. On the one hand, as Justice Robert H. Jackson in *Brown v. Allen* (1953, 543) stated, "[S]ome say denial means nothing, others say it means nothing much. . . . Perhaps the profession could accept denial as meaningless before the custom was introduced of noting dissents from them. Lawyers and lower judges will not readily believe that Justices of this Court are taking the trouble to signal a meaningless division of opinion about a meaningless act." On the other hand, as Felix Frankfurter noted, "All that a denial of a petition for a writ of certiorari means is that fewer than four members of the Court thought it should be granted . . . such a denial carried with it no implication whatever regarding the Court's views on the merits of a case which is has declined to review" (*State of Maryland v. Baltimore Radio Show* [1950], 917–919).

3. Letter from Harry A. Blackmun to William H. Rehnquist, August 6, 1991. Marshall Papers, Box 525. Originally quoted in Tinsley E. Yarborough, *The Rehnquist Court and the Constitution* (Oxford University Press, 2000).

4. We recognize that by focusing on the memos we are missing information that can be obtained from other sources and thus that our analysis may not be as comprehensive as we would like. However, most of the justices rely on pool memos as opposed to reading through all of the briefs. We examine the notes written by Blackmun's clerks as a check on the pool memos and find that, unlike the pool memos, they were more likely to include strategic and political analysis. Consequently, we believe that pool memos, with the exception of strategic and political considerations, accurately reflect the information available to the justices at the time they must decide to grant or deny certiorari.

5. The memos come from the collected papers of Justice Harry A. Blackmun housed at the Manuscript Division of the Library of Congress. The Blackmun Archives are available online at http://epstein.usc.edu/blackmun.php, which includes Blackmun's papers for the 1986–1993 terms. From those available dates, we randomly selected the 1989 term.

CHAPTER 6

1. Seven years later, the Supreme Court revisited this issue in *Scott v. Illinois* (1979), in which it clarified the *Argersinger* ruling, stating that the Sixth Amendment Right to Counsel is activated only if imprisonment is a potential outcome, even if imprisonment is authorized under the controlling statute. Interestingly, the Court specifically pointed out in *Scott* that the *Argersinger* ruling was in fact "reasonably workable" in relation to the concerns initially expressed by Justice Powell.

APPENDIX

1. 5–4 and 4–3 decisions were coded 1; 5–3 and 6–3 decisions were coded 2; 5–2, 6–2, and 7–2 decisions were coded 3; 4–1, 5–1, 6–1, 7–1, and 8–1 decisions were coded 4; and 5–0, 6–0, 7–0, 8–0, and 9–0 decisions were coded 5.

Bibliography

Aberbach, Joel D., Ellis S. Krauss, Michio Muramatsu, and Bert A. Rockman. 1990. "Comparing Japanese and American Administrative Elites." *British Journal of Political Science* 20:461–488.

Anderson, Christopher J., and Christine A. Guillory. 1997. "Political Institutions and Satisfaction with Democracy: A Cross-National Analysis of Consensus and Majoritarian Systems." *American Political Science Review* 91:66–81.

Annas, George J. 1994. "Death by Prescription." *New England Journal of Medicine* 331:1240–1243.

Bailey, Michael A., and Forrest Maltzman. 2008. "Does Legal Doctrine Matter? Unpacking Law and Policy Preferences on the U.S. Supreme Court." *American Political Science Review* 102:369–384.

Barnes, Robert. 2009. "Court Reveals Customary Divide in Wrestling with Anti-Bias Law." *Washington Post*, April 30.

Bartels, Brandon L. 2009. "The Constraining Capacity of Legal Doctrine on the U.S. Supreme Court." *American Political Science Review* 103:474–495.

——. 2011. "Choices in Context: How Case-Level Factors Shape the Magnitude of Ideological Voting on the U.S. Supreme Court." *American Politics Research* 39:142–175.

Baum, Lawrence. 1994. "Symposium: The Supreme Court and the Attitudinal Model." *Law and Courts Newsletter* 4:3–5.

——. 1997. *The Puzzle of Judicial Behavior.* Ann Arbor: University of Michigan Press.

——. 2006. *Judges and Their Audiences: A Perspective on Judicial Behavior.* Princeton, NJ: Princeton University Press.

——. 2007. *The Supreme Court*, 9th ed. Washington, DC: CQ Press.

Benesh, Sara. 2003. "Harold J. Spaeth: The Supreme Court Computer." In *The Pioneers of Judicial Behavior*, edited by Nancy Maveety, 116–147. Ann Arbor: University of Michigan Press.

Bergara, Mario, Barak Richman, and Pablo T. Spiller. 2003. "Modeling Supreme Court Strategic Decision Making: The Congressional Constraint." *Legislative Studies Quarterly* 28:247–280.

Best, Bradley J. 2002. *Law Clerks, Support Personnel and the Decline of Consensual Norms on the United States Supreme Court, 1935–1995.* New York: LFB Scholarly Publishing.

Bickel, Alexander M. 1986. *The Least Dangerous Branch: The Supreme Court at the Bar of Politics*, 2nd ed. New Haven: Yale University Press.

Biskupic, Joan. 2010. "High Court Weighs Fairness of Tax Credits for Religious School Students." *USA Today*, November 4.

Black, Ryan C., and Ryan J. Owens. 2009. "Agenda Setting in the Supreme Court: The Collision of Policy and Jurisprudence." *Journal of Politics* 71:1062–1075.

Bonneau, Chris, Thomas Hammond, Forrest Maltzman, and Paul J. Wahlbeck. 2007. "Agenda Control, the Median Justice, and the Majority Opinion on the U.S. Supreme Court." *American Journal of Political Science* 51:890–905.

Boucher, Robert L., Jr., and Jeffrey A. Segal. 1995. "Supreme Court Justices as Strategic Decision-Makers: Aggressive Grants and Defensive Denials on the Vinson Court." *Journal of Politics* 57:812–823.

Boyd, Christina L. 2010. "Federal District Court Judge Ideology Data." http://clboyd.net/ideology.html.

Brace, Paul, Laura Langer, and Melinda Gann Hall. 2000. "Measuring the Preferences of State Supreme Court Judges." *Journal of Politics* 62:387–413.

Brenner, Saul. 1979. "The New Certiorari Game." *Journal of Politics* 41:649–655.

Brenner, Saul, and Theodore S. Arrington. 1987. "Unanimous Decision Making on the U.S. Supreme Court: Case Stimuli and Judicial Attitudes." *Political Behavior* 9:75–86.

Brenner, Saul, and John F. Krol. 1989. "Strategies in Certiorari Voting on the United States Supreme Court." *Journal of Politics* 51:828–840.

Brenner, Saul, and Harold J. Spaeth. 1988. "Majority Opinion Assignments and the Maintenance of the Original Coalition on the Warren Court." *American Journal of Political Science* 32:72–81.

Brenner, Saul, and Marc Stier. 1996. "Retesting Segal and Spaeth's Stare Decisis Model." *American Journal of Political Science* 40:1036–1048.

Breyer, Stephen. 2010. "Justice Breyer: The Court, the Cases and the Conflicts." Interview with Terry Gross, *Fresh Air*, NPR, September 14. http://www.npr.org/templates/story/story.php?storyId=129831688.

Brudney, James A., and Corey A. Ditslear. 2005. "The Elusive Quest for Neutral Reasoning: Canons of Construction in the Workplace Law Jurisprudence of the Supreme Court." *Vanderbilt Law Review* 58:1–116.

Caldeira, Gregory A., and John R. Wright. 1988. "Organized Interests and Agenda-Setting in the Supreme Court." *American Political Science Review* 82:1109–1127.

———. 1990. "The Discuss List: Agenda Building in the Supreme Court." *Law & Society Review* 24:807–836.

Caldeira, Gregory A., and Christopher J. W. Zorn. 1998. "Of Time and Consensual Norms in the Supreme Court." *American Journal of Political Science* 42:874–902.

Collins, Paul M., Jr. 2008. "Amici Curiae and Dissensus on the United States Supreme Court." *Journal of Empirical Legal Studies* 5:143–170.

———. 2009. *Friends of the Supreme Court: Interest Groups and Judicial Decision Making*. New York: Oxford University Press.

Cook, Beverly Blair. 1995. "Justice Brennan and the Institutionalization of Dissent Assignment." *Judicature* 79:17–23.

Cordray, Margaret Meriwether, and Richard Cordray. 2001. "The Supreme Court's Plenary Docket." *Washington & Lee Law Review* 58:737–794.

Corley, Pamela C. 2009. "Uncertain Precedent: Circuit Court Responses to Supreme Court Plurality Opinions." *American Politics Research* 37:30–49.

——. 2010. *Concurring Opinion Writing on the U.S. Supreme Court*. Albany, NY: SUNY Press.

Cross, Frank B. 1997. "Political Science and the New Legal Realism: A Case of Unfortunate Interdisciplinary Ignorance." *Northwestern University Law Review* 92:251–327.

Danelski, David J. 1960. "The Influence of the Chief Justice in the Decisional Process of the Supreme Court." Paper delivered at the annual meeting of the American Political Science Association, New York, September 8–10.

——. 1964. *A Supreme Court Justice Is Appointed*. New York: Random House.

——. 1980. "The Influence of the Chief Justice in the Decisional Process of the Supreme Court." In *Constitutional Law and Judicial Policy Making*, edited by Joel B. Grossman and Richard S. Wells, 147–160. New York: John Wiley.

Danelski, David J., and Joseph S. Tulchin, eds. 1973. *The Autobiography of Charles Evans Hughes*. Cambridge, MA: Harvard University Press.

Douglas, William O. 1963. Transcript of conversations with Walter F. Murphy, April 5, Cassette 14, Princeton University Library.

——. 1980. *The Court Years, 1939–1975*. New York: Random House.

Dworkin, Ronald. 1978. *Taking Rights Seriously*. Cambridge, MA: Harvard University Press.

——. 1986. *Law's Empire*. Cambridge, MA: Harvard University Press.

Easterbrook, Frank. 1982. "Ways of Criticizing the Court." *Harvard Law Review* 95:802–832.

Edelman, Paul H., David E. Klein, and Stefanie A. Lindquist. 2008. "Measuring Deviations from Expected Voting Patterns on Collegial Courts." *Journal of Empirical Legal Studies* 5:819–852.

——. 2012. "Consensus, Disorder and Ideology on the Supreme Court." *Journal of Empirical Legal Studies* 9:129–148.

Ely, John Hart. 1980. *Democracy and Distrust: A Theory of Judicial Review*. Cambridge, MA: Harvard University Press.

Epstein, Lee, and Joseph F. Kobylka. 1992. *The Supreme Court and Legal Change: Abortion and the Death Penalty*. Chapel Hill: University of North Carolina Press.

Epstein, Lee, and Jack Knight. 1998. *The Choices Justices Make*. Washington, DC: CQ Press.

Epstein, Lee, Jack Knight, and Andrew D. Martin. 2001. "The Supreme Court as a Strategic National Policy Maker." *Emory Law Journal* 50:583–611.

Epstein, Lee, and Jeffrey A. Segal. 2000. "Measuring Issue Salience." *American Journal of Political Science* 44:66–83.

Epstein, Lee, Jeffrey A. Segal, and Harold J. Spaeth. 2001. "The Norm of Consensus on the U.S. Supreme Court." *American Journal of Political Science* 45:362–377.

Epstein, Lee, Jeffrey A. Segal, Harold J. Spaeth, and Thomas G. Walker. 2007. *The Supreme Court Compendium: Data, Decisions & Developments*. Washington, DC: CQ Press.

Epstein, Lee, Andrew D. Martin, Jeffrey A. Segal, and Chad Westerland. 2007. "The Judicial Common Space." *Journal of Law, Economics, & Organization* 23(2):303–325.

Eskridge, William N., Jr. 1991. "Overriding Supreme Court Statutory Interpretation Decisions." *Yale Law Journal* 101:331–417.

Feldman, Stephen M. 2005. "The Rule of Law or the Rule of Politics? Harmonizing the Internal and External Views of Supreme Court Decision Making." *Law & Social Inquiry* 30:89–135.

Ferren, John M. 2004. *Salt of the Earth, Conscience of the Court: The Story of Justice Wiley Rutledge*. Chapel Hill: University of North Carolina Press.

Frank, Jerome. 1936. *Courts on Trial: Myth and Reality in American Justice*. Princeton, NJ: Princeton University Press.

Frankfurter, Felix. 1953. "Chief Justices I Have Known." *Virginia Law Review* 39:883–905.

Gely, Rafael, and Pablo T. Spiller. 1990. "A Rational Choice Theory of Supreme Court Statutory Decisions with Applications to the *State Farm* and *Grove City* Cases." *Journal of Law, Economics & Organization* 6:263–300.

George, Alexander L. 1980. "Domestic Constraints on Regime Change in U.S. Foreign Policy: The Need for Policy Legitimacy." In *Change in the International System*, edited by Ole R. Holsti, Randolph M. Siverson, and Alexander L. George, 223–262. Boulder, CO: Westview Press.

George, Tracey E., and Lee Epstein. 1992. "On the Nature of Supreme Court Decision Making." *American Political Science Review* 86:323–337.

Gerber Scott D., and Keeok Park. 1997. "The Quixotic Search for Consensus on the U.S. Supreme Court: A Cross-Judicial Empirical Analysis of the Rehnquist Court Justices." *American Political Science Review* 91:390–408.

Gibson, James L. 1991. "Decision Making in Appellate Courts." In *The American Courts: A Critical Assessment*, edited by John B. Gates and Charles A. Johnson, 255–278. Washington, DC: CQ Press.

Giles, Micheal W., Virginia A. Hettinger, and Todd Peppers. 2001. "Picking Federal Judges: A Note on Policy and Partisan Selection Agendas." *Political Research Quarterly* 54:623–641.

Gillman, Howard. 1993. *The Constitution Besieged: The Rise and Demise of Lochner Era Police Powers Jurisprudence*. Durham, NC: Duke University Press.

——. 1996. "More on the Origins of the Fuller Court's Jurisprudence: Reexamining the Scope of Federal Power over Commerce and Manufacturing in Nineteenth-Century Constitutional Law." *Political Research Quarterly* 49:415–437.

——. 1999. "The Court as an Idea, Not a Building (or a Game): Interpretive Institutionalism and the Analysis of Supreme Court Decision-Making." In *Supreme Court Decision-Making: New Institutionalist Approaches*, edited by Cornell W. Clayton and Howard Gillman, 65–90. Chicago: University of Chicago Press.

——. 2001. "What's Law Got to Do with It? Judicial Behavioralists Test the 'Legal Model' of Judicial Decision Making." *Law & Social Inquiry* 26:465–504 (review of Spaeth and Segal's *Majority Rule or Minority Will*).

Gillman, Howard, and Cornell W. Clayton. 1999. "Beyond Judicial Attitudes: Institutional Approaches to Supreme Court Decision-Making." In *Supreme Court*

Decision-Making: New Institutionalist Approaches, edited by Cornell W. Clayton and Howard Gillman, 1–14. Chicago: University of Chicago Press.

Goldman, Sheldon. 1969. "Backgrounds, Attitudes, and the Voting Behavior of Judges: A Comment on Joel Grossman's 'Social Backgrounds and Judicial Decisions.'" *Journal of Politics* 31:214–222.

———. 1975. "Voting Behavior on the United States Courts of Appeals Revisited." *American Political Science Review* 69:491–506.

Graber, Mark A. 1991. *Transforming Free Speech: The Ambiguous Legacy of Civil Libertarianism*. Berkeley: University of California Press.

Grossman, Joel B. 1967. "Social Backgrounds and Judicial Decisions: Notes for a Theory." *Journal of Politics* 29:334–351.

Grossman, Joel B., and Richard S. Wells. 1989. *Constitutional Law and Judicial Policy-Making*. New York: Longman.

Hagle, Timothy M., and Harold J. Spaeth. 1993. "Ideological Patterns in the Justices' Voting in the Burger Court's Business Cases." *Journal of Politics* 55:492–505.

Haley, John O. 1992. "Consensual Governance: A Study of Law, Culture, and the Political Economy of Postwar Japan." In *The Political Economy of Japan, Volume 3: Cultural and Social Dynamics*, edited by Shumpei Kumon and Henry Rosovsky, 32–62. Stanford, CA: Stanford University Press.

Halpern, Stephen, and Kenneth Vines. 1977. "Institutional Disunity, the Judges' Bill and the Role of the United States Supreme Court." *Western Political Quarterly* 30:471–483.

Hand, Learned. 1958. *The Bill of Rights*. Cambridge, MA: Harvard University Press.

Harlan, John M. 1958. "Manning the Dikes." *Record of the N.Y.C. Bar Association* 13:541.

Harvey, Anna, and Barry Friedman. 2006. "Pulling Punches: Congressional Constraint on the Supreme Court's Constitutional Rulings, 1987–2000." *Legislative Studies Quarterly* 31(4):533–562.

Haynie, Stacie L. 1992. "Leadership and Consensus on the U.S. Supreme Court." *Journal of Politics* 54:1158–1169.

Hellman, Arthur D. 1996. "The Shrunken Docket of the Rehnquist Court." *Supreme Court Review* 1996:403–438.

Hensley, Thomas R., and Scott P. Johnson. 1998. "Unanimity on the Rehnquist Court." *Akron Law Review* 31:387–408.

Hettinger, Virginia A., Stefanie A. Lindquist, and Wendy L. Martinek. 2004. "Comparing Attitudinal and Strategic Accounts of Dissenting Behavior on the U.S. Courts of Appeals." *American Journal of Political Science* 48:123–137.

———. 2006. *Judging on a Collegial Court: Influences on Federal Appellate Decision Making*. Charlottesville: University of Virginia Press.

Hettinger, Virginia A., and Christopher Zorn. 2005. "Explaining the Incidence and Timing of Congressional Responses to the Supreme Court." *Legislative Studies Quarterly* 30:5–28.

Hoekstra, Valerie, and Timothy Johnson. 2003. "Delaying Justice: The Supreme Court's Decision to Hear Rearguments." *Political Research Quarterly* 56:351–360.

Howard, Robert, and Jeffrey A. Segal. 2004. "A Preference for Deference? The Supreme Court and Judicial Review." *Political Research Quarterly* 57:131–143.

Hurwitz, Mark S., and Drew Lanier. 2004. "I Respectfully Dissent: Consensus, Agendas and Policymaking on the U.S. Supreme Court, 1888–1999." *Review of Policy Research* 21:429–445.

Hutchinson, Dennis J. 1998. *The Man Who Once Was Whizzer White: A Portrait of Justice Byron R. White*. New York: The Free Press.

Jeffries, John C., Jr. 1994. *Justice Lewis F. Powell, Jr.* New York: Charles Scribner's Sons.

Johnson, Charles A., and Bradley C. Canon. 1984. *Judicial Policies: Implementation and Impact*. Washington, DC: Congressional Quarterly.

Johnson, Timothy R. 2003. "The Supreme Court, the Solicitor General, and the Separation of Powers." *American Politics Research* 31:426–451.

Johnson, Timothy R., James F. Spriggs, II, and Paul J. Wahlbeck. 2005. "Passing and Strategic Voting on the U.S. Supreme Court." *Law & Society Review* 39: 349–377.

Kagan, Robert A., Bliss Cartwright, Lawrence M. Friedman, and Stanton Wheeler. 1978. "The Evolution of State Supreme Courts." *Michigan Law Review* 76:963–1005.

Kalman, Laura. 1996. *The Strange Career of Legal Liberalism*. New Haven, CT: Yale University Press.

Katznelson, Ira. 2005. *When Affirmative Action Was White: An Untold History of Racial Inequality in Twentieth-Century America*. New York: W.W. Norton.

Keck, Thomas M. 2004. *The Most Activist Supreme Court in History: The Road to Modern Judicial Conservatism*. Chicago: University of Chicago Press.

Kerr, Orin. 2009. "Legal Ambiguity, Empathy, and the Role of Judicial Power." *The Volokh Conspiracy*, May 13. http://volokh.com/artiches.archive_2009_05_10-2009_05_16.shtml#1242251518. Accessed September 27, 2009.

Klein, Mitchell S. 1984. *Law Courts and Policy*. Englewood Cliffs, NJ: Prentice Hall.

Kluger, Richard. 1977. *Simple Justice*. New York: Vintage Books.

Kritzer, Herbert M. 2010. "Re: Attitudes, Legal Rules, and What Else?" LawCourt listserv, September 15. LAWCOURT-L@TULANE.EDU on behalf of Bert Kritzer, kritzer@UMN.EDU.

Kritzer, Herbert M., J. Mitchell Pickerill, and Mark Richards. 1998. "Bringing the Law Back In: Finding a Role for Law in Models of Supreme Court Decision-Making." Paper presented at the 1998 Annual Meeting of the Midwest Political Science Association, Chicago, April 23–25.

Krol, John F., and Saul Brenner. 1990. "Strategies in Certiorari Voting on the United States Supreme Court." *Western Political Quarterly* 43:335–342.

Kronman, Anthony T. 1993. *The Lost Lawyer: Failing Ideals of the Legal Profession*. Cambridge, MA: Harvard University Press.

Lanier, Drew Noble. 2003. *Of Time and Judicial Behavior: United States Supreme Court Agenda-Setting and Decision-Making, 1888–1997*. Selinsgrove, PA: Susquehanna University Press

Lax, Jeffrey R. 2007. "Constructing Legal Rules on Appellate Courts." *American Political Science Review* 101:591–604.

Lazarus, Jeffrey, and Amy Steigerwalt. 2009. "Different Houses: The Distribution of Earmarks in the House and Senate." *Legislative Studies Quarterly* 34:347–373.

Liebman, Lance. 1972. "Swing Man on the Supreme Court." *New York Times*, October 8.

Lindquist, Stefanie A., and David E. Klein. 2006. "The Influence of Jurisprudential Considerations on Supreme Court Decisionmaking: A Study of Conflict Cases." *Law & Society Review* 40:135–161.

Lindquist, Stefanie A., and Rorie Spill Solberg. 2007. "Judicial Review by the Burger and Rehnquist Courts: Explaining Justices' Responses to Constitutional Challenges." *Political Research Quarterly* 60:71–90.

Linzer, Peter. 1979. "The Meaning of Certiorari Denials." *Columbia Law Review* 79:1227–1305.

Liptak, Adam. 2008. "A Second Justice Opts out of a Longtime Custom: The 'Cert. Pool.'" *New York Times*, September 26.

———. 2010. "A Sign of Court's Polarization: Choice of Clerks." *New York Times*, September 17.

Llewellyn, Karl. 1930. *The Bramble Bush: On Our Law and Its Study*. Dobbs Ferry, New York: Oceana Publications.

———. 1962. *Jurisprudence: Realism in Theory and Practice*. Chicago: University of Chicago Press.

Maltzman, Forrest, and Paul J. Wahlbeck. 1996. "Strategic Policy Considerations and Voting Fluidity on the Burger Court." *American Political Science Review* 90:581–592.

Maltzman, Forrest, James F. Spriggs, II, and Paul J. Wahlbeck. 1999. "Strategy and Judicial Choice: New Institutionalist Approaches to Supreme Court Decision-Making." In *Supreme Court Decision-Making: New Institutionalist Approaches*, edited by Cornell Clayton and Howard Gillman, 43–64. Chicago: University of Chicago Press.

———. 2000. *Crafting Law on the Supreme Court: The Collegial Game*. Cambridge: Cambridge University Press.

Martin, Andrew D., and Kevin M. Quinn. 2002. "Dynamic Ideal Point Estimation via Markov Chain Monte Carlo for the U.S. Supreme Court, 1953–1999." *Political Analysis* 10:134–153.

Mason, Alpheus Thomas. 1956. *Harlan Fiske Stone: Pillar of the Law*. New York: Viking Press.

———. 1964. *The Supreme Court from Taft to Warren*. New York: W.W. Norton.

McGuire, Kevin T. 1998. "Explaining Executive Success in the U.S. Supreme Court." *Political Research Quarterly* 51:505–526.

McGuire, Kevin T., Georg Vanberg, Charles E. Smith, Jr., and Gregory A. Caldeira. 2009. "Measuring Policy Content on the U.S. Supreme Court." *Journal of Politics* 71:1305–1321.

Meinhold, Stephen S., and Steven A. Shull. 1998. "Policy Congruence between the President and the Solicitor General." *Political Research Quarterly* 51:527–537.

Miller, Charles E. 1989. "The Social Psychological Effects of Group Decision Rules." In *Psychology of Group Influence*, edited by Paul B. Paulus, 327–355. Hillsdale, NJ: Lawrence Erlbaum.

Mooney, Christopher Z., and Mei-Hsien Lee. 2000. "The Influence of Values on Consensus and Contentious Morality Policy: U.S. Death Penalty Reform, 1956–82." *Journal of Politics* 62:223–239.

Moorhead, R. Dean. 1952. "Concurring and Dissenting Opinions." *American Bar Association Journal* 38:821–884.

Motley, Constance Baker. 1979. "From *Brown* to *Bakke*: The Long Road to Equality." *Harvard Civil Rights-Civil Liberties Law Review* 14:315–327.Murphy, Walter F. 1964. *Elements of Judicial Strategy.* Chicago: Chicago University Press.

Newman, Roger K. 1994. *Hugo Black: A Biography.* New York: Pantheon.

O'Brien, David M. 1996. *Storm Center: The Supreme Court in American Politics*, 4th ed. New York: W.W. Norton.

——. 1997. "The Rehnquist Court's Shrinking Plenary Docket." *Judicature* 81:58–65.

——. 1999. "Institutional Norms and Supreme Court Opinions: On Reconsidering the Rise of Individual Opinions." In *Supreme Court Decision-Making: New Institutional Approaches*, edited by Cornell W. Clayton and Howard Gillman, 91–113. Chicago: University of Chicago Press.

——. 2005. *Storm Center: The Supreme Court in American Politics*, 7th ed. New York: W.W. Norton.

Orren, Karen, and Stephen Skowronek. 2004. *The Search for American Political Development.* New York: Cambridge University Press.

Palmer, Jan, and Saul Brenner. 1988. "The Time Taken to Write Opinions as a Determinant of Opinion Assignments." *Judicature* 72:179–184.

Perry, H. W. 1991. *Deciding to Decide: Agenda Setting in the United States Supreme Court.* Cambridge, MA: Harvard University Press.

Pickerill, J. Mitchell. 2004. *Constitutional Deliberation in Congress: The Impact of Judicial Review in a Separated System.* Durham, NC: Duke University Press.

Pierson, Paul. 2004. *Politics in Time: History, Institutions, and Social Analysis.* Princeton, NJ: Princeton University Press.

Posner, Richard A. 1992. *Economic Analysis of Law.* Boston: Little, Brown.

——. 1996. *The Federal Courts: Challenge and Reform.* Cambridge, MA: Harvard University Press.

——. 2005. "The Supreme Court, 2004 Term—Forward: A Political Court," *Harvard Law Review* 119:31-102.

Post, Robert. 2001. "The Supreme Court Opinion as Institutional Practice: Dissent, Legal Scholarship, and Decisionmaking in the Taft Court." *Minnesota Law Review* 85:1267–1390.

Pound, Roscoe. 1908. "Mechanical Jurisprudence." *Columbia Law Review* 8:605–623.

Pritchett, C. Herman. 1941. "Divisions of Opinion Among Justices of the U.S. Supreme Court, 1939–1941." *American Political Science Review* 35:890–898.

——. 1948. *The Roosevelt Court: A Study in Judicial Politics and Values, 1937–1947.* New York: Macmillan.

——. 1954. *Civil Liberties and the Vinson Court.* Chicago: University of Chicago Press.

Provine, Doris Marie. 1980. *Case Selection in the United States Supreme Court.* Chicago: University of Chicago Press.

Rasmusen, Eric. 1994. "Judicial Legitimacy as a Repeated Game." *Journal of Law, Economics & Organization* 10:63–83.

Rehnquist, William H. 1987. *The Supreme Court: How It Was, How It Is*. New York: William Morrow.

Richards, Mark J., and Herbert M. Kritzer. 2002. "Jurisprudential Regimes in Supreme Court Decision Making." *American Political Science Review* 96: 305–320.

Richardson, Bradley M., and Scott C. Flanagan. 1984. *Politics in Japan*. Boston: Little, Brown.

Rohde, David W., and Harold J. Spaeth. 1976. *Supreme Court Decision Making*. San Francisco: W.H. Freeman.

Rohlen, Thomas P. 1989. "Order in Japanese Society: Attachment, Authority and Routine." *Journal of Japanese Studies* 15:5–40.

Rosen, Jeffrey. 2007a. "Roberts's Rules." *Atlantic Monthly* 499:104–113.

——. 2007b. "The Dissenter." *New York Times Magazine*. September 23.

Rosenberg, Gerald. 1991. *The Hollow Hope*. Chicago: University of Chicago Press.

Roy, Dona, and Donald R. Songer. 2010. "Does the Attitudinal Model Explain Unanimous Reversals?" *Justice System Journal* 31:342–372.

Sala, Brian R., and James F. Spriggs, II. 2004. "Designing Tests of the Supreme Court and the Separation of Powers." *Political Research Quarterly* 57:197–208.

Salokar, Rebecca M. 1992. *The Solicitor General: The Politics of Law*. Philadelphia: Temple University Press.

Samuels, Richard. 1987. *The Business of the Japanese State: Energy Markets in Comparative and Historical Perspective*. Ithaca, NY: Cornell University Press.

Savage, David G. 2010. "Kagan Advances, with Just One GOP Supporter." *Philadelphia Inquirer*, July 21.

Schubert, Glendon. 1961. "A Psychometric Model of the Supreme Court." *American Behavioral Scientist* 5:14–18.

——. 1962. "Policy without Law: An Extension of the Certiorari Game." *Stanford Law Review* 14:284–327.

——. 1965. *The Judicial Mind: The Attitudes and Ideologies of Supreme Court Justices, 1946–1963*. Evanston, IL: Northwestern University Press.

Schweiger, David M., William R. Sandberg, and James W. Ragan. 1986. "Group Approaches for Improving Strategic Decision Making: A Comparative Analysis of Dialectical Inquiry, Devil's Advocacy, and Consensus." *Academy of Management Journal* 29:51–71.

Segal, Jeffrey A. 1984. "Predicting Supreme Court Cases Probabilistically: The Search and Seizure Cases, 1962–1984." *American Political Science Review* 78:891–900.

——. 1988. "Amicus Curiae Briefs by the Solicitor General during the Warren and Burger Courts: A Research Note." *Western Political Quarterly* 41:135–144.

——. 1997. "Separation-of-Powers Games in the Positive Theory of Congress and Courts." *American Political Science Review* 91:28–44.

——. 2003. "Glendon Schubert: The Judicial Mind." In *The Pioneers of Judicial Behavior*, edited by Nancy Maveety, 78–100. Ann Arbor: University of Michigan Press.

Segal, Jeffrey A., and Albert Cover. 1989. "Ideological Values and the Votes of U.S. Supreme Court Justices." *American Political Science Review* 83:557–565.

Segal, Jeffrey A., Lee Epstein, Charles M. Cameron, and Harold J. Spaeth. 1995. "The Ideological Values and Votes of U.S. Supreme Court Justices Revisited." *Journal of Politics* 57:812–823.

Segal, Jeffrey A., and Harold J. Spaeth. 1993. *The Supreme Court and the Attitudinal Model*. New York: Cambridge University Press.

———. 1996. "The Influence of Stare Decisis on the Votes of United States Supreme Court Justices." *American Journal of Political Science* 40:971–1003.

———. 1999. *Majority Rule or Minority Will: Adherence to Precedent on the U.S. Supreme Court*. New York: Cambridge University Press.

———. 2002. *The Supreme Court and the Attitudinal Model Revisited*. New York: Cambridge University Press.

Slotnick, Elliot E. 1978. "The Chief Justice and Self-Assignment of Majority Opinions: A Research Note." *Western Political Quarterly* 31:219–225.

Smith, Kevin H. 2005. "The Jurisprudential Impact of *Brown v. Board of Education*." *North Dakota Law Review* 81:115.

Smoke, Richard. 1994. "On the Importance of Policy Legitimacy." *Political Psychology* 15:97–110.

Songer, Donald R. 1982. "Consensual and Nonconsensual Decisions in Unanimous Opinions of the United States Courts of Appeals." *American Journal of Political Science* 26:225–239.

Songer, Donald R., and Stefanie A. Lindquist. 1996. "Not the Whole Story: The Impact of Justices' Values on Supreme Court Decision Making." *American Journal of Political Science* 40:1049–1063.

Songer, Donald R., and Julia Siripurapu. 2009. "The Unanimous Decisions of the Supreme Court of Canada as a Test of the Attitudinal Model." *Canadian Journal of Political Science* 42:65–92.

Spaeth, Harold J. 2007. *The United States Supreme Court Judicial Database, 1953–2006 Terms*. East Lansing: Michigan State University, Department of Political Science. scdb.wustl.edu.

Spiller, Pablo T, and Rafael Gely. 1992. "Congressional Control or Judicial Independence." *RAND Journal of Economics* 23:463–492.

Spriggs, James F., II, and Thomas G. Hansford. 2001. "Explaining the Overruling of U.S. Supreme Court Precedent." *Journal of Politics* 63:1091–1111.

Starr, Kenneth W. 2006. "The Supreme Court and Its Shrinking Docket: The Ghost of William Howard Taft." *Minnesota Law Review* 90:1363–1385.

Stevens, John Paul. 2009. Interview by Brian Lamb, C-SPAN, June 24. http://supremecourt.c-span.org/assets/pdf/JPStevens.pdf.

"Supreme Court Bar Publishes Memorials to William H. Rehnquist." 2007. *Supreme Court Historical Society Quarterly* 28:1–16.

Tamanaha, Brian. 2006. *Law as a Means to an End: Threat to the Rule of Law*. New York: Cambridge University Press.

———. 2010. *Beyond the Formalist-Realist Divide: The Role of Politics in Judging*. Princeton, NJ: Princeton University Press.

Tanenhaus, S. Joseph, Marvin Sehick, Matthew Muraskin, and Daniel Rosen. 1963. "The Supreme Court's Certiorari Jurisdiction: Cue Theory." In *Judicial Deci-*

sion Making, edited by Glendon Schubert, 111–132. New York: The Free Press of Glencoe.

Time. 1974. "The Supreme Court: A Unanimous No to Nixon." August 5. http://www.time.come/time/magazine/article/0,9171,879409,00.html. Accessed November 11, 2010.

Tybor, Joseph R. 1987. "Powell Departure Creates a Void in Center of Court." *Chicago Tribune*, June 28.

Ulmer, S. Sidney. 1970. "Dissent Behavior and the Social Background of Supreme Court Justices." *Journal of Politics* 32:580–598.

——. 1972. "The Decision to Grant Certiorari as an Indicator to Decision 'On the Merits.'" *Polity* 4:429–447.

——. 1984. "The Supreme Court's Certiorari Decisions: Conflict as a Predictive Variable." *American Political Science Review* 78:901–911.

——. 1986. "Exploring the Dissent Patterns of the Chief Justices: John Marshall to Warren Burger." In *Judicial Conflict and Consensus: Behavioral Studies of American Appellate Courts*, edited by Sheldon Goldman and C.M. Lamb, 50–67. Lexington: University Press of Kentucky.

Unah, Issac, and Ange-Marie Hancock. 2006. "Supreme Court Decision-Making, Subissue Salience and the Attitudinal Model." *Law & Policy* 28:295–320.

Urofsky, Melvin. 1991. *Felix Frankfurter: Judicial Restraint and Individual Liberty*. Boston: Twayne Publishers.

Wahlbeck, Paul J. 1997. "The Life of the Law: Judicial Politics and Legal Change." *Journal of Politics* 59:778–802.

——. 2006. "Strategy and Constraints on Supreme Court Opinion Assignment." *University of Pennsylvania Law Review* 154:1729–1755.

Wahlbeck, Paul J., James F. Spriggs, II, and Forrest Maltzman. 1999. "The Politics of Dissents and Concurrences on the U.S. Supreme Court." *American Politics Research* 27:488–514.

Walker, Thomas G., Lee Epstein, and William J. Dixon. 1988. "On the Mysterious Demise of Consensual Norms in the United States Supreme Court." *Journal of Politics* 50:362–389.

Ward, Artemus, and David L. Weiden. 2006. *Sorcerers' Apprentices: 100 Years of Law Clerks at the United States Supreme Court*. New York: New York University Press.

Warren, Earl. 1977. *The Memoirs of Earl Warren*. Garden City, NY: Doubleday.

Westerland, Chad. 2003. "Who Owns the Majority Opinion?" Paper presented at the annual meeting of the American Political Science Association, Philadelphia, August 28–31. (Manuscript on file with authors.)

Whittington, Keith E. 2000. "Once More Unto the Breach: Postbehavioralist Approaches to Judicial Politics." *Law & Social Inquiry* 25:601–634.

Wilkinson, J. Harvie, III. 1974. *Serving Justice: A Supreme Court Clerk's View*. New York: Charterhouse.

Williams, Richard. 2006. "Generalized Ordered Logit/Partial Proportional Odds Models for Ordinal Dependent Variables." *Stata Journal* 6(1):58–82.

Wood, Sandra L., and Gary M. Gansle. 1997. "Seeking a Strategy: William J. Brennan's Dissent Assignments." *Judicature* 81:73–75.

Woodward, Bob, and Scott Armstrong. 1979. *The Brethren: Inside the Supreme Court*. New York: Simon and Schuster.

Yates, Jeff. 2002. *Popular Justice: Presidential Prestige and Executive Success in the Supreme Court*. Albany: State University of New York Press.

Zorn, Christopher. 2002. "U.S. Government Litigation Strategies in the Federal Appellate Courts." *Political Research Quarterly* 55:145–166.

Index

abortion, 55, 88
acquiescence, 39–44, 86–87
addition of syllabus. *See* syllabus
agenda setting. *See* certiorari process
amicus curiae briefs, 65, 70–71, 143. *See also* Collins, Paul M., Jr.; legal certainty
Argersinger v. Hamlin, 117, 164
assisted suicide, 4, 167
attitudes. *See* attitudinal model
attitudinal model: description of, 5–6, 51–52, 61; explanation for unanimity, 76–77, 78, 101, 125; interaction of legal certainty and, 65–76, 109–112, 135–136; measurement of, 76–80, 82; test of, 101, 105–106, 125, 129. *See also* consensus, theory of; ideological polarization

bad vehicle, 150–151, 154–155. *See also* certiorari process
Bailey, Michael, 6, 54–55, 57–58, 69
Baltimore City Department of Social Services v. Bouknight, 149–150
Bankruptcy Code, 102
Bartels, Brandon L., 57–58, 66, 69, 70, 91
Baum, Lawrence, 6, 54, 55, 65, 66, 68, 160
Betts v. Brady, 20
Bill of Rights, 45
Black, Hugo, 18, 20, 24–25, 28–29, 34–37, 40–41, 42–43, 87, 90
Black Lung Act, 154
Blackmun, Harry, 84–88, 117–118, 145–147, 152, 156–158
Blackmun Archives, 146–147, 184n5
Blystone v. Pennsylvania, 158
Board of Comm'rs of Jackson County v. United States, 37
Booth v. Maryland, 10
Bowers v. Hardwick, 117–118
Brandeis, Louis, 25–26, 39, 42, 46
Bray v. Alexandria Clinic, 88
Brennan, William, 84–88, 117–118
Brenner, Saul, 56, 60–61, 82, 147
Breyer, Stephen, 2, 164
Brown v. Allen, 184n2
Brown v. Board of Education, 8, 80, 149, 167
Burger, Warren E., 3, 8–9, 49–50, 65, 81, 83–86, 96–97, 108, 117–118, 120, 126. *See also* Burger Court
Burger Court, 37, 47, 86–87, 89, 143–144
Burton, Harold H., 35, 80, 90
Bush, George W., 164
Bush v. Gore, 149
Butterworth v. Smith, 155
Byrnes, James, 18, 25, 33, 41

case-specific factors: measurement of, 91–93; test of, 98, 107, 121–122, 131
cert pool, 12, 89; formation and description of, 144–146, 158, 166. *See also* certiorari process; pool memo
certiorari process: description of, 143–146; factors explaining, 147–152; unanimity and, 142–143. *See also* cert pool
certworthiness. *See* certiorari process
Chaplinsky v. New Hampshire, 22
Chesapeake & Ohio v. Leitch, 39
chief justice, 83–86; as majority opinion writer, 81–82, 98, 123, 129–131; opinion assignment, 32–33; self-assignment, 35–36, 81, 84–85
circuit split. *See* conflict, lower court
civil liberties and rights, 23, 71, 89, 91, 107, 121, 131–132, 140
Clarke, John H., 23
Clayton, Cornell W., 167
Claytor, Graham, 46
Clinton v. Jones, 4, 167
collegiality, 25–29, 84–86

Collins, Paul M., Jr., 65, 71
Commerce Clause, 21–22, 25, 36, 55
Commissioner of INS v. Jean, 156
Commissioner of Internal Revenue v. National Alfalfa Dehydration and Milling Co., 65
concurrence, 4–5, 33–38, 40–44, 115–140. *See also* opinion writing practices
Conference, 16–17, 36–40; discussions, 29–32, 83–86, 88, 147, 155, 167
conflict, lower court, 71–72, 132, 142; relation to certiorari, 148–149, 152. *See also* certiorari process; legal certainty
confusion, lower court, 150, 154. *See also* certiorari process
consensus. *See* unanimity
consensus, theory of, 62–93, 95, 160, 162–165. *See also* legal certainty
consensus era, 16–17
constitutional interpretation. *See* statutory interpretation
Contract Clause, 28
Coolidge v. Long, 27
County of Sacramento v. Lewis, 114–115

Davis v. United States, 40
death penalty, 10, 55, 158
Debt Collection Act of 1928, 108
Department of Agriculture, 108
Department of Social Services, 149
discretionary docket, 22–24, 29
discuss list, 82–83, 143–144, 149
dissensus path, 20
dissensus revolution, 11, 15–16, 47–48, 56
dissent assignment. *See* opinion assignment
distinguishable events, 11
docket size, 88–89, 100, 124, 157. *See also* certiorari process; consensus, theory of; institutional context
Douglas, William O., 11, 14, 18, 20, 25, 28, 30–36, 40–43, 83–85, 88, 90, 117, 161
Driscoll v. Edison Light & Power Co., 38
Due Process Clause, 25, 49–50, 55, 117
Dworkin, Ronald, 51, 56–57, 65

East Carroll Parish School Board v. Marshall, 182
Eaton v. City of Tulsa, 86
eBay Inc. v. MercExchange, L.L.C., 164
Eighth Amendment, 117
Elwood, Courtney, 85
Enforcement Act of 1870, 43
Environmental Protection Agency (EPA), 155
Epstein, Lee, 4, 6, 16–17, 52–53, 55, 60, 61, 77, 78, 79, 80, 81, 83, 91, 116, 118, 146, 160
Equal Access to Justice Act, 156
error correction, 151, 155–156. *See also* certiorari process
Establishment Clause, 2
Ex parte Quirin, 22
Ex Post Facto Clause, 4
extreme lower court decision, 78–79, 106, 125

Federal Employees Liability Act, 39
Federal Power Commission v. Hope Natural Gas, 28, 41–42
Federal Torts Claims Act (FTCA), 126
Federal Trade Commission v. Eastman Kodak Co., 25
Ferguson v. Moore McCormack Lines, 115
Fifth Amendment, 94, 150
First Amendment, 58, 155
Food Stamp Program, 108
Foreign Sovereign Immunities Act of 1976, 132
Foremost Insurance Co. v. Richardson, 152
Formalization of Dissent Assignment, 87–88
Fourteenth Amendment, 49–50, 114, 117
Fourth Amendment, 94
Franchise Tax Board v. Alcan Aluminum Ltd., 157
Frankfurter, Felix, 18, 20, 24–25, 28, 30–32, 34–42, 44, 46, 87, 90, 115
Free Exercise Clause, 150
Free Speech, 23, 29, 32, 55, 58, 87, 89, 100, 168
freedom of expression, 29
Fuller Court, 16–17, 33

Garcia v. Elf Atochem North America, 1
gay marriage, 168
gay rights, 54
General Motors Corp. v. United States, 154–155, 157
Gideon v. Wainwright, 164
Gillman, Howard, 55–56, 167
Ginsburg, Ruth Bader, 145

Golden State Transit Corp. v. City of Los Angeles, 158
Goldman, Sheldon, 60, 73
good vehicle. *See* bad vehicle
Gregg Cartage & Storage Co. v. United States, 41
Guantanamo Bay, 164

Hamdan v. Rumsfeld, 164
Hand, Learned, 60, 89
Harris, Crampton P., 29
Hawk v. Olson, 34–35
Higgins v. Smith, 30
Hiibel v. Sixth Judicial District Court of Nevada, 94
Hirabayashi v. United States, 21
Holmes, Oliver Wendell, 39, 42
Hughes, Charles Evans, 26–27, 30–31, 34, 90, 144. *See also* Hughes Court
Hughes Court, 16–18, 42

ideological polarization, 77, 101, 106, 109, 112, 125, 129, 134, 136, 162. *See also* attitudinal model; consensus, theory of
incorrect lower court decision. *See* error correction
institutional changes, external developments, 22–25
institutional context, 52, 79, 82–83; measurement of, 83–90; test of, 100–101, 107, 124–125, 131, 140
Interstate Commerce Commission, 41, 151
issue importance, 142–143, 149–150, 152–154. *See also* certiorari process

Jackson, Robert, 18, 20–22, 25, 28–29, 33–34, 36–37, 41, 168
Jewell Ridge Coal Corp v. United Mine Workers of America, 29
Jimmy Swaggart Ministries v. Board of Equalization of California, 150
John Doe Agency v. John Doe Corp., 150
Judges' Bill of 1925, 23, 88–89, 141
Judicial Common Space scores, 78–79
judicial ideology, measures of, 77–79
judicial review, 79–80, 99, 123–124. *See also* consensus, theory of; strategic model
Judiciary Act of 1925. *See* Judge's Bill of 1925
jurisprudential regimes, 57–58, 70

Keller v. State Bar of California, 157
Kennedy, Anthony M., 118
Kokoszka v. Belford, 102
Korematsu v. United States, 20, 43
Kritzer, Herbert, 6, 57–58, 68, 69, 75

law. *See* legal certainty
law clerks, 89–90, 100, 124; Blackmun's, 156–159; role in certiorari process, 144–146. *See also* certiorari process; consensus, theory of; institutional context
Lawrence v. Texas, 54, 118
Leach v. Peirson, 39
legal certainty, 50, 65–69, 162–163, 166–168; certiorari process and, 152; explanation of, 50, 65–69, 162–163; interaction of attitudes and, 6–7, 65–68, 75–76, 109–112, 135–136; measurement of, 69–75; test of, 101–105, 125, 129. *See also* consensus, theory of
Legal Certainty Index. *See* legal certainty
legal complexity, 70, 108, 132. *See also* consensus, theory of; legal certainty
legal model, 6, 54–59, 68
legal realism, 15–17, 22, 24, 29, 38, 47, 51, 161, 169
liberal decision, 61, 77, 91–92, 107, 131–132, 160
Little v. Streater, 49
lower court dissensus, 72–74. *See also* consensus, theory of; legal certainty
Lynce v. Mathis, 4

majority coalition, 39–42, 74, 82, 88
Maltzman, Forrest, 6, 52–53, 54–55, 57–58, 69, 70–71, 81–82, 93, 118
Marbury v. Madison, 168
Marshall, Thurgood, 52, 87, 118, 145, 160
Marshall Court, 16
Martin-Quinn scores, 182
Maryland v. Pringle, 94, 183
McCoy v. North Carolina, 158
McReynolds, James, 26
median justice, as opinion author, 81–82, 98, 106–107, 123, 131
Medo Photo Supply Corp. v. Labor Board, 43
Mercoid Corporation v. Mid-Continent Investment Co., 41–42
Military Force Act, 164
Minersville School District v. Gobitis, 25, 34
Minnesota v. Olson, 151
minority coalition, 42–44, 47

Moore v. City of East Cleveland, 50
Morehead v. New York ex rel. Tipaldo, 25
Motor Carrier Act of 1935, 41
Municipal Investors Assn. v. Birmingham, 28
Murdock v. Pennsylvania, 21, 158
Murphy, Frank, 18, 20–21, 25, 34–36, 40, 42–44, 52, 65, 90
Murphy, Walter F., 52, 65, 83

National Broadcasting Co. v. United States, 34
National Labor Relations Act, 158
New Deal, 16, 24–25, 89
New York Herald Tribune, 44–46
NLRB v. Boeing Co., 84
Nobelman v. American Savings Bank, 102
norm of consensus, 11; theory of breakdown of, 15–16, 60, 95, 161
notation, 86–87

Oklahoma Press Publishing Co. v. Walling, 35–36
Olmstead v. United States, 25
Oncale v. Sundowner Offshore Services, 1
opinion assignment, 32–33, 83–85, 90; dissents, 87–88, 100, 131
opinion circulation, 16, 33–36, 47, 161
opinion consensus, 116–140, 163–165; compared to unanimity, 132–135; definition of, 5, 95–96, 116; fully unanimous, 119; rates of, 120–121; UOC, 119; UOCD, 119–120
opinion writing practices: influence on consensus, 17, 32–36; separate, 25–27, 34–38, 40–41, 93. *See also* chief justice; median justice
Origination Clause, 155

Payne v. Tennessee, 10
per curiam, 40, 85–86
Polish National Alliance v. Labor Board, 39–40
pool memo: description of, 146; results of, investigation, 152–159, 166. *See also* cert pool; certiorari process
Powell, Lewis, 3, 84, 87–88, 117–118, 144, 164
precedent, 55–56; overturning of, 79–80, 99, 123–124
Preseault et ux. v. Interstate Commerce Commission, 151
Pritchett, C. Herman, 18, 46, 60, 68, 162, 195–196; explanation for unanimity, 7–8, 51–52
privacy, 24, 89, 117

Racketeer Influenced and Corrupt Organizations Act (RICO), 150, 153–154
Railroad Retirement Board v. Alton Railroad Co., 25
reargument, 36–37
Reed, Stanley, 18, 20, 25, 28, 35–36, 41, 44, 90
Rehnquist, William, 3, 10, 52, 84–86, 87–89, 92, 94, 96–97, 100, 108, 117, 120, 150–151. *See also* Rehnquist Court
Rehnquist Court, 3–4, 18, 47, 61, 89, 92, 120
Republic of Argentina v. Weltover, Inc., 132
reversal, 78–79
Richards, Mark, 6, 57–58, 69, 75
Richards v. Wisconsin, 4
Roberts, Owen, 20–21, 27–28, 30, 41, 43
Roe v. Wade, 87
Roosevelt, Franklin D., 18, 22–23
Roosevelt Court, 14–48; collegiality on, 25–29; definition of, 14, 18; external changes during, 22–28; internal changes during, 29–38; level of dissensus on, 15, 16, 18, 22–23, 36–37, 42
Rule 10 (of the Federal Rules of Civil Procedure), 147–148
Rule 11 (of the Federal Rules of Civil Procedure), 160
Rutledge, Wiley B., 18, 21–22, 25, 32, 35–36, 40, 43, 44

salience, 71, 75, 91, 98, 107, 121. *See also* case-specific factors; legal certainty; statutory interpretation
Sanford, Edward T., 25
Scalia, Antonin, 1, 115, 132, 160
Schneiderman v. United States, 42–43
Schubert, Glendon, 52, 60, 143
Scott v. Illinois, 184
Segal, Jeffrey A., 5–6, 16–17, 52, 55–56, 60, 61, 81, 83, 91, 118, 146, 147, 160
Selvage v. Collins, 151
separate opinions. *See* opinion writing practices
Sisson v. Ruby, 141, 151–152
Sixth Amendment, 117, 164

Skinner v. Oklahoma, 21
Smith v. Allwright, 41
solicitor general (SG), 25, 80–81, 98–99, 106, 123, 131, 147, 149
Sorrells v. United States, 25–26
South Carolina v. Gathers, 10
Spaeth, Harold, 5–6, 16–17, 52, 55–56, 60, 61, 70, 71–73, 82, 83, 118, 121, 147, 160. *See also* Spaeth dataset
Spaeth dataset, 70, 72–73, 96, 121, 182
Special Assessment on Convicted Persons statute, 155
Specter, Arlen, 2
Spriggs, James F., II, 6, 10, 52–53, 70, 71, 80, 81–82, 93, 118
State of Maryland v. Baltimore Radio Show, 184
statutory interpretation, 74–75. *See also* consensus, theory of; legal certainty
Stevens, John Paul, 86, 88, 115, 117–118, 145, 152, 158
Stewart, Potter, 87, 117
Stone, Harlan Fiske, 11, 14–47, 87, 90, 161. *See also* Roosevelt Court
Stone Court. *See* Roosevelt Court
strategic model: certiorari process and, 157–159; description of, 6, 52–54, 79, 82; explanation for unanimity, 79; measurement of, 79–82; test of, 98–100, 106, 123–124
Sutherland, George, 23
Swann v. Charlotte-Mecklenburg Board of Education, 8
syllabus, 86–87, 100, 124

Tafflin v. Levitt, 150, 153–154
Taft, William Howard, 25, 27, 29. *See also* Taft Court
Taft Court, 17–18, 23, 29
Takings Clause, 151
Tamanaha, Brian, 56–57, 65–68
Taylor v. United States, 154
Texaco v. Hasbrouck, 151, 153
Texas v. Florida, 37
Thomas, Clarence, 54, 115
time, 92–93, 121–122
Tinker v. Des Moines, 87
Title VII (of the Civil Rights Act of 1964), 1, 155
Truman, Harry S., 28

unanimity, 98–112, 121–136; compared to opinion consensus, 132–135; existing explanations for, 60–61; highly consensual, 4, 96–97, 103; impact of Conference discussions on, 29–32; measurement of, 96, 103; media coverage of, 1–3, 44–46; puzzle of, 1–4, 50–51, 94–95; rates of, 3–4, 17–22, 96–97; value of, 7–10, 44–46, 118–119
unanimous decisions. *See* unanimity
Uniform Code of Military Justice, 164
United States Department of Labor v. Triplett, 154
United States Supreme Court Judicial Database, 1953–2006 Terms. *See* Spaeth dataset
United States v. Boyle, 108
United States v. Classic, 43
United States v. Munoz-Flores, 155
United States v. Nixon, 7–8
United States v. Orleans, 126
United States v. Southeastern Underwriters Assn., 21
United States v. Texas, 108
Utah v. Aldrich, 34

Vacco v. Quill, 4
Varnum v. Brien, 168
Venegas v. Mitchell, 154
Vinson, Fred M., 83, 86, 89–90, 144
Vinson Court, 37

Wahlbeck, Paul, 6, 52–53, 56, 70, 71, 81–82, 93, 118
Waite, Morrison, 16
Walker, Thomas G., 4, 15, 116
Warren, Earl, 8, 80, 83, 86–87, 89, 90, 96–97, 161, 167. *See also* Warren Court
Warren Court, 37, 47, 82, 97, 120
Washington v. Glucksberg, 167
West Virginia State Board of Education v. Barnette, 20, 25, 34, 168
White, Byron, 3, 10, 84, 87, 117, 158. *See also* White Court
White Court, 17–18
Wickard v. Filburn, 22, 36
Willy v. Coastal Corp., 161
Wilson, Woodrow, 23
writ of certiorari. *See* certiorari process

Yellow Freight System v. Donnelly, 155